800 nr
U

D0955690

FORESTRY
IN
COMMUNIST
CHINA

FORESTRY
IN COMMUNIST CHINA

BY S. D. RICHARDSON

THE JOHNS HOPKINS PRESS
Baltimore, Maryland

Dedicated to the memory of
KING CANUTE
who also attempted the impossible

PREFACE

PEOPLE WHO write books about foreign countries based on visits of only a few weeks' duration have never greatly impressed me; now that I have joined their ranks, I feel duty-bound to offer some self-justification.

My reasons for writing a book on forestry in communist China are several. Firstly, there is a remarkable dearth of factual information available to the Western world on this vital—and possibly even limiting —factor in the Chinese economy. From time to time, brief accounts of China's vast afforestation projects filter through the bamboo curtain; usually they are statistical and concerned more with areas or numbers of trees planted than with silvicultural practices and problems. Their validity is questionable and they provide little information that is of direct interest elsewhere. Yet forestry in China contains much that is relevant to other countries: her native tree flora is among the richest in the world and has yielded many species of horticultural and economic importance; as a source of plantation forestry species, however, it remains virtually unexploited. The Chinese are planting trees for production and protection forestry, with feverish haste and on an unprecedented scale; while their efforts have frequently been mis-directed and they have experienced widespread failures, foresters are rapidly accumulating a wealth of silvicultural experience (and expertise) that could be used with advantage in many other countries. Therefore, an account of some of that experience, however brief and inadequate, may have some value.

But forestry is not concerned merely with planting trees. Recently, the 1965 H. R. MacMillan lecturer (Mr. J. C. Westoby) at the University of British Columbia drew attention to a feature of developing countries that many economists have tended to overlook: the fact that the agricultural and industrial sectors of the economy are closely interdependent—progress in the one determines and is in turn conditioned by progress in the other. He continued: "In the light of this interdependence . . . forestry and forest industry activities take on a particular significance. At one end they reach back into the rural economy; at the other, they penetrate into many branches of the industrial sector." This dual role of forestry is nowhere better illustrated than in the developing country of China. Agricultural productivity depends on water conservancy and, hence, on catchment afforestation and shelter planting, while timber resources are vitally important in the development of communications and industry, which must provide the base for agricultural progress. There are, in fact, few aspects of the economy which are not affected by the forest policy, many of them crucially. A consequence of this pervasive influence is that any attempt to evaluate the role of forestry in China demands consideration of social, political, economic, and technological aspects of the country that a biologist is scarcely qualified to judge or comment on. (Sincere recognition of my limitations in this respect has prompted the Dedication of this volume.)

Yet the forester visiting present-day China has opportunities to investigate some of these features that are not given to many better-qualified visitors. Since his interests lie outside the cities and the populated regions, he gets to parts of the country that are remote from the beaten tourist track and where socio-economic conditions are more representative than the environs of the International Hotels and "show-place" communes. Also, visiting foresters are extremely rare in China and there are no established itineraries for them (as there are for journalists, politicians, agriculturalists, social scientists, and other professional groups); consequently, while I have no doubts that the Chinese, like all good hosts, wanted to show me only the best aspects of forestry in their country, I at no time felt that the projects I visited were in any way artificially contrived. Of six specific areas that I asked to visit, I travelled to five—from Yunnan to Manchuria. I felt quite free at all times and (apart from performances of Peking opera!) in no way oppressed; except during air travel, I had virtually unlimited opportunities to take photographs (most of the ones included here were taken by me; those supplied by the Ministry of Forestry, Peking, are so acknowledged in the captions). I also found Chinese foresters and scientists (in contrast to the political cadres and administrators) perfectly willing to discuss their work freely and critically. It is my hope, therefore, that my comments and evaluation may be somewhat more objective than those of more restricted visitors.

The invitation extended to me to visit China developed from contact between the Royal Society of London and the *Academia Sinica* in Peking; my appreciation of the courtesies shown me by both learned societies is heartfelt. I am particularly indebted to Chu Ko-ching, Kuo Chin-tse, and Cheng Wan-chun of the *Academia*. The last named, who is also Vice-Director of the Academy of Forest Science, and a stimulating and immensely knowledgeable dendrologist, accompanied me to Manchuria. Visits to forestry operations and research institutes have placed me in the debt of Chinese scientists too numerous to list by name; I am grateful to all of them, as to my able interpreters, Peng Sien-tse and Wu Pao-lo. In collecting background information for this book, I have received help from many sources; acknowledgment is especially due to the Reuters correspondent in Peking (Mr. A. Kellett-Long) who gave me access to translations of many official Chinese news releases relating to forestry, and to the staff of the British Foreign Office. The interpretation of information received, however, is entirely my own responsibility. I also wish to record my thanks to the New Zealand Forest Service and its Director-General (Mr. A. L. Poole) whose moral support enabled me to make the visit; to the University of Wisconsin for the invitation to serve as visiting professor during the academic year 1964–65, which provided me with time and facilities to write this book; and to Mr. H. R. Orman and Mr. E. H. Bunn, who, in my absence, have done my job for me in New Zealand.

Finally, it is both my pleasure and my duty to acknowledge the assistance given me by my secretary, Ruth Gill. Her patience and ability to decipher the incoherencies which I committed daily to a tape recorder while in the People's Republic—usually after midnight and in some highly improbable situations—far exceed my own; as a result this book contains a record of on-the-spot impressions, rather than experiences only dimly remembered long after the event.

An article incorporating some of the material presented here, was published in the February, 1965, issue of *American Forests* and two reports in technical journals have made use of these data.

S. D. Richardson

Madison, Wisconsin
April, 1965

CONTENTS

xi

Contents

FIGURES

TABLES

CONVERSION FACTORS

To ENABLE the statistical information presented in this volume to be readily compared with data published by other countries, metric measurements have been employed throughout. The conversion factors given below can be applied to obtain units in common American usage. It should be noted, however, that the use of cubic meters in connection with yields per unit area refers to total tree volume; to obtain merchantable volumes in cubic feet by U.S. utilization standards, the metric volume per hectare must be reduced by about 10 per cent.

1 cu. m. sawn lumber	=	424 bd. ft.
1 cu. m. roundwood	=	221 bd. ft. (6 bd. ft./cu. ft.)
1 cu. m. per ha.	=	14.29 cu. ft. per acre
	=	89.32 bd. ft. per acre
	=	0.159 cords per acre
1 cu. m. (solid volume)	=	35.3145 cu. ft.
	=	0.3924 cords
1 ha.	=	2.47 acres
1 m.	=	39.37 inches
	=	3.28 ft.
1 km.	=	0.621 miles
1 sq. m.	=	10.76 sq. ft.
1 kg.	=	2.205 lbs.
1 metric ton	=	2,204.6 lbs.
1 kg. per ha.	=	0.892 lbs. per acre

FORESTRY
IN
COMMUNIST
CHINA

CHAPTER I.

THE ECONOMIC BACKGROUND

THE People's Republic of China covers an area of 9.6 million sq. km., spanning 50° of latitude (including the tropical islands within Chinese territorial waters) and 62° of longitude. This vast section of the Eurasian land mass amounts to one-fourteenth of the total land area of the globe and supports nearly one-fourth of the world's population. It is characterized by immense variation in topography, climate, soils, ecology, and ethnic features. In altitude it extends from almost 300 m. below sea level in the Turfan depression of northern Sinkiang to over 8,800 m. on the peak of Everest in the Himalayas. The climate ranges from the humid tropics of Kwangtung and Taiwan, with a mean annual rainfall of over 250 cm. and mean annual temperatures in excess of 25°C., through periglacial conditions on the Tibetan plateau, to the arid deserts of Inner Mongolia, northern Kansu and Sinkiang, where the mean annual precipitation may be less than 1 cm., the mean annual temperature below 5°C., and the annual temperature range greater than 45°C. Edaphically, most of the major soil types of the world are represented, from chernozems and chestnut soils of the Manchurian steppes to tropical laterites and terra rossa. China's flora is among the richest in the world, including more than 5,000 woody species in almost 700 genera; moreover, the vegetation pattern is unique in Eurasia in that the natural forest extends in an unbroken sequence of communities from tropical rain forest in the south to montane-boreal coniferous forest in the northeast. The native fauna, though much depleted, is almost as varied.

The inhabitants of present-day China are as diverse as their country. Made up of more than forty nationalities, they differ widely in ethnic type, culture, language, and religion. Muslims, Lamaist and Southern

1

Buddhists, and Taoists now co-exist with nominal Christians of all denominations; the still nomadic Mongols of the north are aligned with peoples who had developed a settled agriculture by 10,000 B.C. and who cultivated silkworms on a commercial scale 3,000 years ago.

As if the political problems of unifying this polyglot nation were not enough, China's economy is, at the present time, undergoing rapid and far-reaching changes, planned and directed by a stable, powerful, and resourceful central government. To evaluate the role of forestry and forest industries in the economy of China, it is necessary to appreciate the extent of these changes and to understand the background of them.

PHYSICAL GEOGRAPHY AND CLIMATE

China is a country of mountains, high plateaus, deserts, and river plains. On a topographic map, it is the high country that is most conspicuous. In the west, and covering nearly half the land area, lie the sparsely populated plateaus, depressions, and lofty mountains of Tibet, Sinkiang, and Tsinghai—an area largely without external drainage and accessible only via high mountains or, in the north, through the Kansu corridor. From the Pamirs, in the extreme northwest, a series of mountain ranges radiates to the eastern edge of the Tsinghai–Sinkiang–Tibetan plateau; one such—the Tsinling range—continues across central China, throwing the major rivers apart and increasing the latitudinal climatic differences between the north and south of "China proper."* A second conspicuous mountain chain runs southwest from the Greater Khinghan range in northwest Manchuria to the Yunnan-Kweichow plateau. Somewhat lower ranges form the north, northeast, and southeast borders of Manchuria and run through the southeast coastal provinces. The major rivers run west-east from the interior highlands and include three of the longest in the world—the Yangtze, the Yellow, and the Amur.

---

* Traditionally, there were two Chinas—"China Proper," which comprised the eighteen provinces within the Great Wall, and "Outer China," made up of dependencies beyond the Wall (Manchuria, Mongolia, Sinkiang, and Tibet). Outer China covered almost two-thirds of the land surface of the country but contained only 5 per cent of the population. The distinction is no longer officially acceptable in China but, in news releases aimed at overseas readers, reference is occasionally made to "China Proper" and to its former subdivisions of North, Central, and South China.

China east of the Greater Khingan ridge, therefore, is a land of hills, plains (including the Manchurian and the so-called North China plains), and river deltas. The northern part of the ridge merges with the Tsinling mountain range to act as a barrier between the green, humid rice lands to the south and the dry loess hills and sand deserts further north. It also forms the limit of the monsoon air-flow system drawing moist air during early summer from the Pacific region, and the prevailing dry and dust-laden winds from the west, which, by the time they reach China, have long since dropped their moisture.

In general, the climate of China is affected by interrelationships between the arid north and northwestern interior, the monsoon zone of the south and southwest, and the Tibetan plateau. The chief characteristic of the temperature is its mild variation between north and south in summer and great fluctuations in winter. Rainfall is heavy in the southeast, decreasing in intensity to the north and becoming increasingly unreliable. In addition, the provinces south of the Yangtze are always subject to summer typhoons. Details of the more important climatic factors are included in Table 1.

PHYTOGEOGRAPHY AND SOILS

A comprehensive study of the natural vegetation of China, together with a brief review of earlier publications, was recently issued by Wang (1961). He points out that many of the major plant communities were recognized as long ago as the fifth century and that the early Chinese literature contains many descriptions of plants and habitats, providing valuable records of land-use patterns and vegetational changes. These have been supplemented by numerous regional surveys, including descriptive material contributed by the late nineteenth- and early twentieth-century professional plant hunters from Europe and America. The efforts of these collectors have been outlined by Cox (1945). From the prolific (if somewhat humorless) Robert Fortune—who left England in 1843, equipped "with fowling piece and pistols and a Chinese vocabulary"—to the *doyen* of them all, Frank Kingdon Ward, the catalogue is an impressive one. It includes men like Pratt, Wilson, Forrest, Farrer, and the French missionaries David, Delavy, Soulie, and Ducloux. The collectors operated mainly in the southern and southwestern provinces and it is through their efforts that these areas became better known, from the standpoint of their flora, than the much simpler regions of the north and northeast.

Perhaps, too, it is because they were interested in China primarily as a source of horticultural and garden material for Europe, rather than as a field for scientific study, that few attempts have been made until recent times to describe and interpret the broad phytogeographical patterns of the land mass. Modern attempts at such classification have been both physiognomic (Tsou and Chien, 1925) and floristic (Handel Mazzetti, 1930; Walker, 1944; Liou, 1934; 1936). In particular, the forest regions have been studied (Wang, 1935; Cheo and Kuo, 1941; Teng, 1948; Wu, 1950) and up to twelve separate zones delineated. Wang (1961) recognizes three major forest formations and nine forest types. He describes the general characteristics of each type and includes notes on habitat, soil, climate, structure, composition, succession, etc. In a series of regional treatises, he provides detailed floristic descriptions of types and subtypes, and discusses the origin and segregation of the forest communities. Wang's monograph runs to over 300 pages and is, undoubtedly, the most complete modern synthesis available in English. For present purposes, however, it has limitations in that the author deliberately avoids any serious attempt to relate vegetation type to soil such as those made, for instance, by Thorp (1936) and Hwang (1940; 1941), or to climate (Wang, 1935; Chien *et al.*, 1956), believing that "one should make enquires that are independent of presumed causal relations." Also, Wang oversimplifies and makes much of the division between woodland in eastern China and the grassland-desert complex in the western inland regions. As a background to an understanding of land use in China, a paper by Hou *et al.* (1956) is more relevant. These authors divide China into twelve phytogeographical regions, the natural vegetation and land-use patterns of which can be broadly correlated with physical geography, climate, and soil type. The distribution of vegetation types is illustrated in Figure 1, and in Table 1 their salient features (in so far as they are of interest to foresters) are summarized. They are described more fully in Chapter II.

Very broadly, in south and east China, the natural forest distribution is determined by soil type; in the arid west and northwest, climate-induced steppe, semidesert, and desert dominate the vegetation types. In the mountain and plateau regions, vertical zonation of soils and vegetation is marked.

The greater part of China's natural forests has, of course, been destroyed over the years, resulting in acute soil-erosion problems and in a shortage of forest produce that has to be experienced to be believed. Virgin forest in the northeast remains only in the horseshoe formed

Figure 1: The Vegetation-Soil Regions of China (Source: Hou *et al.*, 195[

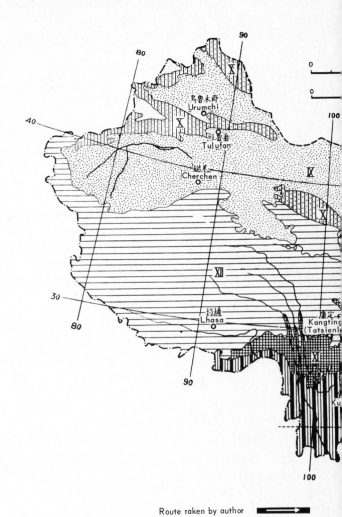

Route taken by author

I The coniferous forest—podzolic soils region

II The region of mixed coniferous and deciduous broadleaved forests — podzolic soils and brown forest soils

III The deciduous broadleaved forest — brown forest soils and Korichnevie soils region.

IV The region of mixed deciduous and evergreen broadleaved forests—yellow podzolic soils and yellow Korichnevie soils

V The evergreen broadleaved forest — yellow podzolic soils and red podzolic soils

(1) The eastern evergreen broadleaved forest—yellow podzolic soils and Rendzina soils subregion

(2) The western evergreen broadleaved forest—red podzolic soils and *terra rossa* soils subregion

VI The tropical monsoon rain forest—yellow lateritic soils region

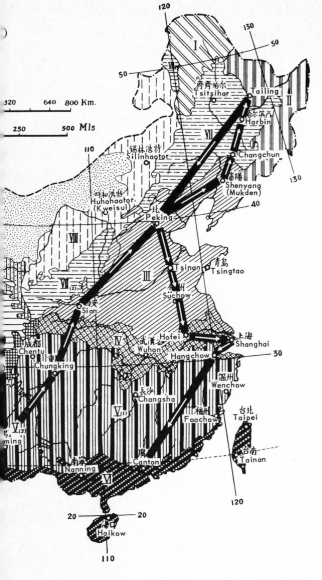

120 130 50

I

齊齊哈尔
Tsitsihar   Tailing

II

哈尔滨
Harbin

VII

长春
Changchun

50

锡林浩特
Silinhaotor

130

呼和浩特
Huhohaotor.
(Kweisui)

北京
Peking

沈阳
Shenyang
(Mukden)

40

VIII

VII
(2)

III

济南
Tsinan   青岛
Tsingtao

徐州
Suchow

西安
Sian

IV

武汉
Wuhan   合肥
Hofei   上海
Shanghai

汉口
Hangchow

成都
Chentu

重庆
Chungking

30

温州
Wenchow

长沙
Changsha

V
(1)

福州
Foochow   台北
Taipei

昆明
ming

V
(2)

南宁
Nanning   广州
Canton

VI

台南
Tainan

120

20   20

海口
Haikow

110

320   640   800 Km.

250   500 Mls

110

by the eastern margin of the Mongolian plateau, the Greater and Lesser Khinghan mountains, and the Changpaishan massif in Manchuria. This region contains some 60 per cent of China's total timber reserves. Significant, though generally inaccessible, areas of natural forests are to be found also in the provinces of Yunnan, Kwangtung (on the island of Hainan), Kiangsi, Fukien, Kweichow, and Szechuan; in the Tsinling mountains; and on the eastern edge of the Tibetan plateau. Over most of China, however, the primary forest vegetation is indicated only by groves surrounding the ubiquitous Buddhist temples and shrines.

ECONOMIC GEOGRAPHY AND RESOURCE DEVELOPMENT

It can be argued that forestry is of greater importance in present-day China than in any other country of the world. The validity of this argument rests on three features of her national economy: firstly, the extent to which agricultural productivity depends on water conservancy and, hence, on afforestation; secondly, the importance of timber resources in the development of communications and industry; and, thirdly, the existence of an acute shortage of forest products throughout most of China. The key to an understanding of why these features are of overriding importance lies in an appreciation of China's economic development since 1949.*

Agriculture

As might be expected in a country with a population of more than 700 million, the traditional basis of the economy is agriculture, and it is likely to remain so for a good many years. Agriculture does more than feed the population: it is a source of raw material for major textile industries; it provides many locally used products such as timber, tobacco, fish, soap, cooking oils, and handicrafts; and, most importantly, until recently farm products made up some 40 per cent (by value) of China's exports. Yet the total cultivated area amounts to only 11 per cent of the entire country. Because the climate enables more than one crop to be raised annually on much of this land, however, it is equivalent to perhaps 16 per cent of the land area. Agriculture is extremely intensive, supporting a population of 600/sq. km. of cultivated land (compared with figures of 110 in the United States and about 230 in Great Britain). About 10 per cent of the rest of the

---

* Since this section was written, some support for the evaluation of forestry as a limiting factor in the Chinese economy has been provided by a radio broadcast from Peking in January, 1965, which described timber production as being "the weak link in the national economy."

land surface is under forest (natural and artificial) and the remainder is sparse grazing land or barren, mountainous, and eroding country.

When the Communists achieved national control in 1949, their primary aim was to increase agricultural productivity, which, after almost forty years of civil disorder, war, and natural calamities had fallen to a low level. Attempts at currency stabilization and the revitalization of moribund industry, involving stringent economic and political regimentation, placed severe strains on the rural economy. Widespread floods in the latter half of 1949, the outbreak of the Korean War, and the prohibition in 1950 of imports of rice and wheat (reversing a trade flow of more than fifty years' standing) provided the incentive for collectivization of agriculture and the formulation of the first five-year plan in 1952. The initial pronouncements of the Communists emphasized intensive farming, land reclamation, and the mechanization of agriculture. There is something of a paradox here, and one that China is still far from solving. In order to increase agricultural output, mechanization (and, by implication, industrialization) is deemed essential; but in China's present condition (with many of her exports in the form of foodstuffs), increased agricultural output is a *sine qua non* of industrialization. Mao Tse-tung expressed this paradox in 1955 as follows:

> As everyone knows, the amount of marketable grain and industrial raw materials produced in our country today is very low, while the State's demands for these items grow year by year. Therein lies a sharp contradiction. If, in a period of roughly three five-year plans, we cannot fundamentally solve the problem of agricultural co-operation if we cannot jump from small-scale farming to large-scale farming with machines, which includes State-sponsored land reclamation carried out on a large scale by settlers using machinery, ... we shall fail to resolve the contradiction between the ever-increasing demand for marketable grain and industrial raw materials and the present generally poor yield of staple crops. In that case, our socialist industrialization will run into formidable difficulties; we shall not be able to complete socialist industrialization.

China's initial answer to the contradiction was to allocate a disproportionate amount of state investment to industry. During the first five-year plan (1953–57), 58 per cent of all state investment was earmarked for industry, heavy industry receiving much the greater part (85 per cent). Industrial output certainly rose (and continued to rise during the period of the second five-year plan) but the rise was not a smooth one. It became increasingly clear that the level of agricultural production simply could not sustain the targets for industrialization. Unexpected and widespread floods emphasized the need for a drastic tactical revision. A large budget deficit in 1956, a vastly increased rate of lending by the Bank of China (on the strength of previous budget surpluses), and an increase in the wage bill of U.S. $1,080,000,000 led to inflationary pressures that could only be relieved by retrenchment.

The campaign to this end was ushered in by the "hundred flowers" speech of Mao Tse-tung in February, 1957, when criticisms of the administration were invited and expressions of liberal political opinion encouraged ("Let a hundred flowers bloom and a hundred schools of thought contend"). A major demand made by the workers was for a reduction in unproductive staff at all levels of administration and was followed not only by a marked decrease in national expenditure and investment but also by a decentralization policy. Regulations on industrial control published in November, 1957, placed many of the enterprises controlled by the economic ministries under the aegis of provincial and local bodies, with profit-sharing in the ratio of 20 per cent to the local authority and 80 per cent to the central government. By the following year, some 80 per cent of former government enterprises had been handed over to local bodies; these authorities were empowered to raise capital by bond issues and to retain certain taxes and excess profits. These sweeping changes heralded the Great Leap Forward, the formation of the communes, and the startling proliferation of back-yard industries manufacturing everything from ball bearings to toilet paper.

Realization that industrial retrenchment was necessary was also reflected in the first specific plan for agriculture, issued in 1956. This twelve-year plan emphasized the need for higher yields per hectare of crops, livestock, and fish. The country was divided into three "output" zones according to grain yield potential and the 1967 targets indicate that the aim was to raise the yield per hectare by at least 100 per cent.

The first of these output zones lies to the north of the Yellow river and the Tsinling mountains and extends into the arid northwest. With a 60-cm. annual rainfall in the northeast, falling to only 10 cm. in the northwest, the growing season is limited to four to five months; in consequence, cultivated land forms a single-crop area for spring wheat, barley, millet, sorghum, and soya beans, with small areas of maize, oats, cotton, flax, sweet potatoes, tobacco, and fast-maturing paddy rice. On the mountains and plateaus of the north and northwest, extensive—but low-density—grazing lands support cattle, sheep, and horses. Historically, the area has always been one of marginal settlement. Except on the Manchurian plains—which feed industrial areas developed during the Japanese occupation—isolation from markets, political instability, and the uncertain, scanty rainfall have discouraged long-term agricultural developments. Soil erosion of the unstable loess plateaus and sand deserts is rife.

The second zone lies between the Yellow and the Hwai rivers, taking in the alluvial flats of the North China plain. With a 60-cm. to 75-cm. annual rainfall and a growing season of seven to eight months, this region forms China's biggest production area for cotton, winter wheat, peanuts, sesame seed, millet, maize, and tobacco. It is the zone made famous by Pearl Buck in her book *The Good Earth* and has long been known for floods, drought, famine, and banditry. Though limited to the three provinces of Shantung, Honan, and Kiangsu, it contains some 25 per cent of the total population.

South of the Hwai river and the Tsinling range, lies the third zone, the traditional area of rice and fish. With an annual rainfall in the cultivated areas of 200 cm. and a growing season varying from eight months in the north to twelve months in the south, subtropical and tropical crops thrive. Rice (double-cropped), wheat, cotton, beans, maize, jute, hemp, tobacco, tea, citrus fruits, mulberry, rubber, coconut, and sugar cane flourish and, in the Upper Yangtse valley lies the most fertile area in the world—the red basin of Szechuan—containing about sixty million people. It is the great "rice bowl" of China. Elsewhere in the south, however, soils tend to be acid, intensively leached, and deficient in nitrogen.

In all these zones, increased productivity per unit area and per man was called for; somewhat paradoxically, the plan also heralded a reduction in the cultivated area, with the realization that ambitious schemes for the reclamation of marginal land would not succeed. Even in 1956, it had been suggested that "our country will not in the near future . . . be in a position to carry out reclamation of waste land to any great extent, or rapidly to end flood and drought" (NCNA, Suppl. No. 248, 10/1/56). In 1957–58, the cultivated area of Shansi was reduced by one-third, and by a further third in 1958–59; half the cultivable area of Inner Mongolia was abandoned. Over-all, the cultivated area declined by four million hectares in 1958 and by a further million in 1959. Increased productivity was to be achieved by concentrating resources of capital and labor on areas known to be fertile— "higher output on a smaller quantity of land." Ma Yin-chu's eight-point charter for agriculture (deep ploughing, fertilizers, water conservation, seed improvement, close planting, protection from pathogens, improved management, and improved tools) was revived and adopted by Mao Tse-tung.

Justification for the partial abandonment of a land-reclamation policy is not hard to find in China; it lies in the marked increase in soil erosion triggered by indiscriminate cultivation of unstable soil. Of all countries in the world, China has had most reason historically to be aware of erosion hazards (see e.g. Sowerby, 1924; Cressey, 1955); yet many of the development projects of the early years of communist control were put into effect with an almost complete failure to appreciate the consequences.

By 1958, then, a significant shift in national economic policy was apparent: agricultural productivity was to be encouraged by all possible means and at the expense of heavy industry. The withdrawal of Russian technical assistance and financial aid (beginning in 1957) also doubtless influenced the pace of industrialization and brought into focus, all the more sharply, the need to develop agricultural output, since only by providing an exportable surplus of agricultural products could the Chinese pay for industrial equipment which they were now forced to purchase abroad.

The year of the Great Leap Forward (1958), while it undoubtedly lived up to its name, demonstrated the impracticability of combining agriculture and back-yard industry in the communes; and from 1959 on, the two sections of the economy were rigorously segregated. Major industrial areas were centered on a number of iron and steel "complexes" (including one at Paotow, in the heart of a sparsely settled pastoral region of Inner Mongolia), while some 24,000 communes (averaging 4,200 ha., 5,000 households, and 10,000 laborers) provided the agricultural base. Further decentralization of agricultural organization occurred in 1959, with the production brigade (averaging 250 households) forming the key unit.

It has long been recognized in China that agricultural productivity is inseparable from water regulation. Irrigation has been practiced since 2,000 B.C. and, with widespread cultivation of the relatively high-yielding paddy rice, terrace cultivation and similar dry-land farming practices are well established. Inevitably, therefore, attempts to increase production demanded increased irrigation works and properly co-ordinated water-conservation measures, particularly in the two northern output zones. China's rivers, however, do not flow peacefully; the major catchments are enormous and for the most part steep, barren, and located in areas of uncertain and maldistributed rainfall. The rivers flood easily, inundating the densely populated coastal plains. They are known the world over for the heavy silt loads they carry. In summer months the Yellow river, for example, carries up to 40 per cent solids by weight, and the King river as much as 50 per cent when in flood. The Yangtze river carries away more than 700 million cu. m. of soil annually. The task of creating storage reservoirs, building dams, stopbanks, new canals, and irrigation channels on the scale required was truly a Gargantuan one. Some measure of its success (and of the impetus given to water conservation from 1956 on) can be obtained from Chinese claims of increases in irrigated areas. From 1949 to 1955, the area is said to have increased by over two million ha. annually, from 1956 to 1959 by eleven million annually and from 1960 to 1962, by five million annually. The reduced rate reported from 1960 to 1962 was allegedly due to "incomplete statistics" and to concentration on large-capital, multipurpose projects. Changes in objective are also apparent. Thus, the principal projects during the period of the first five-year plan were designed to regulate river flow onto the North China plain, while, from 1958 to 1962, the main emphasis was on long-term development of the northwest. Projects included forty-six large dams on the upper reaches of the Yellow river, an 800-mile irrigation canal in eastern Kansu, major irrigation projects in the Tien mountains of Sinkiang, and the transfer of water from the headwaters of the Yangtze (on the eastern Tibetan plateau) to Kansu and Inner Mongolia. To be successful, these ambitious projects required extensive catchment-afforestation schemes and shelter belt establishment. There is abundant evidence that, by 1957, the Chinese had begun to appreciate the folly of attempting water-conservancy projects and land-reclamation schemes without proper regard for the revegetation of areas subject to virtually constant wind or water erosion.

The withdrawal of land from cultivation, already mentioned, was also accompanied by ambitious plans for protection forestry. Between 1956 and 1957, some 100 million ha. of "waste land and desert" were to be afforested. And this was to be only a start; the Minister of Forestry announced that ". . . to plant trees on 100 million ha. of land in twelve years is only a beginning. There will still be 70 million or 100 million, or even 200 million ha. of barren mountains for us to afforest." Following these pronouncements, the project for establishing the "great green wall"—a shelter belt covering 1.6 million ha. intended to serve as a protective barrier around the Gobi desert—was accelerated; a 600-km. belt skirting the Tengri desert was initiated; and, in 1958, there was a call for one-third of the entire cultivated area of China to be planted in trees. Recent communiqués continue to highlight shelter planting and attacks upon the "sand dragon." There can be no doubt that the Chinese now fully appreciate the dependence of agricultural development on water, the necessity, in water-conservation works, for catchment stability, and the value of plantation forestry in revegetation programs (these topics are discussed further in Chapter VI).

Industry

For present purposes, the industrial economy of China can be treated very briefly. Before 1949, significant industrial development was limited to the eastern seaboard and (under Japanese control) the central lowlands of Manchuria. With few exceptions, industrial centers were remote from their raw materials, which it was often cheaper to import than to supply from the hinterlands. When the Communists came to power, their first concern was to rehabilitate existing industrial centers and then, under the first five-year plan, to establish new centers in northern China based on mineral resources. Vigorous expansion occurred in Manchuria (utilizing known resources of coal, power, and iron); in north China at Taiyuan, Shihchingshan, and Paotow, based on coal and iron; and in the northwest (Sinkiang, Kansu, Shensi, and Tsinghai) to exploit nonferrous metals and oil resources. These developments (coupled with an effective ban on major food imports) demanded a vastly increased interchange of the products of industry and agriculture, and the stimulation of internal trade among the various regions of China.

Political considerations, also, undoubtedly conditioned the government's determination to promote interregional economic integration. One reason why previous regimes in China have lost effective national control is that local self-sufficiency, encouraged by poor communications, allowed the authority of local officials and war lords to become virtual independence. "The Communist Government have been anxious from the start to restore and to maintain the unity of the country. It was partly in order to obviate the fissiparous tendencies which had endangered previous regimes that they have made such efforts to ensure that every part of the country should be firmly linked with all others and thus merged, economically as well as politically, in a single integrated and organic unit" (Hughes and Luard, 1959). In this

connection, developments in the northwest take on a special significance, since Chinese control of that area has for many decades been
precarious, and the location there of a substantial force of nonindigenous Chinese has enabled both effective political control and
the discovery and development of natural resources.

The significance of forestry in China's industrial adolescence lies in
the overriding importance of communications development and, in
particular, of railways. With the main industrial potential in the
sparsely populated north and northwest, and with the area south of
the Yangtze best fitted climatically for agricultural production, present-
day China is experiencing a sweeping change in economic geography,
involving mass population shifts and mass transport of industrial and
agricultural products, which demands an extensive railway network.
(At China's present stage of development, lacking adequate motorized
transport, railway construction is of far greater importance than road-
building.) Of a total railway length of around 33,000 km., more than
50 per cent has been built since 1949. Much of it is through difficult
country in the west and northwest, in the latter case requiring protective afforestation along hundreds of kilometers.

The construction of a kilometer of single railway track requires 285
cu. m. of roundwood for manufacture of ties. In most parts of China
ties last only about five years (in the south, where termites abound,
they last only one or two years if untreated, and six or seven years
when surface treated with creosote or tung oil; less than half the ties
laid in 1961 were treated with a preservative). Concrete and other
timber substitutes have not proved satisfactory, with the result that
current replacements and construction of new track require some
2,500,000 cu. m. of timber annually. The greater part of this must be
supplied from the virgin forests of Manchuria, since only here is there
a softwood resource adequate to produce the size of log required. It
can plausibly be argued that railway construction in China is currently limited, not by a lack of iron and steel, as is often supposed
(see e.g. Watt, 1961), but by the availability of suitable timber for the
manufacture of ties. Recent government exhortations to use concrete
and steel as timber substitutes lend weight to this contention.

Another important consequence of China's vigorous attempts to in-
dustrialize is her increased requirement for mining timber. Production of coal and ferrous ore is probably around 220 million tons per
annum, requiring some 5,500,000 cu. m. of timber in pit props alone.
The total mining-timber requirement, therefore, is of the order of 8
million cu. m. (roundwood equivalent). It can, however, be cut from

smaller logs than those demanded for railway ties and the use of substitute materials (steel or concrete-filled bamboo) is possible.

The same argument applies to timber for construction purposes which, although greater in total requirement than railway and mining timbers together (currently, about 15 million cu. m. of roundwood annually), is of less significance in long-term industrialization, since in this case a greater range of substitutes (concrete, steel, bamboo, composite wood products, and strawboard) is available, and the possibility of eventual local supply from new plantations is greater.

Of the other two major end uses for forest produce in China—fuelwood and paper—little need be said. The requirement for the first is difficult to estimate (few statistics are available) but is probably at least 100 million cu. m. annually; its influence on industrial development is impossible to gauge. In all probability, however, it will decrease rather than increase. The requirement for paper and paper products, on the other hand, is likely to increase rapidly and could exercise considerable influence. China's heroic and much-publicized efforts in several fields of education (see e.g. Snow, 1963), her massive propaganda campaigns, both within and outside China, and her alarming population increase (2 per cent a year) imply a demand for paper that will rise exponentially. The withdrawal of Russian technical assistance will intensify the need for technological (and, probably, ideological) education, and add even more to the requirement. As with industrial wood, however, plantations established during the last ten years or so will eventually contribute to the pulpwood resource (especially in southern China).

In all fields, the existing demand for forest produce highlights the present maldistribution of China's timber resources and re-emphasizes her dependence on the improvement of communications.

Timber Resources

The considerations outlined above suggest that the limiting factor in China's timber economy as it affects industrialization is the production and rational utilization of large logs. There is, however, a patent dearth of all kinds of forest products in China which undoubtedly has far-reaching effects on almost every aspect of the economy. In Appendix I, available data relating to the production and consumption of forest products in China, and future requirements, are analyzed in some detail.

Timber resources in China amount to more than 7 billion cu. m. (all species)—most of it far removed from consumption centers; 60 per cent is in Manchuria and Inner Mongolia. Perhaps 75 per cent of the total resource will eventually prove to be accessible. The Chinese claim an average annual requirement over the period 1960–90 of 150 million cu. m. and that their afforestation program is geared to self-sufficiency by the time the existing resource runs out (about 1990). In recent years, however, the annual cut (which rose from 28 million cu. m. in 1957 to 40 million cu. m. in 1959) has dropped to about 30 million cu. m. (as against 40 million planned in 1962). This reduction is undoubtedly associated with a slackening in the rate of industrialization (aggravated by maldistribution of the timber resources), and with the realization that afforestation programs have in large measure failed and cannot be relied upon to supplement production from the natural forests as early as was hoped. It has been accompanied by far-reaching legislation designed to conserve timber and by exhortations to use substitute materials wherever possible. The result is that, in a country with a net population increase of 2 per cent per annum (or, expressed more graphically, of 26.6 bodies per minute), the annual consumption of forest products is less than 0.05 cu. m. per capita. This compares with a figure of 1.88 for the United States. Paper and paperboard consumption in China amounts to 3 kg. per capita compared with 196 kg. in the United States. The acuteness of this shortage is apparent everywhere in China. Bamboo, bagasse, straw, and grass are used in building construction and in paper manufacture (only 20 per cent of the raw material for paper production is wood pulp); jointed transmission poles are a regular feature of the landscape; every kind of vegetable matter is used for fuel (millions of newly planted trees are uprooted for firewood almost before they have had a chance to strike); and virtually every established plantation tree is mutilated by reckless pruning for the same purpose. Perhaps the most horrific illustration is provided by the fact that, in some areas, used toilet paper is collected and returned to the mill for repulping!

Even in regions of extensive virgin forest, timber is not wasted. Logging operations provide an object lesson in clean harvesting and close utilization. After clear felling and saw-log extraction, branch wood down to a 3-cm. diameter is harvested for mining timber, pulpwood, handicrafts, charcoal, and, in the case of hardwoods, manufacture into blocks for tractor fuel; finally, twigs and foliage are collected and dried for fuel and animal fodder.

During the past fifteen years, China has attempted to bring about social, agrarian, and industrial revolutions at one and the same time; and, however suspect many of her claims may be, there can be no doubt that her rulers have cause to be well satisfied with progress to date. A backward economy, with little capitalization and poor in both agricultural and industrial techniques, has been considerably transformed. Nevertheless, in comparison with the modern industrial powers, China is still a backward and relatively undeveloped nation. The extent to which her economy can continue to expand will depend to a great extent on her ability to increase agricultural production, to accelerate industrialization, and to contain and capitalize on her enormous population; the importance of protection and production forestry in these endeavors may well be crucial.

CHAPTER II.

THE NATURAL VEGETATION, SOILS, AND LAND USE

THE CLASSIFICATION of vegetation types outlined in this chapter follows that presented by Hou *et al.* (1956). In detailing specific composition of forest communities, however, it relies heavily on Wang (1961) and, where appropriate, on personal observation in China.

For convenience, the classifications of Hou *et al.* and Wang are presented below in Table 2; their affinities can readily be appreciated.

Table 2. Phytogeographical Regions of China

Hou, et al., 1956	Wang, 1961
The Forests of the East	**Montane-Boreal Coniferous Forests**
1. The northern coniferous forests	1. Montane spruce-fir forests
2. The mixed coniferous and deciduous broadleaved forests	2. Montane larch forests
3. The deciduous broadleaved forests	**Deciduous Broadleaved Forests**
	3. Mixed Northern hardwoods— birch
4. The mixed deciduous and evergreen broadleaved forests	4. Mixed Northern hardwoods— maple, lime, and birch
5. The evergreen broadleaved forests	5. Deciduous oak forests
6. The tropical monsoon rain forests	6. Mixed mesophytic forests
	Evergreen Broadleaved Forests
The Steppes and Deserts of the Northwest and Northeast	7. Evergreen sclerophyllous broadleaved forests
7. The forest steppes	8. Evergreen broadleaved forests with secondary *Pinus massoniana*
8. The steppes	
9. The desert and semidesert	9. Evergreen broadleaved forests with secondary *Pinus yunnanensis*
Mountains and Plateaus of the West and Southwest	10. Rain forests
	11. Littoral forests
10. The NW. Mountains	12. Grassland
11. The E. Tibetan mountains and plateaus	13. Desert vegetation
	14. Saline vegetation
12. The Tibetan plateau	15. Tundra and alpine vegetation

THE FORESTS OF THE EAST

In general terms, that part of China which lies east of an imaginary line drawn between Tengchung (Yunnan), Peking, and Hailar (Heilungkiang)—but excluding the Manchurian plains—has a climax vegetation which is essentially high forest. Natural forest extends in an unbroken sequence of communities from tropical monsoon rain forest in the south to montane coniferous forest in the north.

The Northern Coniferous Forest

Located in the extreme north of Manchuria, this region includes the northern part of Ta Hingan Ling (Greater Khingan mountains)—the long and narrow ranges of gneiss and granite which form the uplifted eastern margin of the Mongolian plateau. Administratively, the area covers some 200,000 sq. km. and embraces parts of Heilungkiang province, the Inner Mongolian autonomous region, and the autonomous districts of Orochon and Evenki.

In elevation, the northern coniferous forest ranges from 450 m. to 1,100 m., with peaks reaching 1,400 m. It is very cold, with a mean annual temperature from −1.2°C. to −3.2°C. and an extreme minimum of −50.1°C. January temperatures are around −25°C. and those for July about 18°C., giving a mean annual range of 43°C. Precipitation varies from 35 cm. to 60 cm. at the higher altitudes. As might be expected, the soils are podsolic, the degree of podsolization varying with the relief.

The major tree species in the region are *Larix dahurica* (syn. *L. gmelini* and *L. kamtchatica*) and *Pinus sylvestris*, with *Picea obovata, P. microsperma, Pinus pumila,* and *Juniperus dahurica* locally dominant. Secondary species include *Betula platyphylla, B. dahurica,* and *Populus davidiana,* while, in the understory, *Alnus mandshurica, Vaccinium vitis-idaea, V. uliginosum, Ledum palustre, Rhododendron dahuricum,* and *Linnaea borealis* are frequent. The herbs of the forest floor include several *Pyrola* species, *Trientalis europaea, Mitella nuda,* and *Goodyera repens.* This vegetation type is strongly reminiscent of the northern coniferous forests of Europe and North America, with many common or closely related species. It is distinguished, particularly at the lower elevations, by the large size of the trees and their stocking density.

The region is almost entirely forest, with the tree line at about 1,100 m. Occasional meadows, characterized by such species as *Carex schmidtii, Calamagrostis hirsuta, Sanguisorba parviflora, Eriophorum vaginatum, Iris sibirica, Lilium dahuricum, L. pulchellum, Veratrum dahuricum, Geranium,* and *Pedicularis* spp., and wet swamps of *Populus suaveolens, Betula fruticosa, Chosenia macrolepis, Salix rorida, S. brachypoda, S. sibirica,* and *S. myrtilloides.* etc., support a scattered indigenous population of prospectors and hunters, with small groups of Orochons in the autonomous districts, who live by raising reindeer and cultivating crops of potatoes and barley. Climatically, the area has virtually no potential for agricultural development, but it forms an extensive reservoir of high-quality timber with few exploitation problems other than lack of communications and long hauls to markets.

The Mixed Coniferous and Deciduous Broadleaved Forest

This type forms a transition between the coniferous forest in the north of Manchuria and the deciduous broadleaved forest in the south. It covers much of the Siao Hingan Ling (Lesser Khingan mountains), the Changkwansai mountains, and the Changpaishan massif north of Korea. The latter consists of several parallel ridges, generally between 450 m. and 1,100 m., but with peaks rising to almost 2,750 m. In the Siao Hingan Ling, the topography is rolling and generally below 600 m. The river valleys and alluvial flood plains of the Sungari and the Ussuri rivers (tributaries of the Amur) form an extensive area of low-lying land to the east. Some 300,000 sq. km. in area, the type covers parts of Heilungkiang and Kirin provinces and the Korean autonomous districts of Yen-pien and Ch'ang-pai.

The climate is both milder and moister than that of the far north. Annual precipitation ranges from 50 cm. to 75 cm. in the Siao Hingan Ling to 100 cm. in the eastern plains. Below 600 m., the mean annual temperature is from 0.5°C. to 5.5°C., with mean temperatures in January from −16°C. to −25°C. and in July from 20°C. to 24°C. The extreme winter minimum ranges from −32°C. to −45°C. but the length of the growing season (average number of frost-free days) is more than 125 days.

The soils include moderately leached podsols derived from pre-Cambrian metamorphic rocks in the mountains, brown forest soils of low base-status on the lower slopes, and deeper and richer alluvial soils in the plains, with local areas of gleyed peat. The pattern again resembles that in Europe and North America, often showing local catenas with sharply differentiated topographic components. The author examined such a sequence in an area northeast of Tailing in

Heilungkiang province and was struck by the similarity to that in, for example, parts of Upper Deeside in Scotland. Over a distance of perhaps 200 m., and an altitude range of 50 m., the soil type changed from a shallow podsol at the top of the slope to a deep brown forest soil half way down, and then to a strongly gleyed alluvium in an area of impeded drainage at the bottom.

Turning to vegetation, the relative richness of the flora distinguishes it from similar European forest types. At higher elevations, *Pinus koraiensis* is the characteristic species, but *Abies nephrolepis, Picea jezoensis, P. koyamai* var. *koraiensis, Larix olgensis,* and *Abies holophylla* are frequent among the conifers. The broadleaved species include *Betula ermani, B. platyphylla, B. costata, Sorbus pohuashanensis, Acer tegmentosum, A. mono, A. pseudo-sieboldianum, Tilia amurensis, Fraxinus mandshurica, Syringa amurensis, Phellodendron amurense, Juglans mandshurica, Populus koreana, P. ussuriensis,* and *Maackia amurensis.* Shrub layers are characterized by *Sorbaria sorbifolia, Spiraea salicifolia, Corylus mandshurica, Crataegus maximowiczii, Aralia mandshurica, Acanthopanax senticosus, Prunus maximowiczii, Viburnum* spp., *Ribes* spp., *Lonicera* spp., *Vitis amurensis, Schizandra chinensis, Actinidia kolomicta,* and *Celastrus flagellaris.*

On the brown forest soils at lower elevation, the dominant *Pinus koraiensis* is supplemented by *P. densiflora* and *Abies holophylla,* with *Acer, Populus,* and *Betula* spp., *Corylus heterophylla, Lespedeza bicolor, Quercus mongolica,* and *Q. liaotungensis* common. The broadleaved trees predominate on the well-drained alluvial soils, while, in areas of impeded drainage and a fluctuating water table, the sedges *Carex rhynchophysa* and *C. meyeriana, Calamagrostis* spp., *Iris ensata, Trollius ledebourii,* and *Pogonia japonica* assume dominance; *Larix olgensis* is frequent.

To a greater extent than in the coniferous forest region (where the limiting factors are climatic), vegetation and soil patterns determine cultural practices in this zone. Production forestry is by far the most important land use since, in terms of quantity, quality, and accessibility, China's richest timber resources are located here. As long ago as 1913, Sowerby visited Manchuria and was impressed by the seemingly endless tree cover (Sowerby, 1922–23) and, in spite of later settlement and occupation by the Japanese, vast forests remain which provide some 30 per cent of China's present day timber requirements. Settlement and agricultural development have been mainly confined to the river valleys and plains, where crops of potatoes, soybeans, spring wheat, maize, barley, kaoliang, millet, rice, and cabbage are raised.

The growing season is also adequate for cucurbits such as pumpkin, watermelon, and cucumbers. In addition, some plantation forestry (using, mainly, *Pinus koraiensis, P. sylvestris* var. *mongolica,* and *Larix dahurica*) has recently been started.

The Deciduous Broadleaved Forest

This zone skirts the southwestern end of the Manchurian plain to take in the peninsulas of Shantung and Liaoning, the North China plain, the northern slopes of the Tsingling mountains and the western half of the Shansi highlands. It covers almost 1 million sq. km. in the provinces of Kirin, Liaoning, Hopeh, Shansi, Shantung, Kiangsu, Anwhei, Honan, and Shensi, including the autonomous districts of Fou-hsin, Ko-la-Chin, and Peking. The plains are low-lying (below 150 m.) but the Shansi highlands and the Tsinling mountains range generally between 450 m. and 2,500 m., with ridges and peaks over 4,000 m. Local areas rising to 900 m. are also found in Shantung and Liaoning.

The climate is uniformly subcontinental, with hot, wet summers and cold, dry winters, and is noted for the big fluctuations from year to year in amount of precipitation. In general, however, the rainfall is between 50 cm. and 85 cm., falling over periods of about 120 days in the north and 65 days in the south. The mean annual temperature ranges from 7°C. in the north to 16°C. in the south, with extreme minima varying from −33°C. to −15°C. The January mean is from −13°C. to 0°C. and the July mean from 22° to 29°C. The length of the frost-free season varies from 150 days in the north to 240 days in the south. This mildness, together with dry-farming practices, enables double-cropping in many southeastern parts of the region.

Not surprisingly, parent materials and soils show considerable variation through the area. The soil-forming materials on the intensively cultivated plains are ancient alluvial deposits sometimes overlain with loess and giving rise to the so-called Korichnevie soils; they are alkaline or neutral. Calcareous Korichnevie soils (often leached) are also found on the limestone mountains and loess-covered hills of Shansi. The granite and gneiss hills of Shantung and Liaoning, on the other hand, form acid brown forest soils sometimes slightly podsolized. Solonchaks containing easily soluble chlorides occur along the eastern seaboard and, in local inland depressions, soils containing mixed chlorides and sulphates affect the vegetation.

The primary vegetation on the brown forest soils comprises several species of *Quercus, Ulmus,* and *Acer* (including *Quercus liaotungensis, Q. dentata, Q. variabilis, Q. aliena, Q. acutissima,* and *Acer truncatum), Tilia amurensis, Pterocarya stenoptera, Lindera obtusiloba, Sorbus alnifolia,* and *Fraxinus rhynchophylla.* The shrubs include *Callicarpa japonica, Clerodendron trichotomum, Grewia biloba* var. *parviflora, Styrax obassia, Celastrus orbiculatus, Rhododendron micranthum,* and *Lespedeza bicolor.* Destruction of the forest may give rise to dense thicket growth of *Corylus heterophylla, Crataegus pinnatifida, Zizyphus sativa* var. *spinosa, Vitex chinensis, Prunus humilis, Pyrus betulaefolia, Symplocos paniculata,* and *Periploca sepium.* On dry sites, *Pinus tabulaeformis* is common, together with *Biota orientalis* and *Pinus densiflora.* According to Wang (1961), the first two of these conifers may represent climax species and not simply seral stages.

The Korichnevie soils of the plains are almost entirely cultivated and the specific composition of the natural vegetation is somewhat conjectural. Remnants of forest occur on surrounding hilly country and in protected reserves around villages and temples. These have been studied intensively by Yang (1937), who recognized four types of oak forest, two birch associations, and a *Tilia-Betula* type. Following Wang (1961), the components of the oak forests are listed in Table 3, together with those of the higher elevation *Tilia-Betula* and *Pinus tabulaeformis* types. The Betula types (comprising *Betula fruticosa, B. japonica* var. *mandshurica, B. alba* var. *chinensis,* and *B. chinensis,* with admixtures of *Populus tremula* var. *davidiana, Sorbus, Prunus,* and *Salix* species) are found at higher altitudes still. The original cover of the North China plain itself may have been grassland, wooded steppe, or forest. Wang (1961) concludes that it was forest, on the grounds that the existing gallery forest of *Salix matsudana, S. babylonica, Populus simonii, P. suaveolens,* and *P. tomentosa* is not confined to watercourses and that, furthermore, many species now growing in plantations or in seminatural stands have been present on the plain since the third century A.D. Because the status of these species may be important in evaluating the effectiveness of China's artificial protection forests they are listed in Table 4 (from Wang, 1961).

The limestones of the high mountains and the loess-covered hills are also very rich in woody species. *Quercus liaotungensis, Q. variabilis, Tilia mongolica, Fraxinus chinensis, Acer truncatum,* and *Biota orientalis* of the deciduous oak forests (see Table 3) are enriched with *inter alia, Quercus acutissima, Prunus armeniaca, Oxytropis davidiana, Carpinus turczaninowii, Acer pictum* var. *parviflorum, Cotinus coggy-*

Table 3. Components of the Deciduous Oak Forests

Plant Name	Forest Type and Altitudinal Distribution (meters)					
	1 (700 m.)	2 (500 m.)	3 (400– 1,000 m.)	4 (700– 1,000 m.)	5 (1,100– 1,400 m.)	6 (1,400 m.)
Quercus aliena	1**		1 r			
Q. dentata	1 f		1**			
Q. variabilis		1**				
Q. liaotungensis				1**	1 f	11 f
Pinus tabulaeformis						1**
Fraxinus chinensis	1**	1 r	1 o	1*		
Biota orientalis		1 r				
Cornus walteri	1 r					
Evodia danielii	1 f					
Populus tremula var. *davidiana*				1 o	1 f	1 f
Ulmus macrocarpa			1 r	1 r	1 o	
Betula fruticosa				1 f		
B. dahurica					11 o	
B. japonica var. *mandshurica*				11 r	1 f	
B. chinensis				11 r		
Carpinus turczaninowii	11**	11 r	1 r			
Acer mono	11 f			11 f	11 r	11 f
A. truncatum		11 r				
Tilia mandshurica	11 o			11 f	1*	
T. mongolica	11 o			11 f	1*	11 o
Malus baccata				11 r		
Prunus sibirica				11 o		
Salix phyllicifolia					11 f	
Sorbus pohuashanensis					11 r	
S. alnifolia	11 o					
Pistacia chinensis		1 r				
Celtis bungeana	11 r					
C. koraiensis	11 r					
Chionanthus retusa	11 r					
Hovenia dulcis	11 o					
Picrasma quassioides	11 r					
Pyrus ussuriensis	11 r					
Ulmus japonica	11 r					

Source: Wang, 1961.
1, *Quercus aliena-Fraxinus chinensis*; 2, *Q. variabilis*; 3, *Q. dentata*; 4, *Q. liaotungensis-Fraxinus chinensis*; 5, *Tilia-Betula*; 6, *Pinus tabulaeformis*.
1, trees of the crown layer; 11, second tree layer; **dominant; *abundant; f, frequent; o, occasional; r, rare.

gria var. *cinerea, Pinus bungeana, P. tabulaeformis, Juglans regia,* and *Crataegus pinnatifida.* Calcicolous shrubs are also found, including *Gleditschia heterophylla, Wikstroemia chamaedaphne, Indigofera bungeana, Prinsepia uniflora, Periploca sepium, Lycium halimifolium, Ulmus pumila, Lespedeza floribunda, L. dahurica,* and *Vitex chinensis.*

The coastal vegetation is strongly influenced by the sea. In the littoral zone, *Carex kobomugi, Calystegia soldanella, Ixeris repens,*

Table 4. Species Currently Growing on the North China Plain

Ailanthus altissima	Pinus tabulaeformis
Albizzia julibrissin	Pistacia chinensis
Broussonetia papyrifera	Populus simonii
Castanea mollissima	P. suaveolens
Catalpa bungei	P. tomentosa
Cedrela sinensis	Pterocarya stenoptera
Celtis bungeana	Pyrus betulaefolia
C. koraiensis	Quercus mongolica
Diospyros lotus	Q. serrata
Fraxinus chinensis	Q. variabilis
Gleditschia heterophylla	Salix babylonica
G. sinensis	S. cheilophila
Hemiptelea davidii	S. matsudana
Hovenia dulcis	Sophora japonica
Juglans regia	Ulmus japonica
Juniperus chinensis	U. parvifolia
Koelreuteria paniculata	U. pumila
Morus mongolica	Zelkova sinica
Paulownia tomentosa	Zizyphus vulgaris
Picrasma quassioides	Biota orientalis

Source: Wang, 1961.

Phellopterus littoralis, and Lathyrus maritima are examples of halophytic psammophytes. On the heavier Solonchaks, Suaeda ussuriensis is commonly found in pure communities. Statice bicolor, Artemisia scoparia, Scorzonera mongolica var. putiatae, Puccinellia distans, Tamarix juniperina, Chenopodium glaucum, Atriplex littoralis, Aster tripolium, Polygonum sibiricum, and Suaeda glauca may also be found. In the inland depressions, where the Solonchaks contain sulphates as well as chlorides, the common halophytes include Triglochin palustre, Crypsis aculeata, Halerpestes sarmentosa, Atriplex sibiricum, and Statice aurea.

Most of the accessible forest in the deciduous broadleaved region has been logged and the present potential for timber production is not high. There is scope for plantation forestry in the foothills of the mountains, however, and it is probable that this form of land use will become increasingly important in the future. On the plains, cereal and mixed crops are important—wheat, potatoes, maize, cotton, millet, and kaoliang, with some barley, flax, hemp, beans, soya beans, sweet potatoes, peanuts, etc. on the smaller farm units. In the southeast, with an annual rainfall of 62 cm. to 85 cm. and a growing season of seven to eight months, the provinces of Shantung, Honan, and Kiangsu form China's biggest production area for cotton, winter wheat, peanuts, sesame, millet, maize, and tobacco. This area has a long history of drought and flood, but, like the rest of the plains region, it has been greatly transformed by water-conservancy projects along the Yellow river and in the surrounding highlands. Much of China's agricultural export of soya beans, peanuts, and sesame seeds is produced here and shipped from the coastal ports. There is still an obvious need for protection afforestation in conjunction with water conservancy schemes.

There is also considerable scope for the development of farm forestry and shelter planting on the plains. In fact, Lowdermilk (1932) found "extensive farm woodlots of *Populus simonii* . . . cultivated and irrigated for construction material on farmland" and, in Honan, noted that "forest management is worked out to greater detail in this region than the writer found at any time in Germany." He was impressed by the fact that the North China plain was self-supporting in timber and, also, produced poplar logs for match manufacture elsewhere. This picture has changed considerably during the past thirty years but, at the present time, China has an ambitious reforestation program for the region.

The Mixed Deciduous and Evergreen Broadleaved Forest

This region is a transition between the deciduous and the evergreen broadleaved forest zones and forms a belt of 300,000 sq. km. along the Han Chiang river in the west (a tributary of the Yangtze) and the lower reaches of the Yangtze in the east. It runs through parts of Shensi, Szechuan, Hupeh, Hunan, Kiangsi, Anwhei, Kiangsu, and Chekiang provinces. The western part is very rugged and ranges from 200 m. to 3,500 m.; the eastern region comprises an alluvial plain with hills seldom rising above 1,300 m.

The climate is milder and more humid than further north, with mean annual temperatures from 15°C. to 17°C., and a mean annual range of 23°C. to 27°C. Mean temperatures for January range from 2°C. to 5°C. and, for July, from 26°C. to 30°C. The extreme minimum, however, may be as low as −14°C. The annual rainfall varies from 120 cm. to 200 cm., some 10 per cent of it falling during winter. The average frost-free season is from 230 to 280 days.

Soils are also to some extent transitional. In the hill country to the west, between the Tsinling and Tapa ranges, brown forest soils of low-base status have developed from the acid parent materials, while yellow podzolic soils are found in the mountain foothills and on the hills of the lower Yangtze plains. Over calcareous rocks, the resultant soils are neutral yellow-Korichnevie types. Areas of alluvial soils border the lower reaches of the rivers.

Wang (1961) emphasizes two characteristics of the mixed mesophytic forest formation of this region. Firstly, it is composed of many species, representing a large number of plant families which are not closely related. Secondly, no species or group of species is predominant and, in this respect the forest differs from all other deciduous forest types, resembling, rather, the tropical rain forest of the extreme south of China. The northern boundary of the region coincides with the northern distribution boundary of many evergreen species, including members of the *Rutaceae, Theaceae, Ericaceae, Lauraceae, Fagaceae,* and *Euphorbiaceae*. Together with *Pinus massoniana, Cunninghamia lanceolata, Cryptomeria japonica, Cupressus funebris,* and *Dicranopteris linearis,* they show the close affinity of the region with the evergreen broadleaved types.

The richness of the forest flora is illustrated by the fact that within the canopy more than fifty broadleaved and twelve coniferous genera are represented, only a few of which are localized or rare. Of those known in Europe and North America there are, in this region, over fifty species of *Acer,* nine of *Tilia,* eleven of *Carpinus,* ten of *Fraxinus,* eight of *Ulmus* and thirty-two of *Sorbus*.

Wang (1961) points out that many genera of the deciduous broadleaved forest type are found as small trees in the understory of the zone presently under consideration. He lists the following:

Acer	Gleditschia	Pistacia
Aesculus	Hovenia	Populus
Albizzia	Juglans	Prunus
Alnus	Kalopanax	Pterocarya
Betula	Maackia	Pyrus
Carpinus	Magnolia	Quercus
Castanea	Malus	Salix
Celtis	Morus	Sorbus
Diospyros	Ostrya	Tilia
Evodia	Paulownia	Zelkova
Fraxinus	Phellodendron	

In addition, the following broadleaved genera are found:

Alniphyllum	Cladrastis	Eucommia
Aphananthe	Daphniphyllum	Euptelea
Camptotheca	Ehretia	Fagus
Carya	Elaeocarpus	Firmiana
Cercidiphyllum	Emmenopterya	Gymnocladus

Halesia	Litsea	Pterostyrax
Hamamelis	Mallotus	Rhus
Idesia	Meliosma	Sassafras
Liquidambar	Nyssa	Styrax
Liriodendron	Platycarya	Tetracentron

The twelve coniferous genera of the region are:

Cephalotaxus	Juniperus	Pseudotsuga
Cryptomeria	Nothotaxus	Taxus
Cunninghamia	Pinus	Torreya
Cupressus	Pseudolarix	Tsuga

Several coniferous species are of more than passing botanical interest, including the monotypic *Pseudolasia*, the rare *Larix leptolepis* var. *louchanensis*, and the relict *Ginkgo*, *Metasequoia*, and *Taiwania*. The complexity of the region is indicated by the fact that in spite of relatively intensive botanical exploration in western parts (David, 1872–74; Franchet, 1883–88; Bretschneider, 1898; Potanin, 1899; Wilson, 1913; see also Cox, 1945), two of these conifers (*Metasequoia* and *Taiwania*) are recent discoveries. Indigenous conifers which are being cultivated include *Cryptomeria japonica*, *Torreya grandis*, *Cunninghamia lanceolata*, and *Cupressus funebris*. Of these, the third is the most important timber-producing species of the central and southern provinces of China.

The mixed deciduous and evergreen broadleaved forest type is characterized by understories, also very rich in species. Chen (1936) distinguishes five strata, including many climbers and epiphytes. The bamboos, *Phyllostachys* and *Arundinaria* spp., are important constituents, now widely cultivated.

The existing vegetation, as in most accessible parts of China, has over a long period been modified by man. The alluvial plains and the yellow-Korichnevie soils of the lower Yangtze are intensively cultivated and most of the natural vegetation has disappeared. Densely populated, they form part of the traditional "rice bowl" of China. In addition to rice (double-cropped) are grown barley, wheat, cotton, maize, hemp, sweet potatoes, tobacco, tea, citrus, mulberries, and bamboos. Only the protected areas around the secluded temples in the hills give an indication of the natural vegetation. On limestone, this includes the calcicoles, *Zelkova schneideriana*, and *Pteroceltis tatarinowii*, and such species as *Platycarya strobilacea, Dalbergia hupeana, Pistacia chinensis, Styrax japonica, Celtis sinensis, Quercus acutissima, Q. variabilis, Ulmus parvifolia, Sophora japonica, Gledit-*

schia sinensis, and *Zizyphus sativa.* On the yellow-podsolic soils of the Tsinling and Tapa foothills, forests of *Pinus massoniana* and *Cunninghamia lanceolata* are common; also frequent are the broad-leaved species *Cinnamomum septentrionale, C. camphora, Photinia serrulata, Lindera glauca, Phyllostachys edulis, Thea sinensis, Myrica rubra, Aleurites montana,* and *Liquidambar formosana.* Brown forest soils of the western part of the area now support *inter alia, Pinus armandi, P. tabulaeformis* var. *henryi, P. bungeana, Quercus aliena* var. *acutiserrata, Q. liaotungensis, Q. variabilis,* etc. This western part of the zone has a potential for timber production, once the problems of access have been overcome; meanwhile, there is an almost unlimited choice of species for plantation forestry on the easier country.

The Evergreen Broadleaved Forest

This forest formation is among the most important of eastern Asia, covering as it does, large areas of China, Vietnam, Laos, Thailand, Burma, and Japan. In China it extends in a broad belt some 1,750,000 sq. km. in area across the southern provinces and includes parts of Chekiang, Fukien, Anwhei, Kiangsi, Kwangtung, Hupeh, Hunan, Kweichow, Szechuan, Yunnan, and Chamdo provinces, the Kwangsi Chuang autonomous region, and most of the autonomous districts within these provinces.

It is convenient to subdivide the formation into eastern and western subregions since, climatically and edaphically, they are somewhat different. Floristically they are very similar at the generic level and have many common species; in some genera, however, the species differ. Hou *et al.* (1956) list the following examples:

The Eastern Subregion	*The Western Subregion*
Myrica rubra	*Myrica nana*
Castanopsis hystrix	*Castanopsis concolor*
Machilus pingii	*Machilus yunnanensis*
Rhododendron simsii	*Rhododendron microphytum*
Cyclobalanopsis glauca	*Cyclobalanopsis glaucoides*
Schima superba	*Schima wallichii*
Keteleeria davidiana	*Keteleeria evelyniana*
Pinus massoniana	*Pinus yunnanensis*
Cupressus funebris	*Cupressus duclouxiana*
Cryptomeria japonica	*Cryptomeria kawai*

Eastern Evergreen Broadleaved Forest. This subregion includes the great Red Basin of Szechuan—one of the most fertile areas in the world—the highlands of Kweichow, the South Yangtze hills, the southeastern coast, and the highlands of Kwangtung and Taiwan. The Red Basin fluctuates between 200 m. and 1,000 m. in elevation and is surrounded by mountains of over 5,000 m. The Kweichow highlands range from 600 m. to 3,000 m. and are much dissected by tributaries of the Yangtze and Hsi rivers but, there are level areas at about 800 m. to 1,000 m. To the south and southeast, the country is rolling and generally below 700 m. in altitude, but with coastal hills rising to over 1,000 m.

The climate is very favorable for plant growth, with a mean annual rainfall of 120 cm. to 220 cm., well distributed. Mean annual temperatures range from 15° to 21°C. with the coldest month between 3°C. and 6°C. and the warmest, 21°C. to 31°C. The extreme minimum seldom goes below −7°C. and at least ten months of the year average more than 10°C.

The hills and mountains are mainly acid sandstones, shales, or granite, giving rise to yellow podsolic soils merging into red podsolic soils ("red earths") in the south and east. In the Red Basin and the Kweichow highlands, extensive areas of calcareous parent materials occur, forming Rendzinas or alkaline purple soils.

The type genera of the eastern evergreen—broadleaved forests are the cupuliferous *Quercus, Castanopsis,* and *Pasania;* more than 150 species have been recorded in this belt and, including those of Vietnam, Thailand, and Burma, there are well over 250 species (Wang, 1961). The evergreen oaks occur in mixture with members of the *Theaceae (Schima, Hartia,* etc.), *Lauraceae (Machilus, Phoebe, Beilschmiedia, Cinnamomum,* etc.), *Magnoliaceae (Magnolia, Manglietia, Illicium, Michelia), Hamamelidaceae (Altingia, Bucklandia, Liquidambar)* and others. Although dominated by a few genera, the forests are very rich in species (more so, in fact, than the mixed deciduous and evergreen broadleaved type); nearly 1,000 species have been reported as associates of the community, while the total flora of the region reaches several thousands, including members of the following coniferous genera (Wang, 1961):

Amentotaxus	*Juniperus*	*Pseudotsuga*
Cephalotaxus	*Keteleeria*	*Taxus*
Cryptomeria	*Pinus*	*Torreya*
Cunninghamia	*Podocarpus*	*Tsuga*
Cupressus	*Pseudolarix*	*Cathaya*
Fokienia		

The last of these (*Cathaya*) is a conifer genus only recently described (Chun and Kuang, 1958). Coniferous species of economic importance associated with the eastern evergreen—broadleaved forest include *Pinus massoniana, Cunninghamia lanceolata, Pinus kwangtungensis, Podocarpus javanica, P. neriifolia, Fokienia hodginsii, Taxus chinensis, Cephalotaxus fortunei, Cryptomeria japonica, Keteleeria fortunei, Tsuga longibracteata,* etc.

Many deciduous species also occur, but there is no marked stratification in the forests. In open stands, and in secondary mixed pine and oak stands, xerophytic trees and shrubs (e.g. *Engelhardtia, Albizzia, Phyllanthus,* etc.) are common over a ground cover of grasses. In the dense sclerophyllous forests, there is no obvious understory, though lianes and epiphytes are frequent. Typical of the subsidiary vegetation in the lower altitude forests of southern Hunan, are *Rhododendron, Litsea, Ilex, Photinia, Pittosporum, Lindera, Sapium, Hydrangea, Actinidia,* and the bamboo *Phyllostachys* (see Wang, 1961).

As in the more northern regions, much of the natural forest of this area has been cleared for crop cultivation, but secondary forest (often maintained by uncontrolled burning) occurs in patches, particularly in the west. In southern Kweichow, for example, less than 20 per cent of the natural vegetation remains and the land surface is either bare or covered with secondary forest. According to Yang (1962) it is maintained in this condition by forest fires, "unreasonable practices of tree-cutting and irrational methods of cultivation and reclamation."

The coniferous component is significantly increased in the secondary forests and they comprise mixed *Pinus* species, *Cunninghamia lanceolata,* and hardwoods. *Pinus massoniana* is characteristic, with scattered white pines (*P. kwangtungensis, P. fenzeliana* etc.).

The evergreen-broadleaved forest type is among the most productive agricultural regions of China and a variety of temperate and subtropical crops thrive. Most important, of course, is paddy rice (double-cropped) but a complete list would include tobacco, cotton, jute, ramie, mulberry and tung trees, rapeseed, peanuts, tea, oats, maize, sweet potatoes, kaoliang, sugar cane, millet, soya beans, barley, citrus fruits, and wheat. Of these, tobacco, jute, ramie, sweet potatoes, and barley are the most extensive. The culture of fresh-water fish is also important, and the area is of considerable significance in Chinese plans for plantation establishment, particularly in respect of short rotation "economic" or "industrial" tree crops. In addition to mulberry and tung, these include, in this zone, *Cinnamomum camphora, C. cassia, Thea sinensis, T. oleosa, Sapium sebiferum, Pterocarya stenoptera,*

Quercus acutissima, Castanea henryi, Aesculus chinensis, Sassafras tsuma, Cupressus funebris, Citrus sinensis, C. deliciosa, Bischoffia spp., *Litchi chinensis, Canarium album, Camellia oleifera,* and the bamboos, *Bambusa stenostachys, Dendrocalamus latiflorus, D. giganteus, D. strictus, Sinocalamus affinis, Arundinaria* spp., and *Phyllostachys* spp.

Pinus massoniana is widely planted (or sown) as a production species as is *Cunninghamia lanceolata* to an even greater extent. On a lesser scale, *Cedrela sinensis, Melia azedarach, Cupressus funebris, Cryptomeria japonica, Quercus acutissima, Acacia confusa,* and the exotic *Eucalyptus globulus, E. citriodora,* and *E. exserta* occur in plantations. Growth rates are good; *Cunninghamia lanceolata,* for example, can show mean annual increments (to age twenty years) of 25 cu.m./ha., (see, also, Afanasev, 1959) and *Eucalyptus globulus* as much as 30 cu.m./ha. at the same age. *Cryptomeria japonica, Cedrela sinensis, Eucalyptus citriodora,* and *Melia azedarach* are also impressive and it is scarcely surprising that the Chinese have decided to concentrate some 85 per cent of their production afforestation in the region south of the Yangtze river.

Western Evergreen Broadleaved Forest. The western subregion comprises most of the province of Yunnan and its many autonomous districts, and parts of southwest Szechuan and western Kweichow.

It is extremely variable in topography, climate, and soils. In elevation it ranges from 600 m. to over 5,000 m., with many high-altitude lakes and swift flowing rivers. Much of it is difficult of access and, as a result, the natural vegetation has in many areas survived the predations of man. Significant forest resources (some of them newly discovered) are located here.

Climatically, it is generally drier than the eastern subregion, with a mean annual rainfall of 50 cm. to 150 cm. This difference is reflected in the natural vegetation. Yang (1962) points out that the vegetation of southern Kweichow is sharply differentiated as between east and west, with a more xerophytic flora (including *Schima argentea* and *Alnus nepalensis*) in the east.

The mean annual temperatures range from 8°C. to 23°C. with the coldest month averaging 4°C. to 8°C. and the warmest, 18°C. to 22°C. Eight to ten months of the year have temperatures above 10°C. (except at very high altitudes). The soils include alpine meadow soils (and lithosols and tundra soils) at high altitudes on the edge of the Tibetan plateau, purple-brown forest soils in central Yunnan, and acidic red podsolic soils interspersed with grey-brown podsols; in the east of the subregion, yellow earths predominate, while, over limestone, terra rossas are common.

The evergreen-broadleaved forest is again dominated by the cupuliferous genera *Castanopsis, Pasania,* and *Quercus.* In the north, it forms a transition to montane conifers (*Tsuga, Picea,* and *Pseudotsuga*); further south, it reaches altitudes ranging from 1,200 m. to 3,000 m. and is characterized by the predominance of *Quercus* species. In central and southern Yunnan, the elevation decreases and *Castanopsis, Pasania,* and *Cyclobalanopsis* spp. become more common. In the vicinity of Kunming (central Yunnan), seven associations have been recognized (Hsu, 1950): *Castanopsis delavayi, Quercus schottkyana, Lithocarpus (Pasania) mairei, Quercus franchetti, Pinus armandi, Keteleeria evelyniana,* and *Pinus yunnanensis.* The conifer associations are secondary. Minor constituents of the first four association include *Machilus yunnanensis, Castanopsis concolor, Lindera communis, Schima argentea, Pistacia* spp., *Albizzia mollis, Celtis bungeana,* and *Juniperus formosana.* Climbers are represented by *Hedera sinensis, Smilax* and *Rosa* spp., and, at high elevations in central and southern Yunnan, epiphytic mosses and ferns are abundant. The forests of Yunnan are well described by Wang (1961) who, before the war, carried out considerable field work in the region.

Most of the evergreen cupuliferous species are utilizable timber trees and, where readily accessible, they have been extensively logged. The secondary forest types are coniferous (*Pinus armandi, P. yunnanensis, Keteleeria* spp.) and, particularly in the east of the region (western Kweichow), they now dominate the forest landscape. There is abundant evidence, however, that if left without interference, the forests would quickly revert to evergreen broadleaved associations; one of the problems in coniferous plantation management in Yunnan, for instance, arises from dense regrowth of the hardwoods.

It is, of course, the conifers that are of greatest interest to foresters. In the general area of the western evergreen-broadleaved forest type the following coniferous timber species are exploited:

North	East	South	West
Abies fabri	*Pinus armandi*	*Abies delavayi*	*Abies delavayi*
A. forrestii	*P. yunnanensis*	*Pinus armandi*	*Pinus armandi*
Picea brachytila	*Keteleeria*	*P. yunnanensis*	*P. yunnanensis*
P. likiangensis	*davidiana*	*Keteleeria*	*Keteleeria*
Tsuga chinensis		*evelyniana*	*evelyniana*
T. yunnanensis			*Torreya fargesii*
Larix potanini			*Taiwania*
Pinus armandi			*cryptomeriodes*
P. yunnanensis			

Notwithstanding logging operations and land clearance for agriculture, the western subregion of the evergreen-broadleaved forest type still contains extensive natural forest resources, which have been significantly added to by recent border changes negotiated with Burma. If problems of access can be solved and communication to the north further developed, they could, together with the forests of Szechuan and Shensi, play an important part in the development of northwest China.

Apart from forestry, the accessible areas of the region are cultivated and grow many of the same crop species as the eastern subregion. With an adequate water supply for irrigation, rice can be double-cropped, and the cultivation of tropical fruits holds promise (Yang, 1962). The population of the western subregion, however, is very different racially from that of the east and includes many of China's "national minorities." Agriculture is more primitive and less productive; the principal crops are rice, peanuts, tobacco, rapeseed, cotton, tea, maize, sweet potatoes, kaoliang, sugar cane, millet, soya beans, and barley. Tibetan sheep and goats are grazed extensively in the hill country, while cattle-raising is a feature of the lower altitude grasslands, where fire and past mismanagement have destroyed even the secondary pine forests.

The Tropical Monsoon Rain Forest

Strictly, rain forest forms part of the evergreen-broadleaved formation, but it is distinctive physiognomically and generically; the occurrence of laterites only within the rain forest belt also provides a justification for separating these associations.

The tropical monsoon rain forest type is restricted to south China and forms a narrow belt 250,000 sq. km. in area along the southern edge of Fukien and Kwangtung provinces, Kwangsi Chuang autonomous region, and the autonomous districts of Wen-Shan, Hung-Ho, Ho-Kou, Ping-Pien (all in Yunnan province), and Hai Nan on the island of Hainan (which belongs to the province of Kwangtung). It also includes Taiwan where, as on Hainan, it is restricted to elevations below 500 m. According to Wang (1961) rain forest is also found in northwestern Yunnan, within sight of the permanent snows of southern Chamdo. Hou et al. (1956) and Chang et al. (1962), however, do not extend it north of the Tropic of Cancer, in Yunnan province.

Topographically, the area lies below 500 m., except for the mountain range forming the main divide on Taiwan, isolated peaks on

Hainan, and the southeastern plateau country of Yunnan (800 m. to 1,500 m.). The mean annual rainfall ranges from 130 cm. to 350 cm. and no month of the year is without rain. The winters are comparatively dry, however, with generally less than 10 cm. of precipitation. It is warmer than the evergreen-broadleaved zone, with a mean temperature of 22°C. to 26°C., a July average of 27° C. to 29°C., and a January mean of 13°C. to 21°C. Frost is virtually unknown, even at the higher altitudes. Soils are variable and include grey-brown podsols in the hills, red earths and noncalcareous alluvial soils in the coastal belt (the latter around the river flood plains), purple-brown forest soils in southern Yunnan, and yellow laterites, developed on basalt, granite, gneiss, sandstone, and other acidic materials. Chloride-containing Solonchaks occur along the coast.

The tropical monsoon rain forest is almost entirely evergreen and is rich in epiphytes, lianes, climbing palms, and other parasitic plants. Wang (1961) describes it as "a community of communities" and points out that epiphytes alone "may far exceed in number of species the total flora of simpler types of forest, such as deciduous oaks or even mixed northern hardwoods, of comparable area." It includes all life forms and is unique in the diversity of its flora. He suggests that ". . . the tropical regions in general and the rain forest in particular have been a great reservoir of plant stocks, ancient and modern, primitive and advanced, from which or from whose predecessors all of the other plant communities are derived."

In view of the multiplicity of plant species in the rain forest, a comprehensive description would be beyond both the ability of the author and the patience of the reader. Certain noteworthy features of the Chinese type, however, may be mentioned briefly. Firstly, in comparison with the rest of tropical Asia, the Chinese forests are conspicuously deficient in members of the *Dipterocarpaceae* and their place is taken by genera of the evergreen-broadleaved forest zone— *Michelia, Cedrela, Chukrassia,* and *Dysoxylum.* It is also remarkable that, in spite of the diversity of species, the rain forest community shows considerable floristic homogeneity: Wang (1961) lists sixty genera from the canopy trees of rain forest in southern Yunnan; of these, about 85 per cent are also found on the island of Hainan, and southern Yunnan is over 1,000 km. inland from Hainan. Of twenty-eight genera considered by Merrill (1945) to be characteristic of the primary forests occurring between continental Asia and Australia, twenty-six are represented in the Chinese rain forest.

To some extent, Hainan island forms a distinctive association, with many species which are either endemic or occur only rarely elsewhere. Among them are: *Vatica astrotricha, Alseodaphne rugosa, Pentaphylax euryoides, Tarrieta parvifolia, Hopea hainanensis, Aglaia tetrapetala, Dysoxylum binectariferum, Casearia membranacea, Machilus tsanaii, Cryptocarya densiflora, Xanthophyllum hainanensis, Syzygium hainanense, Schefflera octophylla, Canarium album, Quercus bambusaefolia, Q. blakei, Castanopsis echinocarpa, C. hainanensis, Lithocarpus cornea, Adinandra hainanensis,* and *Ficus championii.* The conifers include *Dacrydium pierrei, Podocarpus imbricata, P. neriifolia,* and *Pinus fenzeliana.*

Conifers, of course, are extremely scarce in the tropical monsoon rain forest type, but *Amentotaxus* also occurs and the deciduous *Glyptostrobus pensilis* is a feature; a monotypic genus, it is endemic to Kwangtung, Kwangsi, and Hainan.

Included by Hou *et al.* (1956) in the tropical monsoon rain forest belt are the littoral forests (mangroves and beach forests) and the vegetation of China's coral islands. The latter is of no economic importance but the mangroves of the swamps (primarily *Rhizophoraceae*) are exploited and the coastal sand dunes are being extensively used for combined protection and production (mainly fuel wood) forestry.

Existing natural forest in the tropical zone is limited to the hills of Fukien, the islands of Taiwan and Hainan, and parts of southern Yunnan. Except for Taiwan, the coastal belt is one of intensive cultivation. The major crops are rice (triple-cropped), barley, wheat, sweet potatoes, sugar cane, mulberries (for silk), tea, and soya beans—with significant areas of millet, maize, peanuts, jute, ramie, rapeseed, and tobacco. Among horticultural crops, bananas, pineapple, lichees, grapes, and tung trees are extensively grown. Pigs, water buffaloes, and poultry are also raised in large numbers.

As in the rest of south China, plantation forestry is assuming prominence (at any rate, in terms of areas planted). The "economic" crops include *Cinnamomum camphora, C. cassia, C. kanahirai, C. micranthum, Morus alba, Citrus* spp., *Casuarina equisetifolia, Bischoffia trifoliata, Sapium sebiferum, Canarium album, C. pimela, Euphoria longana, Mangifera indica, Coffea arabica, Litchi chinensis, Zizyphus spinosa, Ficus lacor, Aleurites cordata,* and bamboos. The principal production forest species are *Pinus massoniana, Cunninghamia lanceolata, Acacia confusa, Eucalyptus exserta, E. citriodora, E. globulus, Liquidambar formosana, Melia azedarach,* and *Schima confertiflora.*

Growth rates of *Eucalyptus* species, *Melia azedarach*, and *Cunninghamia lanceolata* are, again, outstanding—and, in some cases, phenomenal. At the Forest Research Institute, Kwangtung, trial plantations of *Melia azedarach* (clean-cultivated and very carefully nurtured) have reached a mean height of 8 m. and a mean diameter of 12 cm. in three years from establishment by sowing (and following a thinning at two years); *Eucalyptus citriodora* can average 2.5 m. to 3.7 m. height growth per year and reach a breast-height diameter of 25 cm. in five years. Poplars, too, have shown promise on an experimental scale—*Populus robusta* putting on nearly 2-m. annual height growth and reaching a mean diameter of 20 cm. in seven years. Clearly, factors limiting the growth of the exotic production forests in the coastal belt are likely to be edaphic and biotic, not climatic.

The inland regions of the tropical monsoon rain forest zone are, again, more primitive and more restricted as to land use. Apart from natural forests, some rice, tobacco, maize, sweet potato, kaoliang, sugar, and soya beans are grown, and water buffaloes and ponies are raised. Tibetan sheep are grazed in some higher-elevation areas.

THE STEPPES AND DESERTS OF THE NORTHWEST AND NORTHEAST

This formation runs in a broad belt around the southern borders of Outer Mongolia. The steppes form a transition between the forest climax in the east and the northwestern deserts, while the latter give way, more or less abruptly, to the high mountains of the far northwest and the Tibetan plateau to the south. The steppes do not extend south of latitude 33°N. and the western and southwestern limits of the forest climax abut on to the mountain formations along the eastern edges of the Tibetan plateau. The tree and shrub flora of the formation is of interest in the present context because from it, most of the species used in protection forestry in the arid regions of China have been selected.

The Forest Steppes

The forest steppe formations are transitional between the closed forests of eastern China and the true steppe and desert regions of the north and west; they comprise substantial areas of open woodland amid extensive and uniform grasslands. Two subregions may be recognized: that of the northeast, characterized by *Quercus mongolica* and *Betula platyphylla*, and the northwestern forest steppe typified by *Quercus liaotungensis* and *Betula japonica*.

Northeastern Forest Steppe. The first subregion covers nearly 400,000 sq. km. and takes in the Manchurian plains in the provinces of Heilungkiang, Kirin, and Liaoning (including several Mongol autonomous districts), and the Jehol highlands, northeast of Peking, which include parts of the provinces of Hopeh and Liaoning and of the Inner Mongolian autonomous region. These hills form a southward extension of the Greater Khingan mountains, rising to become the eastern edge of the Mongolian plateau. The subregion lies generally below 500 m., however, except at the southwestern end, where the rolling hills give way to mountains of over 1,500 m.

As might be expected, the climate is strictly continental, with very cold, long, and dry winters, and short but mild summers. The mean annual temperature varies from 1.0°C. to 6.4°C., with an annual range of more than 40°. January temperatures decrease from −13.7°C. in the south to −26.9°C. in the north, while the July mean ranges from 21.7°C. in the north to 25.0°C. in the south. The annual precipitation amounts to 65 cm. in the east, decreasing to 47 cm. further west, and is very unevenly distributed during the year. The length of the frost-free season is little more than 100 days.

Hou *et al.* (1956) describe the soils as "unique." While this is not literally true, they are certainly unusual. The soils which have developed under a tree cover are either secondary podsols (grey forest soils) or leached chernozems. The former are characteristic of the Greater Khingan foothills and support, as well as *Betula platyphylla*, various species of willow (e.g. *Salix raddeana, S. chinganica*), *Populus davidiana, Corylus heterophylla, Rosa avicularis,* and *Spiraea media*). The ground vegetation includes *Pteridium aquilinum, Epilobium angustifolium, Polygonum japonicum, Bupleurum dahuricum* and *Adenophora* spp. The leached chernozems are found over basalt and carry dwarf species of the same genera. Thus, willows are represented by *Salix cinerascens,* and *S. mongolica,* poplars by *Populus maximowiczii,* and the genus *Rosa* by *R. dahurica. Quercus mongolica, Tilia amurensis,* and *Lespedeza bicolor* are also frequent, while *Betula platyphylla* and *Corylus heterophylla* are common to both soil types.

Soils of the grassland areas are either calcareous chernozems (with a pH of 8.0 to 8.5) or Solonchaks. On virgin steppe country, *Glycyrrhiza uralensis, Astragalus melitotoides, Aneurolepidium chinense,*

Stipa baicalensis, and *Artemisia* (many species) are characteristic, with local clumps of trees—*Ulmus pumila, U. propinqua, U. macrocarpa, Populus* spp. and *Salix* spp. The Solonchaks support a halophytic vegetation of *Suaeda corniculata, Achnatherum splendens, Cyperus serotinus, Saussurea glomerata, Puccinellia tenuiflora, Triglochin palustre, Nitraria schoberi, Aster tripolium,* and the like. The woodland areas and the Solonchaks have little land-use potential other than for sparse grazing and, in some areas, protection forestry. Cattle, Mongolian sheep, donkeys, horses (including the famous Hailar horse), and, in the southern part of the zone, camels, are raised; but only small areas of these soils are cultivated. The grassland-climax areas, on the other hand, are almost entirely cultivated and undeveloped steppe is difficult to find. Wheat, soya beans, millet, kaoliang, oats, potatoes, and similar northern latitude crops are common, with smaller areas of maize, sugar beet, and barley. The Manchurian plains are ideally suited to large-scale, mechanized farming and the Chinese, following the Russian pattern, have established several state farms in this area. They are highly economic in terms of labor input, with the productivity limited only by the length of the growing season and a shortage of fertilizers. Unlike many state farms in drier regions, the cultivated areas of the northeastern forest steppe subregion are stable and erosion problems are only local.

Northwestern Forest Steppe. This subregion forms part of the loess highlands of Shensi, Shansi, and Kansu provinces and the Ninghsia autonomous region; it covers some 250,000 sq. km. Topography ranges from alluvial plains along the Yellow river and its tributaries, to the loess plateaus (*ca.* 1,000 m.) and the mountains rising to over 2,000 m. above them. The January temperature averages −3.1°C. to −11.3°C. and that for July, 17.9°C. to 25.4°C., giving a mean annual value of from 8.8°C. to 11.3°C. Precipitation ranges from 30 cm. in the west to 60 cm. in the east, approximately half of it falling in summer. Thus, in comparison with the northeastern subregion, the northwestern forest steppe has a milder winter and, generally, a wetter summer, resulting in an effective growing season of about 150 to 180 days.

Soils developed from the loess are the so-called calcareous Ziero-Korichnevie types; they support a sparse natural flora which includes *Dicranostigma leptopodum, Rosa hugonis, R. xanthina, Andropogon ischaemum, Stipa bungeana, S. grandis, Cleistogenes serotina, C. squarrosa,* and *Artemisia* spp. In the ubiquitous eroded gullies,

Zizyphus sativa var. spinosa, Sophora vicifolia, Hippophae rhamnoides, Prinsepia uniflora, and Lycium chinense occur. True forest is
only found at higher elevations, under fairly humid conditions. Essentially, it is deciduous broadleaved, comprising Quercus liaotungensis,
Betula japonica, B. chinensis, Populus davidiana, Tilia paucicostata,
T. mongolica, Acer ginnala, A. mono, Ulumus japonica, U. pumila,
Lonicera ferdinandii, Hippophae rhamnoides, Euonymus alata, Corylus heterophylla, and, locally, many of the species listed earlier as
growing in plantations or seminatural stands on the North China
plain (p. 23). Biota orientalis is found in the high mountains above
the deciduous forest and, even higher, Picea asperata, P. neoveitchii,
and Abies nephrolepis appear.

Formerly rich pastoral country, the flat land of the northwestern
forest steppe zone is now extensively cultivated and grows spring
wheat, oats, maize, millet, peas, potatoes, flax, kaoliang, and beans.
The ravine slopes are terraced and similar crops cultivated, while the
terrace shoulders are frequently planted with trees such as Salix
matsudana, Populus simonii, P. cathayana, and Robinia pseudoacacia.
Away from human settlement, and where soil erosion is not too far
advanced, Mongolian cattle, horses, and Mongolian sheep are grazed.
Unlike the northeastern subregion, however, the northwestern forest
steppe is highly susceptible to erosion by both wind and water; though
fertile, the soils are far from stable, and it is in part from this area
that the Yellow river gets its evocative name. Together with the true
steppe formation, it has a high priority under present-day government policy for water conservation and protection afforestation projects. The species commonly planted are Elaeagnus angustifolia,
Populus simonii, P. pseudosimonii, P. diversifolia, P. euphratica,
Ulmus pumila, U. laciniata, Sophora japonica var. pendula, Robinia
pseudoacacia, Haloxylon ammodendron, Tamarix juniperina, and
various Artemisia spp.

In the near future, significant industrial development is likely to
occur in the western part of this subregion (major untapped coal and
oil resources are located there); the importance of agricultural productivity (and, hence, of erosion control) in this connection need not
be stressed.

The Steppes

The steppe regions in Hou's classification (Hou et al., 1956) cover
an area almost a million square kilometers in extent, running south-

west in a broad belt along the eastern edge of the Inner Mongolian plateau (west of the Greater Khingan range). They also take in the northern boundaries of Hopeh, Shansi, and Shensi provinces, parts of Kansu, and most of the autonomous region of Ninghsia. The greater part of the formation is on flat-undulating country between 1,200 m. and 1,500 m. in elevation.

Climatically, the zone is rigorously continental with a mean annual temperature of −1.8°C. to 2.5°C. in the north and 2.8°C. to 10.5°C. in the south; the July average is 20.9°C. to 21.6°C. in the north and only slightly higher (21.3°C. to 24.1°C.) in the south. January averages, however, are very different, reaching only −29.3°C. to −25.7°C. in the north and −15.1°C. to −4.9°C. in the south. Precipitation ranges from 15 cm. to 40 cm., most of it falling in summer; the frost-free period is from 110 to 140 days.

Edaphically, the region comprises mainly chestnut soils on neutral or slightly alkaline sand dunes and Solonchaks bordering parts of the middle reaches of the Yellow river and in areas without external drainage. With the exception of atypical sites along watercourses (where *Populus cathayana, P. simonii, P. euphratica, Ulmus pumila, Salix matsudana,* etc. survive) and on the stabilized sand dunes of the northeast (which *Pinus sylvestris* var. *mongolica* colonizes), erect trees are absent from the true steppe and woody species are confined to dwarf trees and shrubs. These, however, are fairly abundant, particularly as the steppe approaches the semidesert and desert. They include *Artemisia halodendron, A. frigida, A. adamsii, A. desertorum, A. pubescens, A. sacrorum, A. sibirica, Caragana pygmaea, C. microphylla,* and *Ephedra* and *Atriplex* spp. The prevalance of legumes is also noteworthy (e.g. *Glycyrrhiza uralensis, Astragalus melitotoides, A. adsurgens, Lespedeza dahurica,* and *Thermopsis lanceolata*).

The characteristic species of the formation are, of course, grasses and, in particular, narrowleaved species. *Achnatherum splendens, Stipa* (many species), *Agropyron cristatum, Aneurolepidium pseudoagropyrum, Cleistogenes squarrosa, Elymus dahuricus, Koeleria gracilis, Allium* (many species), *Aster* spp., *Bupleurum* spp., *Medicago ruthenica, Oxytropis grandiflora,* and *Potentilla* spp. are common constituents.

On the chestnut soils of the Yellow river terraces, the *Artemisia* and *Allium* spp. frequently dominate the vegetation type; on the same soil type on the sand dunes of the northeast, however, a greater variety of shrubs occurs. Hou *et al.* (1956) cite the following: *Oxytropis psammocharis, O. aciphylla, Agriophyllum arenarium, Caragana tibe-*

tica, C. microphylla var. *tomentosa, Atraphaxis mandshurica, Artemisia salsoloides, Pugionium cornutum, Salix mongolica, S. cheilophila,* and *Juniperus chinensis,* to which may be added (from Wang, 1961), *Malus baccata* var. *sibirica, Crataegus dahurica, Ribes diacantha, Papaver nudicaule, Scabiosa isetensis, Veronica incana,* etc. Many of these species are characteristic woodland plants.

The Solonchak vegetation is typically halophytic and is strongly affected by relief. Where drainage is good, *Nitraria schoberi, Kalidium gracile, Scorzonera mongolica* var. *putjatae, Lepidium latifolium, Suaeda glauca, Kochia sieversana, Atriplex sibiricum,* and *Salsola collina* are found; where it is poor, the common species are *Phragmites communis, Typha davidiana, Scirpus maritimus, S. compactus, Triglochin palustre, Puccinellia tenuiflora,* and *Glaux maritima.* Aneurolepidium pseudo-agropyrum* and *Puccinellia distans* are common grasses in the transition between the Solonchak vegetation and the *Stipa-Aneurolepidium-Artemisia* steppe.

Traditionally the steppes are the territory of nomadic Mongol and Uighur graziers with some dry-land farming along the great loop of the Yellow river. In spite of substantial industrial development in parts of the region, the land-use pattern has not greatly changed since the advent of the Communists. On the Yellow river terraces, precarious crops of millet, potatoes, flax, barley, oats, and wheat are grown and, where irrigation is practicable, soya beans, peas, and cucurbits. Eleswhere, horses, cattle, Mongolian sheep, and camels are grazed.

Like the forest steppes, the region under consideration is a major target for water conservancy and protection forestry. Wang (1961) points out that the grassland zone has always been of great importance in the national economy and in the minds of the ancient Chinese: "During those early periods the favorite national sport was polo and the national beauty . . . was not the willowy weakling but an agile and rather generously proportioned horsewoman on the rolling steppe." (Cursory examination of the art of the Han dynasty reveals proportions that would have delighted both Rubens and a twentieth-century film producer—Wang's diffident description is a Gargantuan understatement.) If China's current plans in these spheres (i.e., water conservancy and protection forestry) materialize, the steppe area will be considerably transformed. And the buxom horsewoman may again become the symbol of pastoral productivity.

The Semidesert and Desert

Covering more than 1.75 million sq. km. the semidesert and desert associations form the most extensive natural region in China. Administratively, the zone takes in much of the autonomous regions of Inner Mongolia and Sinkiang; part of the province of Kansu and the autonomous districts of A-ko-sai, Pa-li-kun, Mu-lei, I-li (all Kazakh regions), Su-pei, Pay-yin-kuo-leng, Po-erh-ta-la, Ha-pu-ko-sai-erh (Mongol districts); and sundry other minority areas in Sinkiang and Tsinghai. Surrounded on nearly all sides by mountains, the desert basin ranges in height from 300 m. below sea level (in the Turfan depression) to some 2,000 m. in the high desert; the average elevation is 1,300 m. in the north and east, decreasing to 800 m. in Tarim and to 280 m. in Dzungaria.

It is an area of very low rainfall and without external drainage; with a few exceptions, the mean annual precipitation seldom exceeds 10 cm. and may be as low as 0.5 cm. The January mean temperature ranges from −5.7°C. to −19.3°C. and the July average from 23.7°C. to 25.9°C., giving a mean annual value of 4.3°C. to 12.6°C. Noteworthy exceptions are the Turfan and Hami depressions (both below sea level) where the summers are hotter than in the tropics, with a July mean temperature of over 33°C., and a frost-free season of 240 days. In all seasons, sand and dust storms are frequent.

Not surprisingly, the soils are unstable and characterized by a marked lack of organic matter and by high salt contents; they are saline Zierozems and desert, Solonchak, and Solonetz soils. The Zierozem is most common in the semidesert; the climate does not support forest growth and the sparse vegetation is limited to drought-resisting grasses and shrubs, including some halophytes. *Stipa* (many species) *Cleistogenes* spp., and *Allium* spp. are characteristic, with scrub growth of *Artemisia frigida, A. caespitosa, A. xerophytica, A. incana, Tanacetum achillaeoides, T. fruticulosum, T. trifidum, Salsola passerina, Caragana pygmaea, C. bungei, Potaninia mongolica,* and *Sympegma regelii.*

On the true desert soils, the vegetation cover is even more fragmentary. The halophytes include several species from the semidesert (*Tanacetum achillaeoides, Anabasis brevifolia, Salsola passerina, S. ruthenica, S. collina, Sympegma regelii, Eurotia ceratoides, Agriophyllum gobicum, Echinopilon divaricatum,* and *Kalidium gracile*), together with *Salsola arbuscula, Peganum nigellastrum, Nanophyton erinaceum, Haloxylon ammodendron, Calligonum mongolicum, Nitraria sphaerocarpa, N. sibirica, Zygophyllum xanthoxylum, Ephedra przewalskii, Alhagi camelorum,* and *Caragana leucophylla.* The Solonchaks are essentially similar to those of the steppes and support much the same vegetation.

The unbroken extent of China's desert regions is quite remarkable. The Tarim basin for instance covers more than 300,000 sq. km. The Tarim itself is more than 2,000 km. long and drains a catchment of almost 200,000 sq. km. (Tong, 1947). It has no outlet and is entirely absorbed within the basin. Surrounding the central salt lake (the Lop Nor) is the vast Takla Makan desert; its only vegetation comprises two psammophytes, *Agriophyllum arenarium* and *Corispermum hyssopifolium* (this desert supports the only remaining wild camels in the world). The sand plain is bordered by concentric belts of fluvioglacial gravels forming the foothills of the surrounding mountains. Within these gravel belts are found numerous oases which carry remnants of a relatively luxuriant vegetation.

It is, in fact, only around the oases that remnants of a tree flora are found in the desert, and here land use is so intensive that the original vegetation has been much altered. The common species indicate a deciduous broadleaved forest type, and they include *Populus euphratica, P. pruinosa, P. alba, P. nigra, Salix* spp., *Ulmus pumila, Tamarix chinensis, T. hispida, T. juniperina, Myricaria germanica, Morus alba, Elaeagnus angustifolia,* and *Lycium turcomannicum. Juglans fallax, Acer turkestanicum, Prunus divaricata,* and *Celtis australis* were also probably once components of the oasis vegetation.

The oasis at Lolan was once (in the second century B.C.) on the main route from China to Rome and in the first century A.D. had a population of 17,000. Ruins show that the buildings were constructed from logs of *Populus alba,* more than 60 cm. in diameter (Wang, 1961).

The oases support virtually the entire indigenous population of the western deserts. Those of the Turfan depression, for example, have ancient and elaborate irrigation systems and even before the war carried a population of over 90,000 (Hwang, 1944). The climate is such that, with adequate moisture, they can grow cotton, vegetables, grapes, melons, maize, millet, kaoliang, and even some rice. Maize, cotton, and kaoliang are also raised along the Tarim river at the western end of the Tarim basin and there is a spring wheat zone at the western end of the Dzungaria basin. Elsewhere, however, the western deserts support only a sparse, nomadic population of cattle, horse, and sheep graziers. The sheep are mainly Tibetan while the horses include the I-li race. Camels are also raised and on the desert fringes there is a surprisingly extensive native fauna of gazelles, wild asses, and antelopes. The scattered inhabitants of the region are predominantly Buddhists and hunting is rare; as a result, these animals are little disturbed. In view of the extensive industrial development which is taking place along the northern borders of the Tarim basin, in the foothills of the Tien mountains and in Dzungaria, this situation may not continue unchanged. Extensive resources of oil, coal, iron, copper, molybdenum, uranium, etc. have recently been discovered and are being vigorously exploited. As discussed in Chapter I, these developments entail extensive railway construction and mass settlement of nonindigenous Chinese.

The northern deserts contain few oases and, apart from the Ninghsia plain (which, strictly, falls entirely within the steppe region), are virtually uncultivated. Land use is limited to the pasturage of horses, Mongolian sheep, camels, Mongolian cattle, yak, and cattle-yak hybrids (pien riu); productivity is not high.

The fringes of the northern deserts and the communications routes to the northwest have a special importance in China's protection afforestation projects. Attempts to border the Gobi and Tengri deserts with enormous shelterbelt plantings have been widely publicized. Less well-known (but equally Herculean) is a project designed to protect the northwestern railways from the ravages of wind-blown sand. These endeavors have entailed planting trees on a huge scale and on very inhospitable sites, often with species far removed from their native habitats. Not surprisingly, Chinese foresters have encountered many problems, many of which they have yet to solve. These developments are described in Chapter VI.

THE MOUNTAINS AND PLATEAUS OF THE WEST AND SOUTHWEST

With the exception of the greater part of the Tibetan plateau, the montane regions of west and southwest China contain several tree genera of interest to foresters, and it is in this region that substantial timber resources have been discovered in recent years, as a result of surveys carried out by Chinese and Russian expeditions.

The Mountains of Northwestern China

This region covers 400,000 sq. km. and comprises three unconnected mountain ranges—the Chilien mountains, marking the boundary between Kansu province and Tsinghai autonomous region and forming the northeastern edge of the Tibetan plateau; the Tien range to the north of the Tarim basin; and the Altai, north and northeast of the Dzungaria basin. In all three, climate and soils show marked zonation with altitude. The mean annual rainfall ranges from 10 cm. to over 50 cm.; the January temperature from −48°C. to −8°C.; the July temperature from 10°C. to 22°C.; and the mean annual temperature from −4°C. to 10°C. From the desert soils and the steppe Zierozems, the soils change with altitude through the sequence chestnut, grey forest and, above the timber line, alpine meadow soils. In altitude, the Chilien and the Tien mountains reach over 5,000 m. (the Tien, indeed, rise to over 7,000 m.); the Altai range, on the other hand, is nowhere higher than 4,000 m.

The forest zone of the Chilien mountains ranges from 2,200 m. to about 3,800 m. On northerly slopes, *Picea asperata* occurs in pure stands with an understory of *Potentilla, Caragana, Spiraea, Cotoneaster, Lonicera,* and *Berberis* spp. Other conifers are found rarely, including *Picea asperata* var. *heterolepis, P. likiangensis* var. *purpurea,* and *Abies faxoniana*. On southern slopes, *Juniperus tibetica* occupies the zone between 2,700 m. and 3,300 m., with *J. saltuaria* invading the alpine meadow zone for a further 300 m. to 400 m. in altitude. Below about 2,800 m. *Pinus tabulaeformis* var. *gracilifolia, P. tabulaeformis* var. *leucosperma* and *Ulmus pumila* may occur.

The dominant species of the north-facing slopes of the Tien range is *Picea schrenkiana,* occupying chernozem soil types between 1,500 m. and 3,000 m. The trees reach 75 m. in height and 1½ m. in diameter, yielding where accessible an excellent-quality timber. The southern slopes at this altitude are grass covered, with occasional clumps of deciduous forest comprising *Juglans fallax, Pyrus malus, Acer turkestanicum, Prunus divaricata,* and *Celtis australis*. Beneath the spruce forests grow *Populus tremula, Salix* spp., *Betula pubescens,* and *Sorbus tianschanica,* ready to form a secondary broadleaved forest if the spruce is destroyed (as it often is, for summer pasture).

Above the timber line, the alpine meadows may be quite moist and even swampy. Wang (1961) lists the following species: *Erigeron pulchellus, Gentiana algida, Lagotis glauca, Papaver nudicaule, Pedicularis cheilanthifolia, Saussurea involucrata, Saxifraga hirsuta,* and *Seseli athamanthoides*. *Juniperus semiglobosa* is also common on both north- and south-facing slopes.

In contrast to the mountains of the Chilien and Tien ranges, the Altai are richer in tree species (including many more species of *Abies* and, also, *Rhododendron*) but lack *Juniperus* as a subdominant species. The primary components of the coniferous forest zone (2,000 m. to 3,000 m.) are *Larix sibirica, Picea obovata, Abies sibirica, Pinus cembra* var. *sibirica, Betula verrucosa,* and *Populus tremula*. Below the forest, on chestnut soils and chernozems, the vegetation includes *Artemisia, Potentilla, Spiraea, Caragana, Astragalus,* and other steppe species; above it lies a transitional zone of *Betula nana, Cotoneaster uniflora, Lonicera hispida, Ribes fragrans* var. *infracanum,* and *Salix* spp., leading to alpine meadows rich in such species as *Aquilegia glandulosa, Viola altaica, Anemone narcissiflora, Callianthemum rutaefolium,* and *Ranunculus altaicus*.

Land use in the northwestern mountains is restricted to some forest production and grazing. As already mentioned, where the forest is accessible it is being exploited and sometimes converted into summer pasture for cattle, sheep and horses. This is particularly true of the Tien mountains where the pastures are within reach of the oasis farmers of the Tarim basin. Much of the forest, however, is not exploitable with the equipment presently available to the Chinese and it forms a useful reserve for future use.

The Mountains and Plateaus of Eastern Tibet

The east Tibetan borderland contains China's biggest reserves of softwood timber outside Manchuria and forms a zone 300,000 sq. km. in extent, much of which is heavily wooded. It includes parts of the provinces of Yunnan, Szechuan, and Chamdo, and several of the Tibetan autonomous districts (Yu-shu, Kuo-lo, A-pa, Kan-tzu, Ti-ching, Mu-li) and other minority regions (Kung-shan, Li-chiang, Nu-chiang, Ta-li, and Ning-lang). The general level of the plateau is about 4,000 m. but it is deeply incised by river gorges of the Yangtze, Mekong, Salween, Irrawaddy, and Brahmaputra rivers and their tributaries. Furthermore, the high mountain ranges rise to more than 8,000 m. and this variation in relief (together with climatic differences) results in a very rich, if complex, flora, containing many species endemic to the region.

The mean annual temperature ranges from 4°C. in the north to 16°C. in the south, with July and January values of 16°C. to 20°C. and 2°C.

to 10°C. respectively. The annual rainfall varies from less than 20 cm. on the Tibetan plateau to about 120 cm. in the southeast of the region. The length of the growing season varies from 90 to 150 days, but rarely is there a period of more than two months that is completely free of frost. Few studies have been made of the soils of the region, but it is known that they are predominantly podsolic, merging with alpine meadow soils (including lithosols and tundra soils) at high elevations.

The montane coniferous forests of east Tibet comprise many species of *Picea* and *Abies*, with occasional admixtures of *Larix* (*L. potanini* and *L. griffithii*), and *Tsuga* (*T. chinensis, T. yunnanensis,* and *T. dumosa*). The *Picea-Abies* mixture, however, is not a simple one and many species and varieties are found varying in dominance in different parts of the zone. Wang (1961) shows their distribution as follows:

Species	East	North-east	South-east	South-west
Picea asperata	x	x		
P. asperata var. *heterolepis*	x	x		
P. asperata var. *retroflea*	x		x	
P. aurantiaca	x			
P. likiangensis	xxx	x		x
P. likiangensis var. *balfouriana*	xxx			
P. likiangensis var. *hirtella*	x			
P. likiangensis var. *montigena*	x			
P. likiangensis var. *purpurea*		xxx		
P. sikangensis	x			
P. brachytila	x	x	xxx	x
P. complanata	x	x	x	x
P. spinulosa				x
P. neoveitchii		x		
Abies fabri	x		xxx	
A. delavayi	x			xxx
A. chensiensis	x	x		
A. forrestii				x
A. yuana				x
A. faxoniana	x	xxx		
A. georgei	xxx			
A. recurvata	x	x		
A. squamata	xxx			
A. webbiana				x
A. fargesii var. *sutchuenensis*			x	

(xxx = primary forest constituent; x = minor constituent)

Although in general the montane coniferous forest is open, the trees grow to a large size, with heights reaching 50 m. and with one third or more of the trees above 10 cm. in diameter in the 51 to 90 cm. classes (Kuo and Cheo, 1941). The *Picea-Abies* forest reaches its best development on north-facing slopes above 3,500 m. Below it, several species of pine (*Pinus tabulaeformis* var. *densata, P. armandi,* and *P. yunnanensis*) and *Acer-Betula* forest occur sandwiched between the montane coniferous species and the evergreen broadleaved forest at lower elevations. Above the timber line, *Rhododendron* species often form a transition to alpine scrub and meadow plants. The timber line varies from 3,800 m. to about 4,300 m. The south-facing slopes are often characterized by evergreen oaks and junipers, including, in the northeast, the dwarf species, *Juniperus lemeeana, J. przewalskii, J. zaidamensis, J. formosana,* and *J. tibetica.* Regional segregates of the formation are summarized by Wang (1961).

The ground vegetation in these forests is usually sparse and the forest floor is covered only by mosses and shade-bearing shrubs (*Berberis, Ribes, Cotoneaster, Rhododendron,* etc.). Occasional bamboos are found in the south.

With regard to land use, apart from sporadic hunting and some grazing, timber production is a major industry in the forest areas. Though much of the forest is inaccessible (in 1944, some 85 per cent was so regarded [Wang and Chen, 1944]), considerable efforts are being made at the present time to devise techniques of river driving that will enable logs to be extracted. The formation of roads and railways is also proceeding apace.

The Tibetan Plateau

Of little importance in Chinese forestry, the Tibetan plateau is a lofty and inhospitable habitat, covering 1.75 million sq. km. in the provinces of Tibet and Chamdo, the autonomous region of Sinkiang, and the autonomous district of Yu-shu. The average elevation is generally from 4,700 m. to 5,300 m. and it is bounded by even higher ranges—the Himalayas to the south and the Kun Lun to the north. The climate is cold and semiarid, with severe winters and low summer temperatures. Chang *et al.* (1962) give mean annual temperatures of 4°C. to 8°C., with mean January and July values of −5°C. to −16°C. and −6°C. to 10°C. respectively. The higher figures relate solely to the southeastern edge of the region along the upper reaches of the Brahmaputra. In this area, the annual rainfall amounts to over 200 cm. but, in the plateau interior it is never more than 30 cm. and is often less than 10 cm. The length of the growing season at Lhasa (which in comparison with the interior has a mild climate) is 148 days (Wang, 1961).

Forest is developed to some extent in the southeast of the region with evergreen broadleaved species (*Tilia* spp., *Magnolia* spp., and *Quercus* spp.) in the lower valleys and dense montane coniferous associations higher up. Below the snowline at 4,500 m., is a narrow belt of alpine vegetation (including *Betula, Acer,* and *Rhododendron* spp.) above the coniferous zone of *Abies webbiana, Picea likiangensis, Larix griffithii* and *Picea spinulosa.* From 3,000 m. down to 2,400 m., *Tsuga dumosa* is dominant. The soils of the coniferous communities are grey-brown podsols and merge, on the plateau itself, with alpine meadow and desert soils. Here, the drainage is internal and the vegetation halophytic. The common species are *Eurotia ceratoides, Tanacetum tibeticum, Artemisia wellbyi, Capsella thomsoni, Cheiranthus himalayensis, Myricaria prostrata, Astragalus* spp., *Thermopsis inflata, Allium senescens, Ephedra gerardiana, Stipa stenophylla, S. purpurea,* etc. In wetter areas, *Ranunculus tricuspis, Triglochin palustre, Juncus thomsoni,* and *Puccinellia distans* occur.

The vegetation of the outer edge of the plateau is rather different. Along watercourses, *Juniperus, Salix, Ulmus, Populus,* and *Hippophae* occur, while in the semidesert there is a shrub flora of *Berberis, Sophora moorcroftiana, Caragana tibetica, C. jubata, Potentilla fruticosa, Salix biondiana, Spiraea, Rosa, Cotoneaster,* and *Lonicera* spp., etc. The meadow soils, on the other hand, support *Kobresia, Carex, Eriophorum, Helictotrichon, Deschampsia,* and *Poa* spp. among a cosmopolitan variety of herbs and shrubs.

The interior of the Tibetan plateau supports a small nomadic population of graziers and their herds of yaks, goats, cattle-yak hybrids, ponies, and sheep. Large herds of wild asses, gazelles, and antelopes are also found, as in the desert fringes further north. In contrast to the dry interior, the moist-temperate southeastern edge of the region contains numerous permanent pastoral and agricultural settlements such as Lhasa, Gyangtze, and Shigatze. As well as raising yak, yak-cattle hybrids, Sikang horses, sheep, goats, and camels, the population grow crops of maize, millet, barley, tobacco, and tea. Yields are not high, but they are adequate for the low-density population. The forests of this area are not exploited to any extent but, as with the east Tibetan border resources, the development of communications and improved extraction methods may enable these reserves to be tapped.

CHAPTER III

FORESTRY ADMINISTRATION
AND POLICY

IT IS NEVER easy for an outsider to understand the governmental and administrative mechanisms of a foreign state. This is particularly so in a country with a complex political structure in which national executive controls reflect a startling (to a westerner) mixture of empiricism and ideology, and in which regional and local bodies proliferate and flourish with a fecundity unequalled elsewhere. This account of forestry administration, therefore, is necessarily incomplete and, in view of the rapid and sweeping changes which can occur from time to time in China, it should be regarded as applicable only to the situation as it existed in June, 1963.

PLANNING AGENCIES

The supreme organ of state power in China is the National People's Congress, which consists of some 1,200 members of four political parties; of these members, more than 1,000 belong to the Communist party. Congress appoints the State Council which, in theory, plans and promulgates national policies. The State Council is assisted by a number of planning commissions of which the most important in the present context are the State Planning Commission, the National Economic Commission, the Scientific and Technological Planning Commission and the National Committee for Science and Technology. The commissions are primarily staff departments, translating policy decisions into short-and long-term plans. They are not executive bodies but report back to the State Council, which then controls the

49

implementation of the plans through the economic ministries (of which the Ministry of Forestry is one) and various regional and local organizations. In the provinces, the autonomous regions and the autonomous municipalities of Peking and Shanghai, local government organizations parallel those at the national level. There are, for example, provincial people's councils assisted by a number of planning commissions (including committees for science and technology). In general, the economic ministries are concerned with large-scale state enterprises and the provincial councils with small-scale co-operative and commune developments. Figure 2 is a simplified diagram illustrating this structure.

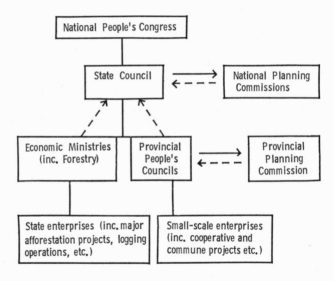

Broken lines show advisory relationships; solid lines show direct supervisory functions.

Figure 2:   Governmental Economic Planning Structure

The extent of co-operation and co-ordination within and between the various national and provincial organizations is difficult to gauge. There are some forty economic ministries, twenty-six provincial people's councils and a multitude of regional, district, and commune committees, all of which are involved to a greater or lesser degree in development and planning of natural resources. Many of them are directly or indirectly concerned with forestry and the forest industries. Thus, the Ministries of Forestry, Water Conservancy, Agriculture,

Land Reclamation, Transport, Coal Industry, Construction, Light Industry (which includes paper manufacture), Railways, and Science all have some interest in the formulation of a forest policy. The provincial organizations, equally, have a stake in the implementation of that policy through manpower and commodity allocation, utilization and distribution of produce, etc.

An added complication is that the various national and regional plans may cover different periods of time. For example, while over-all economic development follows a series of relatively detailed five-year plans (begun in 1952), agriculture works to a twelve year plan (1956 to 1967), and a ten-year plan for forestry is in preparation. References have also been made from time to time to five- and eleven-year plans for afforestation and some thought is being given to a fifty-year program.

As far as this writer could judge, the national long-term plans for particular industries or projects are drawn up by the executive departments (i.e. the ministries) after consultation with the regional planning commissions. They are submitted to one or more of the national planning commissions, which co-ordinate and combine them into an over-all plan for economic development in line with State Council policy. If approved, the plan is issued by the State Council and its implementation is then in the hands of the economic ministries and the provincial people's councils. The ministries draw up regulations designed to achieve the objectives of the plan and assign production targets, etc., which are then promulgated by the State Council to the provincial people's councils. They are usually published in the daily newspapers and, if important, are emphasized by means of editorials. An example of such regulations, together with the editorial which accompanied its publication, is presented in Appendix II and deals with forest protection. The regulations appear to combine the broadest of generalization with very explicit detail. Thus, they require "people's councils at all levels to strengthen propaganda education on loving and protecting forests" and prescribe "severe punishment" for incendiarism; they also lay down precise volume limits for timber felling within commune forests and the levels of approval required. Some months before the promulgation of these regulations (May, 1963) provincial forestry staff had been warned that they were being prepared and had been given an indication of their importance by the ministry in Peking. According to the chief forestry administrator in Kwangtung province, "important" regulations are issued about four times in a year; the example under discussion, however, since it gave effect to a distinct policy change (reducing the emphasis on afforestation and affording priority to conservation and management of existing forest resources), he regarded as the most important directive issued since 1960.

The people's councils and their planning commissions are responsible for the provision of labor and materials required to implement the regulations.

THE STATE FOREST SERVICE

The Ministry of Forestry is the executive body responsible for all afforestation, management, and exploitation in the national forests. It is a combination of two former ministries—forestry and exploitation. These ministries were separately established in 1956, the latter under one of the few non-Communists to hold a ministerial portfolio under the present regime. In 1957, the two ministries amalgamated and the department was reorganized. At present, there are a Minister and eight Deputy Ministers, with responsibilities as follows: machinery and material supply (two deputies); afforestation and management of artificial plantations (two deputies); research; planning and finance; forest industry; and forest management (one deputy each). The deputy ministers are nontechnical administrators and work through professionally qualified divisional directors.

In each of China's twenty-six provinces or autonomous regions, there is a "conservancy" organization under the ministry. Depending on the importance of forestry in the province, it is divided into administrative regions and further subdivided into management and protection districts (based on topography and forest type) and working units.

The administrative region of Tailing in Heilungkiang province can serve to illustrate this breakdown in an area where exploitation, management and reforestation are all important and well advanced. It comprises some 120,000 ha. made up as follows: primary forest, 80,000 ha.; secondary forest, 20,000 ha.; artificial plantations, 12,000 ha.; nonforested land (including some agriculture), 8,000 ha. It has an annual planting program of 1,200 ha. to 1,600 ha. (1,280 in 1963) and a felling plan covering approximately 800 ha. (720 in 1963). There is a small local sawmill and a 20- ha. nursery. There are seven management districts covering three forest types and ranging in area from 4,000 to 24,000 ha., depending on the scope and intensity of operations. In each district there are from two to twelve working units (ninety in total) of 400 ha. to 2,000 ha., each worked by a forest foreman, drawing upon the labor pool for the entire region. In addition, and super-imposed on this organization, each management district is divided into twelve "protection" districts of from 4,800 to 10,000 ha. for fire control and policing purposes.

The labor force totals 3,560 and, of this number, 52 are university graduates in forestry and 12 have university diplomas. Since Tailing is by way of being a "model" forestry region and also includes a number of experimental forests, it is undoubtedly better served by technically qualified personnel than most regions. In the whole of China, there are said to be 3,215 forestry "centers" under the ministry, of which some two-thirds are concerned largely with afforestation and one-third are management units. The total labor force is about 300,000, providing an average of 100 men per center. It is clear, therefore, that with 3,500 men, the Tailing region is under very intensive forest management. This is scarcely surprising, in view of its location in the rich montane-boreal coniferous forests of Manchuria. At the other ex-treme, however, there are vast areas in some provinces in which the only tasks of the regional foresters are to provide technical advice to commune management committees and to carry out general extension and policing work. The administrative organization is illustrated in Figure 3.

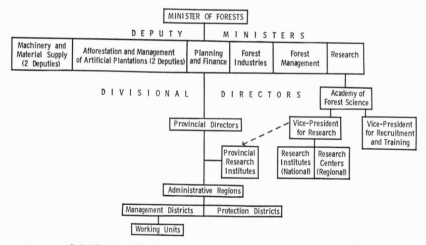

Broken line shows indirect relationship; solid lines show direct supervisory functions.

Figure 3: Administrative Organization of the State Forest Service

"PRIVATE" FORESTRY

Of some 96 million ha. of forest land in China, about 80 per cent is *de facto* state forest; the remainder is controlled by communes, municipalities, autonomous districts, and other administrative subdivisions. In terms of activity, the most important of these local bodies are the communes (production brigades and production teams), of which more than 10,000 are said to be engaged in forestry projects. In this context, "forestry" includes the cultivation of what are variously described in the Chinese literature as "economic" or "industrial" trees; they include bamboos, *Thea* oil trees, camphor, *Lindera*, tung, tallow trees (*Sapium sebiferum*), and other short-rotation crops (see Table 7, Chapter V). The major "forestry brigades" are located in the provinces south of the Yangtze river where the climate is conducive to rapid growth and where afforestation can be financed by the communes themselves out of income. In such cases, technical service is provided free of charge by the State Forest Service or by cadres of agrotechnical extension stations, (see Chao, 1961).

Standing timber may be sold to the state service or exploitation may be carried out by contractors. Before felling any timber for sale, however, the brigades must obtain permission from the State Forest Service. Felling for the individual needs of the brigade is subject to approval from the local people's council at a level determined by the amount to be cut. Similarly, replanting (which is mandatory) after felling is supervised by the State Forest Service and may be carried out with stock provided at cost by the state service.

In areas where short-term returns provide insufficient incentive for communal forestry or where large-scale afforestation is required for protective purposes and land reclamation, projects are planned and supervised by the State Forest Service, but carried out by the production teams either on a labor contract or financed by interest-free or low-interest-rate loans (1 per cent to 2 per cent, depending upon the economic strength of the commune). The plantations become the property of the commune but they must be managed according to plans approved by the state service. Supervisory control by either the state service or local bodies is fairly close, but it is not always clear just where the ultimate authority lies.

It is this writer's impression, based on visits to production teams in several provinces and on discussions with provincial forest officers, that control of so-called private forests by the state service is tightening.

Moreover, since 1958, the area of forest under national rather than regional control has increased from 65 per cent to 80 per cent of the total. The move toward more state control (which contrasts with the decentralization policy adopted toward industry) is most probably due to the inadequate technical supervision exercised by local administrators over many of the earlier afforestation schemes. As will be shown later, Chinese labors in afforestation have been prodigious, but much of this effort has been nullified by poor maintenance; in many commune projects, survival, in terms of number of trees, is less than 10 per cent. Since 1960, therefore, regulations designed to ensure proper treatment and adequate protection have been issued in abundance and it is significant that it is usually the State Forest Service that is called upon to enforce them.

FOREST POLICY DEVELOPMENTS, 1949–63

As soon as the Communists achieved national control in 1949, all forest land (except that attached to certain Buddhist temples, which was not taken over until 1951) was nationalized and a Ministry for National Development drew up interim utilization plans. An immediate aim was to rehabilitate and expand the sawmilling plant in Manchuria (which before the war was, of course, in Japanese hands and much of which had been dismantled by the Russians after 1945) in order to survive the initial shock of a virtual cessation of timber imports from 1950 onward. At the same time, Liang Hsi, professor of forestry at Nanking University and later to become the first Minister of Forestry, was invited to prepare a series of guidelines to serve as a basis for a forest policy. His program (*Far East Econ. Rev.*, 1950; *Petrov*, 1952) recognized the value of protection afforestation in soil conservation, the need to regulate felling in the Manchurian forests, and the potential role of short-rotation tree crops in the southern provinces. However, little in the way of a forest policy emerged before 1952 when the Ministry of Forestry was fully established and drew up a "Directive on Mass Afforestation, Cultivation of Forests and Protection of Forests" which was promulgated by the State Council in September, 1953. This document called for the establishment of organizations to introduce fire control in the natural forests and for vigorous afforestation of hills and wasteland. It never became a formal part of the first five-year plan, though the Chinese claimed to have planted more than ten million ha. under this plan.

Following these initial pronouncements on afforestation, the ministry, in 1954, set up an organization to prepare a national forest inventory. This survey is extremely ambitious and, although originally scheduled for completion by 1962, at the present rate of progress it is unlikely to be concluded before 1970. Concentrating initially on the forest areas of greatest economic value (Heilungkiang, Kirin, and Inner Mongolia), it aims at 100 per cent area survey in all provinces, with a varying sampling fraction for volume estimation. For example, in Heilungkiang province, 10 per cent of the forest area has been assessed—allegedly including all trees down to a breast-height diameter of 5 cm.—and the percentage is now being increased to 25. In Kwangtung, 100 per cent of natural forest (except mangroves) is being measured and plantations sampled to the extent of 5 per cent to 10 per cent; some 300 men are said to be employed on survey work in that province alone.

The afforestation program promulgated in 1953 was outlined in general terms only, but it appears to have been directed primarily at protective planting by peasant collectives, rather than state-sponsored production forestry. Some 94 per cent of the planting carried out between 1953 and 1956 was allegedly done by co-operatives (Messines, 1958); by May, 1955, 182,000 "silvicultural co-operatives of various types" were said to exist (Tao, 1955). In spite of the aims of the program, however, the reported achievements of the first five-year plan highlight afforestation for timber production (some 65 per cent of the area claimed [*Peking Review*, 4/22/58]). Since "timber production" includes the "reconstitution of natural forests" and, further, since no indication is given of the stocking densities which constitute "afforestation," area claims are difficult to evaluate. It does seem, however, as if the objectives of the program were somewhat modified during its operation.

During these early years, also, the Chinese experienced some difficulty in designing an effective administrative organization for forest regions under exploitation and in integrating the timber industry with the Ministry of Forestry. For example, Kuo *et al.* (1959) record the changes that have taken place in the titular management of the Ta Hsingan forest region of Inner Mongolia: from 1946 to September, 1947, it came under the East Mongolian Forest Company; from September 1947 to 1948, under the Inner Mongolian Forestry and Mining Bureau; from 1948 to 1950, the Inner Mongolia Bureau of Forestry; from 1950 to 1951, the General Bureau of Forestry of Inner Mongolia; in 1952, the Inner Mongolia Department of Forestry; in

1953, the Inner Mongolia Industry Control Bureau; and in 1954, it was run by the Bureau of Forestry of the Hu-lun-pei-erh League. Such changes foreshadowed the separation of the Ministries of Forestry and Exploitation in 1956 and their recombination in 1957.

Frequent changes in organization and administration of timber exploitation seem to be a characteristic of communist economies; the U.S.S.R. as well as China has had difficulty in co-ordinating forest management and timber harvesting. Prior to 1957 in Russia, the Ministry of Timber Industry was responsible for all phases of forestry but, in that year, management and protection functions were assigned to a division of the Ministry of Agriculture (except in the Latvian and Lithuanian Soviet Republics). In October, 1959, however, all forestry activities in the Russian Soviet were again concentrated in a single organizational unit—the Glavleskhoz—working under the Council of People's Economy (Sovnarkhoz), thus reviving the situation that existed prior to 1957. It appears, therefore, that both Russia and China (like many capitalist countries) are still searching for an efficient means of reconciling the demands of industry with those of forest management and protection.

The first specific forestry program in China clearly based on a resource assessment was set out in the National Plan for Agriculture which was to run from 1956–68; it arose from a national conference on forestry held in December, 1955. The program assumed a total existing resource of 5,400,000,000 cu. m. (derived from figures compiled by the Nationalist government before the war and accepted by Soviet consultants) which would last about 35 years. Average annual requirements over the period 1960–90 were considered to be 150,000,000 cu. m. (see Appendix I). In order to meet requirements when the resource ran out, some 105,000,000 ha. were to be afforested within the twelve-year period, to give a forest cover of 20 per cent of the land surface area. (This figure was revised from a target of 18 per cent set in 1953). As in the previous program, the bulk of afforestation was to be in the form of protection forest and shelter plantations in very difficult country. According to the Minister of Forestry in 1956: "The National Conference on Afforestation . . . demanded that we plant 100 million hectares of barren lands and barren mountains within the next twelve years. If we can overcome all kinds of difficulties and implement such ambitious plans on schedule, we will have written a new page in the forestry history of China, and scored a success unprecedented in the forestry history of the world. Is this not glorious?

"But China has the greatest number of barren hills in the world.
. . . They are salty, alkaline, or sandy lands presenting enormous
technical problems."

In the twelve-year plan, emphasis was also placed on "economic
crops and fast-growing species." As time went on (and, particularly,
after the formation of the communes in 1958) the latter became
increasingly prominent in governmental pronouncements and present
policy is to devote about 50 per cent of the planting area to such
crops. In 1958, also, the decision was made to concentrate the greater
part (85 per cent) of production afforestation in areas south of the
Yangtze river.

The government also at this stage became concerned about standards of protection in the hill forests and called for a more rational
land use policy: "How can we prevent the indiscriminate reclamation
of hilly land and the loss of water and soil? As far as we can see, only
when we are able to make out a proper production plan for the high
country—particularly a plan for using the land rationally and solving
the conflicting needs of agriculture, forestry, and pasturage—can we
point out to the masses the bright future, and can we prevent them
from reclaiming the hills recklessly. . . . Fire is the greatest enemy of
forests. We must resolutely and thoroughly eliminate it; we must stop
shouting slogans; we must take effective measures. . . ." This clarion
call from the Minister of Forestry was followed by a series of measures
designed to improve forest protection and the co-ordination of land-
use policies. As is usual in China—and despite the Minister of Forestry—massive propaganda campaigns formed the first step: news-
paper articles, lectures, theater performances, and ubiquitous car-
toons and posters exhorted the populace to protect the new forests.
Regulations limiting access to afforestation areas and prohibiting fuel-
gathering were issued, and more than 3,000 State Forest Service Centers were established to police them. In 1957, thirty-seven weather
and fire danger forecasting stations were set up and aerial reconnaissance begun, and the closure of forest land to grazing was accelerated (Chieh Wen, 1958). An elaborate organization for collecting
information about tree diseases and insect pests was also established,
along much the same lines as that for agriculture (see Buchanan,
1960); chemical and biological control of forest insects was intensified.

In attempts to rationalize and co-ordinate land-use policy, the
Academia Sinica, reorganized and strengthened in 1955, and the
Scientific Planning Committee (established by the State Planning
Commission in 1956 and amalgamated with the State Technological

Commission to become the Scientific and Technological Planning Commission, in 1958) played increasingly important roles. The *Academia* organized expeditions to the remote parts of China (including timber resource surveys), established research centers in desert regions (see e.g. Chu, 1959a), and began to prepare technical handbooks of soil and water conservation. The Scientific Planning Committee set up a series of regional land-use committees, advisory to the provincial people's councils, and several national bodies such as the Working Committee for the Harnessing of Deserts.

The years 1959, 1960, and 1961 were excessively dry in China and gave rise to severe food shortages (W.K., 1961; Kenji, 1961; Snow, 1963). These calamities drew attention to deficiencies in water conservancy projects and to the results of poor establishment practices in the new forests. Measures adopted to raise standards included the organization of training courses (often by correspondence) for cadres, the establishment of "seed centers" in seventeen provinces, and centralized nurseries under the aegis of the State Forest Service (and, in some provinces, prohibition of the use of seed other than that supplied by the seed centers), legislation requiring afforestation agencies to "guarantee" survival, and the award of certificates to the organizers of successful projects ("Heroes of Afforestation") only when establishment has been demonstrated.

That the government is still concerned about low standards of establishment practice and lack of initial tending, however, can be gathered from an analysis of recent pronouncements by the Ministry of Forestry and from the fact that early in 1963 an additional Deputy Minister was appointed, with responsibility for management of artificial plantations. In government propaganda, exhortations to plant vast areas of wasteland have been only sporadic since 1960 and emphasis has shifted to the tending and maintenance of existing plantations. Of 148 official news releases on forestry collected by the Reuters correspondent in Peking over the years 1958–63, between 1958 and 1961, 66 items refer to afforestation while only 12 make mention of the need for subsequent tending; from 1961 to 1963, however, there were 38 references to plantation management compared with 36 reports on afforestation. In 1962, the afforestation program was reduced to 50 per cent of that in 1960. The "Regulations" governing the protection of forests issued by the State Council on May 27, 1963, and the *People's Daily* editorial which accompanied their publication (see Appendix II) further demonstrate a determination to raise standards of practice and to conserve the national forest resource. As already mentioned, this concern has been accompanied by a reduction in the annual timber cut from 39,000,000 cu. m. in 1960 to 30,000,000 cu. m. in 1962.

There is every evidence, then, that Chinese foresters are by now fully aware of the deficiencies of their mass afforestation schemes and of the need for conservation of the remaining natural forest resource; whether or not they can resist the inevitable industrial demands on that resource remains to be seen.

CHAPTER IV.

PRODUCTION FORESTRY PRACTICE:

AFFORESTATION, SEED COLLECTION, AND NURSERY PRACTICE

ANY STUDY of forestry in China, however brief, leaves two strong impressions in the mind of a visitor: firstly, the extent to which the Chinese approach to afforestation has, until recently, been influenced by practices developed in the Soviet Union and based on the so-called "new Soviet biology," and, secondly, the evident lack of balance between the efforts and resources devoted to afforestation and those afforded to forest management. Criticism of the policies which have engendered these features of Chinese forestry must, however, be tempered by recognition of a third feature—the realization, by professional foresters at any rate, that such policies are detrimental to sound forestry practice. As a result, silvicultural techniques are in a state of considerable flux involving many changing emphases and large-scale experimentation.

A brief review of the history and concepts of Michurinist biology is presented in Chapter VIII. Though practices such as nest sowing of seed, group planting, and ultraclose spacing of trees—which arise from the Michurinist claim that intraspecific competition does not exist— are a prominent feature of the Chinese forestry scene, little attempt is now made to justify them on ideological grounds and the approach is essentially empirical; it is unlikely that in the future Chinese forestry will be significantly influenced by Michurinism. The second impression, relating to the lack of balance between planting and subsequent tending, is of more consequence.

61

THE BALANCE BETWEEN AFFORESTATION AND MANAGEMENT

Many recent visitors to China have attested to the vastness of the scale on which afforestation is being attempted (see Buchanan, 1960; Kinmond, 1959; Greene, 1962; Snow, 1963; etc.), and the claims of the Chinese themselves are truly startling. In Table 5, selected data relating to areas reportedly afforested are presented. For two reasons, however, these data are of little more than academic interest; firstly, because the statistics are contradictory (particularly those relating to 1958) and, secondly, because even in favorable habitats (which the majority of China's afforestation sites are not), failure in plantations has been widespread and management is almost nonexistent. Over

Table 5.   Selected Data (and Sources) Relating to Areas
Reportedly Afforested, 1950–60.

Years	Area Claimed (ha.)	Source
1950	124,000	Petrov, 1952
1951	463,000	Petrov, 1952
1952	692,000	Petrov, 1952
1953	1,000,000	Radio Peking, 1957
1954	1,120,000	*People's China*, 1956
1955	1,700,000	*People's China*, 1956
1956	4,000,000	FAO, undated
1957	3,960,000	NCNA, 1/2/58
1958 To March	11,000,000	NCNA, 4/4/58
To June	21,000,000	Deng, 1959
To October	27,500,000	NCNA, 11/12/58
To November	33,000,000	NCNA, 11/14/58
	("nearly")	
Whole year	>26,000,000	NCNA, 3/5/59
	17,460,000	NCNA, 4/5/60; Auslands Inf., 1960
1959	18,600,000	NCNA, 4/5/60; Auslands Inf., 1960
	18,800,000	*Peking Review*, 1960
Target	26,600,000	*SCMP*, 1960
1960	13,000,000	Ministry of Forestry, 1963
Target	12,000,000	Li Fu Chun, 1960
1962–63 "Current Program"	5,000,000	Ministry of Forestry, 1963
1952–57 (first five-year plan)		
	10,000,000	NCNA, 9/25/57
	11,000,000	Carter, 1958
	10,320,000	NCNA, 2/5/58
	10,300,000	*Foreign Trade Pub.*, 1959; Solecki, 1964
1950–58	33,190,000	NCNA, 9/18/59; Hsu Chien, 1959
1949–58	30,000,000	NCNA, 11/17/58
1949–60	51,834,000	Chang, 1960

vast areas, particularly in dry, hilly country, plantations now provide a ground cover of less than 50 per cent. In many instances survival in terms of number of stems is no more than 10 per cent. In Appendix III, an attempt has been made to illustrate these poor survivals in relation to areas afforested. The data were drawn from estimates of tree cover and survival made during air and rail travel through China, and were supplemented by actual stem counts on 1 chain × 1 chain (0.04 ha.), square plots in various parts of China, which are shown in Table 6. They clearly demonstrate the high mortality which has occurred in plantations.

Chinese foresters invariably claimed survival rates of 70 per cent to 90 per cent, irrespective of species and site conditions (see also NCNA, No. 080907, 1962); except in state forests in Manchuria and in experimental plantations, however, this writer could nowhere confirm these claims. For other reasons, too, official Chinese data relating to survival must be accepted with the greatest reserve; for instance it is not always clear just what the Chinese mean when they refer to survival. On two occasions (once at the Great Wall afforestation project and once in Manchuria) where two forms of group planting had been practiced, the author queried survival figures of 75 per cent to 87 per cent volunteered by the project administrators: it transpired that these values related to the survival of groups containing one or more living trees rather than to individual trees. In such cases, survival in terms of number of living stems might be as low as 5 per cent, while conforming to an 80 per cent group survival. Similarly, when survival percentages are given for aerially sown areas (see e.g. NCNA, No. 080907, 1962) the figures may relate to full stocking rather than actual survival of individuals.

Table 6 illustrates another general impression gained throughout China—the marked difference in success between state and commune afforestation projects. The correctness of this impression was freely admitted by professional foresters. It is, perhaps, not surprising, in view of the way in which communal projects are carried out. Except in southern China, afforestation projects are generally undertaken at the behest of the state service and with finance and materials provided by the state service. A target is set for the season (often in terms of number of trees to be planted, rather than area to be covered) and payments are made on completion. Enormous numbers of people may be involved at any one time. In 1958, for example, when a 1,700-km. long shelter planting was initiated in northern Kansu, the planting gangs

Table 6.   Stocking Density Assessments of Various Plantations in Yunnan, Heilungkiang, Chekiang, and Kwangtung Provinces

Location	Ownership	Species	Age	Stems/ha.	Remarks
Kunming, Yunnan	Commune	*Pinus yunnanensis*	5	150	N. and P. deficient
Kunming, Yunnan	Commune	*P. yunnanensis*	8	75	
Kunming, Yunnan	Commune	*Eucalyptus globulus*	10	50	Very dry site
Kunming, Yunnan	Commune	*Pinus yunnanensis* / *Keteleeria davidiana*	50	1,150	Very poor growth
Wun Tuan, Yunnan	Commune (?)	*Populus yunnanensis*	3	500	
Wun Tuan, Yunnan	Not known	*Pinus yunnanensis*	5	175	Natural regeneration
Tailing, Heilungkiang	State	*P. koraiensis*	6	1,950	Turf planted in groups
Tailing, Heilungkiang	State	*P. sylvestris* var. *mongolica*	6	1,650	Planted 0.3 m. X 0.3 m.
Tailing, Heilungkiang	State	*P. koraiensis*	6	2,875	Planted 0.3 m. X 0.3 m.
Tailing, Heilungkiang	State	*Larix dahurica*	7	2,375	Planted 0.6 m. X 0.3 m.
Tailing, Heilungkiang	State	*L. dahurica*	5	1,950	Planted 0.6 m. X 0.3 m.
Tailing, Heilungkiang	State	*L. dahurica*	7	1,400	Planted 0.6 m. X 0.3 m.
Tailing, Heilungkiang	Commune	*Pinus koraiensis*	5	1,350	"Experimental"
Great Wall, Peking	Municipality	*P. tabulaeformis*	4	875	Trough-planted at ca. 7,500/ha.
Great Wall, Peking	Municipality	*Robinia pseudoacacia*	4	1,300	Trough-planted at ca. 7,500/ha.
W. Lake, Hangchow	Commune	*Pinus massoniana*	12	1,650	Planted 8,750/ha.
W. Lake, Hangchow	Commune	*P. massoniana*	6	875	
Kwangchow, Kwangtung	State	*P. massoniana*	6	1,700	Direct sown
Kwangchow, Kwangtung	State	*Eucalyptus exserta*	5	1,175	
Ting Hu, Kwangtung	Commune	*Pinus massoniana*	4–5	135	
Ting Hu, Kwangtung	Commune	*P. massoniana*	4	300	

exceeded 700,000 men and two-thirds of the belt was completed in a single season. While there are monumental precedents for this kind of an operation in China (the Great Wall and the Grand Canal), when applied to afforestation there is little incentive to achieve a high standard in planting practice, to maintain the plantations, or to ensure survival. Widespread failure is, doubtless, one reason why closer control of afforestation projects by the state is being fostered.

There are, of course, other reasons for poor tree survivals, not the least important of which relates to the harshness of the sites which are being planted. In official Chinese news releases, references to the afforestation of "bare hills," "shifting sands," "barren deserts," etc. are legion. During 1955, 40 per cent of the area afforested was said to be in the form of shelter belts to combat sand movement (*People's China*, 7/16/56), while the twelve-year afforestation plan adopted in 1956 envisaged the bulk of the planting on "wasteland and desert." In 1957, a total of almost 4 million ha. of "barren land" was allegedly afforested (NCNA, 1/2/58). More recent communiqués highlight the huge shelter afforestation projects in the northern provinces: 700,000 ha. of tree belts in the "sand-ravaged" northeast (NCNA, No. 060123, 1961); a 300-km. barrier covering 300,000 ha. against shifting sand in northern Shensi (NCNA, 12/1/61; NCNA, No. 031517, 1962; NCNA, No. 052105, 1963); 100,000 ha. of shelter belts in Kansu, together with plantings on more than 1 million ha. of "barren slopes" (NCNA, No. 082202, 1962); 8,000 ha. of shelter plantations in northern Sinkiang (NCNA 11/21/62); 500,000 ha. of stabilized sand dunes in Inner Mongolia (NCNA, No. 101704, 1962); a 600-km. tree belt to protect farmland from the "sand dragon" in Shantung (NCNA, No. 032908, 1963). Whatever reservations one may have about the areas and successes claimed, there can be no doubts about the problems of site relating to these schemes; climatically and edaphically, sites are intractable, covering vast loess plains and saline desert soils in the dryest parts of the country. Further south, too, depleted sites form major afforestation centers. Thus, shelter belts have been planted in Fukien and Kwangtung on poor coastal sands to act as breaks against typhoons (NCNA, No. 051214, 1961; NCNA, No. 112502, 1962); 10,000 ha. of plantations in Honan have been established on the former bed of the Hwang-Ho river (NCNA, No. 041105, 1963); and, in the spring of 1963, 60,000 ha. of "denuded and eroded hills" in Kiangsi were afforested (NCNA, No. 041312, 1963).

Examples of this sort could be cited almost indefinitely; and observation confirms that, in general, land available for forestry is unstable, subject to a high degree of erosion by water and wind, and poor in nutrients. Phosphate and nitrogen deficiencies are widespread in plantations. With what is, in effect, piecework planting, no blanking, and virtual disregard of plantation maintenance, poor survival is only to be expected.

That poor planting practice may be a significant factor in survival was indicated to the author during rail travel between Hangchow and Kwangchow (see Appendix III). In the same area, good and poor survivals were sometimes sharply differentiated and it was suggested, in explanation, that the boundary was the line of demarcation between plantings of different production teams in the same commune. In a Kwangtung commune on a hot, dry day in June, *Eucalyptus* saplings (2 m. tall) were being planted bare-rooted, with no protection against drying out. While the quality of stock was generally good, its treatment on the planting site was atrocious.

Another factor which may well contribute to the devastated appearance of young plantations is the very real fuel shortage in most parts of China. The great majority of rural Chinese must rely on wood and other vegetable matter for all cooking and heating purposes and, in the deforested areas (where 98 per cent of the population is located), fuel is at a premium. In the rural communes, peasants are allowed to harvest dead trees for burning and they have, thus, a vested interest in early mortality. To tend trees for posterity, while freezing in the present from lack of firewood, demands an altruism scarcely to be expected, even in China; there is evidence, in fact, that, as happens in the new territories of Hong Kong, trees are stolen for fuel almost as soon as they have been planted.

In many parts of China, young plantations are also subject to considerable fire hazards. In the northern provinces, burning of grassland to improve grazing is common and, elsewhere, land reclamation for agriculture involves the use of fire (on a flight from Kunming to Chungking—a distance of *ca.* 600 km.—the writer noted twenty-one fires in scrub-covered hill country). In the south, even the practice of burning paper "money" at ancestral tombs is sufficiently a hazard to warrant legislation controlling it during the fire season (see Appendix II).

SEED COLLECTION AND NURSERY PRACTICE

Seed Collection

Prior to 1958, tree seed collection in China was somewhat haphazard; in general, collections were made by peasants (usually women and children) for sale to co-operatives or to the provincial forestry departments. The formation of the communes in 1958, however, gave a signal boost to so-called "private" forestry and, with the advent of aerial sowing in about 1960 (NCNA No. 082514, 1960; NCNA No. 080907, 1962), seed requirements increased markedly. The need for more systematic methods of seed collection and an improved nursery organization became apparent and, at present, the bulk of seed collection is organized by the State Forest Service through the "seed centers." These operate either by direct employment of collecting teams or by purchasing surplus seed from the production brigades which run communal nurseries. In areas where seed sources are scarce or where it is necessary to introduce new species or strains, collection and interprovincial exchanges are organized by the ministry in Peking.

The establishment of the seed centers (and of centralized nurseries) has enabled longer-term planning (currently, to five-year plans, revised annually) and the rationalization of planting requirements. Closer state control is also said to be helping to improve tree seed quality by imposing more rigorous selection. For example, in Manchuria, one of the establishment problems in the past derived from the great variability in size and quality of nursery stock of *Pinus koraiensis*—a principal reforestation species in the northeast. The seed of this species is edible and is also used commercially for oil extraction. Before seed collection came under the control of the State Forest Service, collections were "creamed" by separation of the biggest seeds for industrial purposes and only the smaller (and lower quality) material was available for nursery sowings. This practice has resulted in a marked lack of uniformity in *Pinus koraiensis* plantations established before 1958, particularly in comparison with *Larix dahurica*.

It is, perhaps, too early to assess the ameliorative effects of the seed centers; outside Kwangtung province, however, the writer saw little evidence of very rigorous standards of seed tree selection in China. Even in Manchuria, seed is generally collected from the most easily accessible stands, many of which were cut over during the Japanese occupation and, in consequence, comprise trees of poor form and growth rate. Elsewhere, collections are often made in arboreta, in roadside and amenity plantations, and in farm woodlots. After extraction and cleaning, seed is screened and some culling effected at the nursery. Seed for aerial sowing is not culled and the degree of nursery selection probably varies considerably, depending on the seed supply relative to requirements.

As in most countries, the establishment of seed orchards has yet to progress beyond the research stage. The most advanced province in this respect is Kwangtung, where the majority of plantations are now established by direct sowing. It is of interest that, in 1962 in Kwangtung, regulations were drafted prohibiting the communes using seed other than that supplied by the State Forest Service.

Nursery Practice

Nursery practice, as befits a country with a long market-gardening and horticultural tradition, appears to be of a high standard. There are about 30,000 ha. of state forest nurseries in China, employing 20,000 people; in addition, many communes have established small, temporary nurseries.

In general, with the exception of temporary plots established on the site of relatively small afforestation projects, state forest nurseries are located on former agricultural soils; they are normally hand cultivated and, where available, organic manure (usually comprising night soil and forest litter) is applied at rates considerably in excess of those used in agriculture. Where "economic" trees are raised, leguminous green-cropping and organic mulches are used; inorganic fertilizers, however, are seldom employed because of their scarcity. As is general practice in crop production, meticulously clean cultivation is general and nurseries are remarkably weed free. Costs, in terms of manpower, however, must be high. Needless to say, mechanization—apart from sundry precarious homemade devices such as irrigation pumps and spray units—is nonexistent.

For the large-scale protection afforestation schemes, seedlings are raised in huge centralized nurseries and transplanted to the plantation site for "acclimatization" one or two years before planting. The value of this practice is, currently, a lively topic of debate among Chinese foresters.

Commune nurseries are less impressive. They are usually established on small areas of "waste" ground (often inter-cropping fruit trees, or in open woodland as a prelude to the growth of agricultural crops), and they receive no fertilizers other than token amounts of wood ash from precultivation burning. Again, however, they are kept relatively weed-free and the quality of the stock raised is surprisingly high.

State Forest Service Nurseries. Of six production forest nurseries visited by the author, that at Tailing, Heilungkiang, is probably typical of the highest standards of practice in Manchuria, having been in operation for twelve years. Situated on the northern outskirts of the town, it comprises some 20 ha., of which 12 were in production in June, 1963, and serves an annual planting program of 1,200 ha. to 1,600 ha. in cut-over virgin forests of the mixed coniferous and decid-uous broadleaved forest zone. The principal species raised are *Pinus koraiensis, Larix dahurica, Pinus sylvestris* var. *mongolica, Fraxinus mandshurica, Tilia amurensis, Juglans mandshurica,* and *Phellodendron amurense.* Of these, the conifers make up 80 per cent of production. The soil is a deep, rich alluvium, formerly in agriculture (vegetable-growing); it is easily worked, with abundant organic matter and a pH range of 5.5 to 6.5.

Seed is generally broadcast by hand in spring at densities ranging from 0.35 kg./sq. m. for *Pinus sylvestris* and *Larix dahurica* (to give *ca.* 300 seedlings/sq. m.) to 0.75 kg./sq. m. for *Pinus koraiensis* (to give *ca.* 400 seedlings/sq. m.). Germination percentage was said to be 60 for *Larix dahurica,* 84 for *Pinus sylvestris,* and "better than 95" for *P. koraiensis.* The pines are held in seedbeds for three years and then either root-pruned or transplanted; after a further year in the nursery they are ready for planting out. *Larix dahurica,* on the other hand, shows more rapid initial growth and 2 + 0 seedlings are out-planted. A consistent regime for the hardwoods has yet to be established; most of this stock goes for "special purpose" planting (shelter belts, erosion control, etc.) in other districts and size requirements were said to vary considerably.

Fertilizer regimes have been more or less standardized. An applica-tion of 20 cwt./ha. of "organic manure"—a mixture of night soil, town refuse, and forest litter—given in autumn, is supplemented by a mixed nitrogenous and phosphatic artificial fertilizer (28 to 38 kg./ha. for *Pinus koraiensis,* 45 kg./ha. for *P. sylvestris,* and 56 kg./ha. for *Larix dahurica* in July). Green-cropping with soya beans is also general—after five years' growth of *Pinus koraiensis;* three years, in the case of *P. sylvestris;* and two years, with *Larix dahurica.* By agricultural standards in China, the fertilizer applications are very generous indeed and the values may be suspect. Not unexpectedly, the nursery is not highly mechanized. A Fordson tractor is available for ploughing and a homemade irrigation system operates (this was proudly demonstrated during a thunderstorm; it is said to be needed for two to three months in the year). Insecticide spraying is also a standard practice, using Russian-manufactured knapsack sprayers and benzene hexachloride. All other operations—seedbed cultivation, sowing, weeding, transplanting, root-pruning, manuring, etc.—are done by hand. The permanent labor force comprises four technical cadres and forty-one laborers (including twenty-seven women) and is supplemented as required by about thirty temporary employees.

As far as could be judged from a one-day visit, the Tailing nursery production is of a high standard, and growth rates, particularly of *Larix dahurica*, are impressive for the area. For example, four-year seedlings of *Pinus koraiensis* averaged 0.6 m.; 2 + 0 *P. sylvestris*, 0.3 − 0.5 m.; and *Larix dahurica* (3 + 0, for amenity planting, raised from selected seed) up to 1.2 m. Occasional beds of *Larix* had suffered slight losses from damping-off, but no evidence of any other pathogens was apparent, nor were there any obvious nutrient deficiencies. The two young ladies assiduously (and ostentatiously) spraying insecticide—also during a heavy rainstorm—appeared to be working quite needlessly.

Compared with Tailing, the "Dragon's Eye" district nursery of Kwangtung province provides a marked contrast in practice, though its standards are also relatively high. Some 8 ha. in extent, it is attached to the provincial Forest Research Institute, though run by the "conservancy" bureau, not by the research branch. The research institute was formerly (until 1959) an extension forestry organization and the nursery is a legacy from that time.

The soil is a heavy, yellow laterite, poor in nutrients and in organic matter; potassium and nitrogen deficiencies are obvious and the trace elements molybdenum and manganese are also said to be lacking. The pH ranges from 5.0 to 6.3. Climatically, coastal Kwangtung is in the humid tropics, though the winters tend to be dry; of a total rainfall of 200 cm., only 10 cm. falls between January and April.

The main coniferous species used in afforestation in the area, *Pinus massoniana* and *Cunninghamia lanceolata*, are generally established by direct seeding, though *Pinus massoniana* is sometimes nursery-sown in January and out-planted in May/June when the typhoon season brings rain; at the time of this visit, therefore, the greater part of the nursery was under economic crop species—*Thea oleosa, T. sinensis, Cinnamomum camphora, Aleurites cordata, Eucalyptus citriodora, E. exserta, Casuarina equisetifolia* (for coastal dune planting), *Melia azedarach, Populus robusta,* and *Salix* spp. Some fruit trees, including the widespread *Litchi chinensis,* were also being grown, but *Eucalyptus* spp. and *Salix* spp. made up some 50 per cent of the nursery production.

Regimes for the different species vary. Thus, poplars are grown from seed and willows from 15-cm. cuttings rooted at about 15-cm. spacing in February/March and planted out (often by the local commune) after some six months' growth. *Thea* and tung trees, after sowing to give a density of 200 seedlings/sq. m., are transplanted after one year to a spacing of 0.4 m. to 0.6 m. and left in the nursery for another year before out-planting; growth of *Eucalyptus* spp., on the other hand, is much more rapid and they are planted out bare-rooted at eight to nine months after autumn sowing. A small area of *Pinus massoniana* had been nest-sown (eight seeds/nest) and intact clumps would be planted out three to five months after germination. Germination percentage for *P. massoniana* was about 95 and for *Melia azedarach,* 75; figures for other species were not available.

Soil fertility was said to be maintained by an annual application of 25 cwt./ha. of litter, hand-dug into the seed beds at the time of cultivation. *Thea,* tung, and *Cinnamomum camphora* are also mulched with chopped rice straw, sugar-cane waste, or bamboo leaves after germination and a general application of a "trace-element solution" (composition unknown) is given to all the broadleaved species beds. Every three years a third of the nursery is green-cropped with peas or beans in an attempt to improve the nitrogen status; no inorganic fertilizers are used, however.

Clean cultivation is general and the nursery was remarkably free of weeds; there were, however, many more pathogenic problems here than in the Tailing nursery. In particular an unknown species of nematode is proving troublesome with *Thea, Tortrix* attacks on *Pinus massoniana* had been severe, and both *Melia azedarach* and *Eucalyptus citriodora* suffered from a seedling root rot.

The nursery work force comprises two technical cadres and thirty laborers; the abundant labor market in Canton doubtless accounts for the apparently excessive labor force and the absence of even the token mechanization seen at Tailing. All operations are performed manually, even the presowing "deep cultivation" (to 45 cm.)—another point of Mao Tse-tung's "Charter for Agriculture."

In spite of apparent nutritional disorders and the effect of pathogens, initial growth rates in the "Dragon's Eye" nursery were startling, as the following examples will illustrate: *Eucalyptus exserta*, 1.5 m. to 2.0 m., nine months after sowing; *Pinus massoniana*, 1.0 m. at four months; *Cunninghamia lanceolata*, 1.0 m. at five months; *Melia azedarach*, 3.5 m. at one year; and *Populus robusta* and *Salix* sp. 1.5 m. at eight months.

Other Nurseries. Even greater variations in nursery practice are to be found in commune and municipal nurseries. For example, the Great Wall afforestation project, north of Peking, uses two principal species— *Robinia pseudoacacia*, raised in a formal nursery in Peking, and *Pinus tabulaeformis* "acclimatized" by sowing in on-site troughs at an altitude of almost 600 m. These troughs are, in effect, oblong or semi-circular platforms, 2 m. long × 50 cm. at the widest point, cut into the hillside, hand-cultivated, and mulched. The climate is harsh, with 37 cm. to 50 cm. rainfall per year falling largely in July and August; temperatures are low in winter (averaging −20°C.) and, during winter and spring, cold dry winds are frequent. Edaphically, conditions are equally severe; the soil is a shallow sand (25 cm. to 50 cm. deep) overlying shattered granite, with rocky outcrops frequent. It is easily eroded and the afforestation project is designed to combine both protection and production. The area comprises some 2,800 ha. being planted at a rate of 120 ha. to 180 ha. annually.

Seed is sown in lines (two per trough) in spring and at a depth of about 1 cm.; no thinning or transplanting is carried out and seedlings are lifted at three to five years (depending on their size) and out-planted in autumn into precisely similar troughs (six to eight trees in a group, at a planting espacement of about 15 cm.). Fourteen months after sowing seedlings were about 8 cm. tall and chlorotic. A few plants in an abandoned "nursery" were only 0.6 m. tall, six years after sowing. In view of the harsh climate and poor soil conditions, however, it is difficult to judge the success of this method. That it is expensive, though, cannot be doubted.

Visits to commune nurseries were perfunctory only, and details of practices usually not available. At Kunming, where the "West Mountain" commune has planted some 2,000 ha. over the last three years, and in Kwangtung, where the "Ting hu" commune has an afforestation program of 200 ha. per annum, formal nurseries were absent. At Kunming, *Pinus yunnanensis* is grown in cultivated, open patches up to 0.4 ha. in extent, in stagnating, natural stands of *Keteleeria davidiana* and *Cyclobalanopsis glaucoides*, and in semi-natural mixed hardwood forest. Seedlings are grown for two years, then transplanted (together, often, with wilding stock) for a further year before out-planting. The soils are highly calcareous and very dry, and the nursery stock is chlorotic and stunted. These nurseries are reminiscent in form (though not in quality of stock) to the woodland nurseries of Scotland and northern England. The only fertilizer used, however, is wood ash from precultivation burning and, since virtually every twig is removed before burning (for fuel), nutrient additions from this source cannot be very great. After five to six years, the nurseries are taken over for vegetable- and maize-growing.

In addition to the woodland nurseries, in Yunnan many thousands of trees are raised on small patches of land around the commune buildings, along the dykes of the paddy fields, on terrace shoulders, in fruit orchards, and along roadsides and other "waste" ground. Here, cultivation is again intensive and irrigation is often provided. The species are many and varied—*Eucalyptus globulus, Castanopsis delavayi, Populus yunnanensis, Salix* spp., *Cupressus torulosa, Larix potanini, Betula alba* var. *chinensis* among the timber trees; and *Hodgsonia macrocarpa* (an oil-bearing liane, newly discovered by the Kunming Botanical Institute), *Lindera communis* (used for soap manufacture), *Rauwolfia* sp., and *Juglans regia* as economic crops. The Kunming Botanical Institute has a big program of screening native species for possible industrial products, especially essential oils and alkaloids; promising species are released for commune plantations and "backyard" processing.

Similarly, the "Ting hu" commune in Kwangtung is concerned more with cash crops than forestry as such. Seedlings of *Thea oleosa, Aleurites cordata, Cinnamomum camphora, Pasania* spp., *Castanopsis* spp., *Litchi chinensis, Ficus* spp., *Podocarpus imbricata, Pinus fenzeliana, Populus robusta, Eucalyptus* spp., and *Melia azedarach*, etc. are raised on "waste" ground or in orchards, for plantation growth. Practices are very empirical, but the trees looked healthy and vigorous.

In contrast, the Shih Fan production brigade of the West Lake commune at Hangchow works a more formal nursery, raising stock of *Pinus massoniana, Cunninghamia lanceolata*, and *Cryptomeria japonica* for production forestry and some *Populus canadensis* for roadside planting. The commune is primarily concerned with managing extensive tea gardens but, in addition, it has a current tree-planting program of 1,200 ha., of which the Shih Fan production brigade is responsible for 200 ha. annually. The brigade is also "enrichment planting with 9,000 trees per ha." (*sic*) over an area of about 40 ha. per year in cut-over mixed coniferous/hardwood forest. The nursery covers rather less than 2 ha. and is located on the yellow podsolic soils surrounding the West Lake at Hangchow. It is a relatively fertile site and the stock show no obvious nutrient deficiencies, though no fertilizers of any kind are used. A 20° slope and a 150-cm. rainfall promote severe soil erosion in parts of the nursery.

The three coniferous species are all spring-sown to give a seedling density of 200/sq. m. and, after one season's growth, are thinned to 100 in the case of *Pinus massoniana*, 75 for *Cunninghamia lanceolata*, and 150 with *Cryptomeria japonica*. The thinnings are replanted around the tea gardens and other cultivated parts of the brigade's holding. Nursery stock is lifted after two years (*Pinus massoniana* and *Cunninghamia lanceolata*) or three years (*Cryptomeria japonica*). As usual, all operations are carried out manually, including the periodic transport of soil from the bottom of the slope to the top of the nursery. Since the tea gardens are all neatly terraced, it was surprising to find this laborious method of overcoming the effects of soil erosion in the tree nursery. It suggests a relatively recent commitment to afforestation and, possibly, a lack of enthusiasm on the part of the commune managers; the fact that tea production is considerably more lucrative in the short term than forestry may partly explain this attitude.

In spite of the primitive methods employed to raise tree stock in the communes, their contribution to the national afforestation program should not be underestimated. For example, it has been reported that in 1959 in Shantung province, members of one commune raised twenty-five million seedlings along roadsides and around their houses (NCNA, No. 012515, 1959); and the West Mountain commune in Kunming is said to have some ten million seedlings and transplants under cultivation. A peasant in northwest China was recently cited for raising eighteen million "saplings" on one hectare of nursery land (NCNA, No. 042302, 1963)—presumably over a period of years. The same news release referred to the availability of cash loans and chemical fertilizers for commune nurseries. Since there are reputedly 24,000 communes in China and more than 70,000 communal afforestation projects (Chang,

1960), their contribution must be considerable, particularly in high productivity areas south of the Yangtze.

Of all the nurseries visited by the author, the highest levels of technical competence appeared to be reached at the Lon Wha nursery in Shanghai and in nurseries serving botanic gardens. Lon Wha is obviously a "show piece": established in 1954 to raise ornamentals for planting in and around Shanghai municipality, it covers 70 ha., of which 50 are devoted to trees (more than 240 species). As well as raising 150,000 to 200,000 saplings of the common city species (poplars, willows, *Liriodendron tulipifera, Ginkgo biloba,* junipers, etc.), Lon Wha specializes in landscape gardening and in the ancient and highly stylized Chinese art of P'an tsai—the cultivation (and mutilation) of miniature trees. The botanic garden nurseries, on the other hand, serve taxonomic arboreta, orchards for economic trees, "exotic introduction fields," and demonstration areas growing ornamental trees. Examples are described in Chapter IX. Judged by their practices and results, their standards are equal to the highest in America and Europe; and, since these institutions organize training courses for government cadres (including those of the forest service), it is, perhaps, not surprising that, relative to other fields of forestry, nursery practice in China is very impressive.

CHAPTER V

PRODUCTION FORESTRY PRACTICE:

THE MAJOR SPECIES, SILVICULTURE, AND EXPLOITATION

WITH MORE THAN 5,000 indigenous woody species in China, it might seem that foresters are faced with an *embarras de richesse* in deciding what to plant. The problem of species choice is nonetheless formidable and it is not simplified by the fact that substantial areas available for afforestation have not supported tree growth for many decades and, in some cases, not at all. Moreover, even where forest remnants exist to give a guide to the growth habits of the native tree flora, they are often secondary forests, induced by exploitation or fire and, as such, of limited value. Outside Kwangtung province, no part of China had any significant experience of extensive plantation forestry for several decades prior to 1950 and the vast forests which have been planted since then must be regarded as species trials on a scale scarcely to be imagined.

As in other countries, the guiding principle in species choice is local performance, allegedly supplemented by the opinions of "rich-experienced peasants." In China, however, "local performance" has a very limited application and, except in the forested areas of Manchuria, central and southwest China, and Kwangtung (and, to a very limited degree, the North China plain, where farm woodlot management was once highly developed), the approach has, of necessity, been theoretical. This is particularly true of the protection forests of northern China and the Yellow river projects.

Table 7 sets out the principal tree species used in China at the present time, according to region and physical site type. It is based partly

76

on Deng (1959), but is amended according to personal observation in China and discussion of Deng's paper with Cheng Wan-chun, Vice-Director of the Chinese Academy of Forest Sciences and former Chairman of the Forestry Department of Nanking University. Cheng is one of the few Western-trained foresters in China; he achieved an international reputation as a dendrologist in 1948 through his discovery and identification of the "living fossil" tree, *Metasequoia glyptostroboides;* his knowledge of the taxonomy and ecology of Chinese conifers is unparalleled.

In each cell of Table 7 the major timber species are asterisked (one, two, or three asterisks in increasing order of importance), while "economic" crop species and specialty timber trees are indicated by daggers. Divisions into "low" and "high" altitude in Table 7 are relative only; thus, in Yunnan, the boundary comes at about 1,800 m., while in south China and the lower reaches of the Yangtze river it is around 300 m. It is not possible to indicate such divisions more precisely since local climatic and edaphic variations greatly affect species distributions and, furthermore, records of commune plantations are not reliable. For the same reason, the table cannot be considered complete —particularly with regard to "economic" crops.

THE MAJOR SPECIES

Of the 175 species listed in Table 7, the large-scale state afforestation projects for timber production (i.e. excluding protection forests), are limited to some ten major species, as follows: Manchuria—*Pinus koraiensis, Larix dahurica, Pinus sylvestris* var. *mongolica;* North China plain—*P. tabulaeformis;* Yangtze provinces and south China—*Cunninghamia lanceolata, Pinus massoniana;* South China—*Eucalyptus globulus, E. citriodora;* Southwest China—*Pinus yunnanensis, Populus yunnanensis.*

Pinus koraiensis (Red pine, Korean pine, Siberian yellow pine)

Endemic to Manchuria, North Korea, the Russian maritime province, and Japan, *Pinus koraiensis* is a major component of both the mixed coniferous and deciduous broadleaved forests and the decidous broadleaved formation; it is, in fact, an interzonal species and its relationships with either forest type are not entirely clear. As might be expected of a climax species in these communities, however, it is unusually

Table 7. Principal Species Currently Used In Afforestation Projects in China

	"Low" altitude, "easy" country	
Region	General	Wet sites
NW. Inner Mongolia NW. Sinklang N. Kansu N. Tsinghai	*Ulmus pumila* *U. laciniata* *U. japonica* *Populus simonii* *P. suaveolens* *P. euphratica* *P. cathayana* *P. laurifolia* *Prunus armeniaca* *Tamarix chinensis*	*Populus euphratica* *Salix matsudana* *S. phyllicifolia* *S. purpurea* var. *multinervis* *Tamarix chinensis*
E. Sinkiang SE. Kansu Central and S. Inner Mongolia N. Hopeh Liaoning N. Shansi	*Populus canadensis*** *P. tomentosa* *Robinia pseudoacacia** *Cedrela sinensis* *Ailanthus altissima* *Morus alba*† *Sophora japonica*† *Fraxinus chinensis**** *Catalpa bungei*† *Elaeagnus angustifolia* *Acer negundo*	*Salix matsudana* *S. purpurea* var. *multinervis* *Populus canadensis* *P. pyramidalis* *P. simonii*
NE. Inner Mongolia Heilungkiang Kirin	*Pinus koraiensis**** *P. sylvestris* var. *mongolica** *Larix dahurica*** *L. koreana* *Populus cathayana* *P. liaotungensis* *P. simonii* *P. maximowiczii* *Ulmus pumila* *U. laciniata* *Fraxinus mandshurica* *Morus alba*†	*Fraxinus mandshurica* *Salix matsudana*** *S. matsudana* var. *pendula* *Populus canadensis** *P. koreana* *Picea jezoensis* *P. obovata* *Pinus koraiensis* *Larix koreana**** *L. dahurica*
Shantung S. Hopeh S. Shansi Shensi Honan Kiangsu Hupeh Anwhei Chekiang S. Kweichow N. Hunan N. Kiangsi NW. Fukien	*Cedrela sinensis*** *Cunninghamia lanceolata**** *Quercus acutissima*† *Cinnamomum camphora*† *C. kanahirai*† *Zelkova schneideriana*† *Paulownia fortunei* *Cinnamomum cassia*† *Thea sinensis*† *Dendrocalamus strictus*† *Phyllostachys spp.*† *Arundinaria spp.*† *Morus alba*†	*Salix babylonica* *S. glandulosa* *S. wilsonii* *Pterocarya stenoptera*† *Melia azedarach** *Sapium sebiferum*† *Alnus japonica*** *Metasequoia glyptostroboides****

	"High" altitude	Special "problem" sites
Deep soils	Shallow soils	
Ulmus davidiana *U. pumila* *Tamarix pentandra*	*Tamarix pentandra*	Sand dunes: *Haloxylon ammodendron* *Hovenia dulcis* *Tamarix pentandra* *Ailanthus altissima* *Crataegus pinnatifida*
*Pinus tabulaeformis**** *Robinia pseudoacacia*** *Populus cathayana** *Juglans regia†* *Castanea mollissima* *Pyrus malus†* *P. communis†* *Diospyros kaki†* *Zizyphus jujuba†* *Acer negundo*	*Pinus tabulaeformis**** *Robinia pseudoacacia*** *Acer truncatum** *Biota orientalis* *Prunus armeniaca†* var. *ansu* *Sophora japonica†* var. *pendula*	Sand dunes: *Sophora japonica* var. *pendula* *Elaeagnus angustifolia* *Populus simonii* *P. pseudosimonii* *P. diversifolia* *Ulmus pumila* *U. laciniata* Saline soils: *Tamarix chinensis* *Hippophae rhamnoides*
*Larix dahurica*** *L. koreana*** *L. dahurica* var. *olgensis* *Pinus koraiensis**** *P. sylvestris* var. *mongolica** *Fraxinus mandshurica* *Phellodendron amurense†* *Tilia mandshurica†* *T. taquetii†*	*Quercus mongolica**** *Pinus sylvestris*** var. *mongolica* *P. tabulaeformis** *Populus tremula*	Sand dunes: *Salix matsudana* *S. mongolica* *Elaeagnus angustifolia* *Pinus sylvestris* var. *mongolica*
*Cunninghamia lanceolata**** *Cryptomeria japonica** *Cupressus funebris*** *Phyllostachys edulis†* *Sassafras tsuma†* *Quercus variabilis†* *Q. acutissima†* *Castanea henryi†* *C. mollissima†* *Thea oleosa†* *T. sinensis†* *Aesculus chinensis†* *Gingko biloba†*	*Pinus massoniana**** *Liquidambar formosana** *Quercus acutissima*** *Ilex* sp. *Bischoffia javanica†*	Mountain sites: *Pinus tabulaeformis* *Cryptomeria japonica* *Pseudolarix amabilis*

Table 7—Continued

Table 7. Principal Species Currently Used in Afforestation Projects in China—Continued

	"Low" altitude, "easy" country	
Region	General	Wet sites
Szechuan N. Kweichow SE. Tsinghai	*Phoebe nanmu*† *Cedrela sinensis*** *Cupressus funebris**** *Cinnamomum camphora*† *C. cassia*† *Sinocalamus affinis*†* *Pinus massoniana* *Eucalyptus globulus* *E. citriodora* *Morus alba*† *Juglans cathayensis*	*Pterocarya stenoptera*† *Alnus cremastogyne*† *Salix glandulosa** *Melia azedarach**** *Metasequoia glyptostroboides*** *Ginkgo biloba*†
E. Tibet Chamdo NW. Yunnan SW. Szechuan	*Populus rotundifolia**** var. *duclouxiana* *P. lasiocarpa* *P. wilsonii* *P. szechuanica* *P. cathayana* *Larix potanini* *Pinus yunnanensis** *Picea likiangensis*	*Salix wilsonii**** *S. phanera*** *S. rehderiana* *Ulmus bergmanniana** var. *lasiophylla* *Juglans regia*†
Yunnan SW. Kweichow W. Kwangsi	*Populus yunnanensis** *Pinus yunnanensis**** *P. armandi* *Keteleeria davidiana* *Fokenia kawaii* *Catalpa duclouxii*† *Castanopsis delavayi* *Eucalyptus globulus*** *Lindera communis*† *Cupressus torulosa*† *Larix potanini* *Rauwolfia*†	*Populus yunnanensis**** *Salix babylonica*** *S. rehderiana** *Adina racemosa*† *Sapium sebiferum*†
Kwangsi Kwangtung S. Hunan S. Kiangsi S. Fukien	*Cinnamomum camphora*† *C. cassia* *Eucalyptus globulus** *E. citriodora* *Ailanthus altissima* *A. malabarica* *Bambusa stenostachys*† *Dendrocalamus latiflorus*† *D. giganteus*† *Arundinaria amabilis*† *Citrus* spp.† *Morus alba*† *Pinus massoniana**** *Cunninghamia lanceolata*** *Casuarina* sp.†	*Eucommia ulmoides*† *Glyptostrobus pensilis* *Bischoffia trifoliata*† *Sapium sebiferum*†* *Litchi chinensis*† *Eucalyptus exserta**** *Melia azedarach***

"High" altitude		Special "problem" sites
Deep soils	Shallow soils	
Cunninghamia lanceolata*** *Cupressus funebris*** *Phoebe nanmu*† *Pinus armandi** *Juglans regia*† *Thea oleosa*† *T. sinensis*† *Trachycarpus excelsa* *Aleurites fordii*† *Phyllostachys edulis*† *P. bambusoides*† *P. puberula*† *Citrus* spp.†	*Pinus massoniana**** *Cupressus funebris*** *Quercus acutissima** *Q. variabilis* *Phyllostachys bambusoides*† *P. edulis*†	Mountain sites: *Pseudotsuga sinensis* *Castanopsis platyacantha* *Tsuga yunnanensis* *Lithocarpus cleistocarpa*
Larix potanini*** *L. mastersiana* *L. griffithii* *Picea asperata* var. *retroflexa* *P. aurantiaca* *P. likiangensis*** *P. spinulosa* *P. brachytyla* *Abies delavayi** *A. webbiana* *Tsuga chinensis*	*Abies delavayi*** *A. squamata* *A. georgei* *A. recurvata* *Picea sikangensis** *P. likiangensis****	
Pinus armandi*** *Catalpa duclouxii*** *Cupressus funebris*† *Phoebe nanmu* *Actinidia chinensis*† *Coffea arabica*† *Prunus persica*† *Pyrus communis*† *Pinus yunnanensis* *Keteleeria davidiana* *Cedrela toona**	*Pinus yunnanensis**** *Keteleeria davidiana*** *Pterocarpus indica* *Catalpa duclouxii**	
Citrus spp.† *Canarium album*† *C. pimela*† *Euphoria longana*† *Litchi chinensis*† *Coffea arabica*† *Cinnamomum camphora*† *C. kanahirai*† *C. micranthum*† *Zizyphus spinosa*† *Quercus griffithii* *Cunninghamia lanceolata*** *Pinus massoniana**** *Eucalyptus exserta** *Ficus lacor*† *Aleurites cordata*†	*Pinus massoniana**** *Acacia confusa*** *Schima confertiflora** *Liquidambar formosana*	Sand dunes: *Casuarina equisetifolia* *Pandanus odoratissimus* var. *sinensis* Coastal swamps: *Rhizophora mucronata*

ajor timber species (no. of asterisks indicates relative importance).
"Industrial" crop and specialty timber trees.

shade-tolerant for a pine and has obvious affinities with its counterpart in the mixed northern hardwood forests of North America, *Pinus strobus*; it has been reported, in fact, that hybrids of the two species are 100 per cent fertile (Johnson, cited by Wang, 1961). In natural stands, *P. koraiensis* reaches heights of 45 m. to 55 m. with diameters up to 1.3 m. Tree form is good with clean cylindrical boles and well-shaped, almost ornamental, crowns. Mature timber quality is very high; the wood is light (0.4 gm./cu. cm.), soft, straight-grained, and easily worked to a good finish. Strength properties are good; it seasons well, is generally free from defects (except, occasionally, heart rot), and takes paint readily. Red pine is, in fact, the most important general purpose softwood in current use in northern China; it is exported from Manchuria to eighteen provinces (*People's Daily*, 6/9/63) and utilized for construction timber, round produce (poles), joinery, furniture, case material, and veneer production. Sawmill residues are used for chipboard and fiberboard manufacture, for the production of tanning extracts, and for groundwood pulp. Trees from southern exposures are tapped regularly for oleoresin. It is not, however, a durable timber; power poles, for example, in ground contact have an untreated service life of less than three years.

As a plantation species, *P. koraiensis* can be grown on a wide range of sites, though it is difficult to establish on waterlogged soils and grows poorly on shallow, stony soils. It does not tolerate highly calcareous sites. Unlike *P. strobus*, it is a deep-rooting tree and is, consequently, somewhat fire resistant. Climatically, it can withstand very low winter temperatures (down to −45°C.) and a low rainfall (*ca.* 50 cm.) but it needs a minimum growing season (i.e. number of frost-free days) of at least 100 days; it is, however, generally frost-hardy.

In Manchuria, the species is generally established by pit-planting, though turf-planting is common on wet sites; the turfs are 2 m. long × 1 m. broad × 30 cm. deep, and ten trees are planted per turf. On drier sites, planting densities were formerly over 10,000/ha. and large areas have been established at 1 m. × 1 m. spacing; since 1961, however, the usual spacing has been 2 m. × 1 m. Before 1957, *P. koraiensis* covered 39 per cent of the planted area in Manchuria; in the current program, however, it has been reduced to 30 per cent.

Where establishment has been successful, growth rates are good (*ca.* 0.6 m. to 0.7 m. per year at age ten years) but very uneven—particularly in comparison with *Larix dahurica*. The tentative rotation is fifty years. Treatment consists of two weedings in the first year after planting, one to two in the second year, and a thinning (for fuel or pulpwood) at age ten. This first thinning is, of course, a low thinning, some 25 per cent of the trees being removed; beyond this stage, treatments have not yet been defined. Insufficient data are available from thinning plots for the establishment of rigid silvicultural schedules, though it seems likely that, in view of the move to wider initial spacings, later thinnings will be heavier. As is general in China, all trees are axe-pruned for fuel wood (and pruned very badly) at two- to three-year intervals. The aim is to restrict pruning to dead branch whorls, but it is clear that this is not always done.

In general, *Pinus koraiensis* is a promising plantation species, provided that establishment problems can be solved and rational silvicultural schedules evolved.

Larix dahurica (= gmelini) (Dahurian larch)

L. dahurica is one of a group of East Asiatic larches included by many botanists (e.g. Dallimore and Jackson, 1923; Wang, 1961) as geographical varieties of *L. gmelini*. In Chinese forestry, the specific status is maintained though no distinction is drawn between *L. dahurica* and *L. koreana* (= *L. gmelini* var. *olgensis*), in spite of claims by some foresters that *L. koreana* is a superior plantation species.

L. dahurica forms a dense forest cover at altitudes above *ca.* 900 m. in the Greater and Lesser Khingan ranges, the Changpaishan, and in North Korea. It is the most important forest tree of the region (Wang, 1961). *L. koreana*, on the other hand, is a muskeg species (below 1,200 m.) which appears to thrive in waterlogged conditions, often partly inundated. Morphologically the two species are almost identical.

In natural stands, *L. dahurica* reaches a height of 30 m. to 40 m. and a diameter of 1.0 m. to 1.5 m., with a clear, straight bole. The timber is greatly valued for its natural durability (e.g. poles in ground contact have a service life, north of the Yellow river, of twenty to twenty-five years) and its strength properties. Of low density (*ca.* 0.32 gm./cu. cm.), however, it has a tendency to twist during drying and for this reason is less favored than red pine for construction. In China, it is used principally in the round (poles, piles, and pit props) and for railway ties. Minor products include resin, oil, various medicinal bases, charcoal, and pulpwood. It is too coarse grained to peel satisfactorily.

Before 1957, *L. dahurica* was the most extensively planted conifer in Manchuria and it makes up some 52 per cent of existing plantations. At the present time, however, it is losing ground to pines and only 20 per cent of the area currently being planted is in larch. The reasons given for this shift in emphasis are, firstly, the limited utilization potential of larch compared with the pines and, secondly, a policy decision that some 20 per cent of the area shall be planted with allegedly soil-improving broadleaved species. Larch, however, can be grown on a wider range of sites than pine, is easier to establish—particularly in wet areas—grows more rapidly, and, in particular, is much more uniform. The uniformity of *L. dahurica* in plantation, in fact, was, for the author, the most impressive feature of the Manchurian forestry scene. Over blocks, thousand of hectares in extent, it seemed that the height of nine- to ten-year-old larch varied by less than 0.3 m. to 0.5 m. throughout.

Compared with its European counterpart (*L. decidua*), *L. dahurica* tolerates a wide range of soil types from freely drained sands to water-logged swamps; it also stands exposure well and is frost-hardy; in this respect it is closer to *L. sibirica*.

Planting methods with *L. dahurica* in Manchuria vary. On the rich alluvial soils of the river flats, clean cultivation by hand-digging is general followed by notch-planting at less than 1 m. × 1 m. Swampy areas are mounded with turfs 60 cm. × 50 cm., spaced at 1 m. intervals in lines 2 m. apart; two seedlings are planted on each mound. On steep slopes, however, planting spots are screefed (50-cm. squares) and a single tree planted in each spot. The species is also used in cut-over forest and, where there is extensive hardwood regrowth, group planting is practiced with five- or nine-tree groups spaced at 50 cm. within the groups and 5 m. between them. Elsewhere, following line-cutting, trees are pit-planted at 2 m. × 1 m.

It is not possible to assess the extents of the different planting methods; it is the stated policy of the State Forest Service, however, to afford priority in replanting to currently cut-over forest and the easier slopes of older cut-over areas. Probably, therefore, line-planting after hand cultivation is the most common practice; certainly, it was more frequently seen than the other methods.

A silvicultural schedule for *L. dahurica* is taking shape, though it is doubtful whether it is generally applied yet. Except in older cut-over forest, no weeding is necessary and the first treatment is a pruning to 1.0 m. at five years, when the trees are about 3.5 m. tall. At ten years (*ca.* 8 m. to 9 m. mean height), line-planted stands are thinned to 2,500 stems/ha. and pruned to 2.5 m. (all stems). As with pine, the pruned branches are used for fuel, while the first thinnings go for fuel, pulpwood, or stakes (they are 4 cm. to 6 cm. in breast-height diameter at this stage). Regular pruning follows at two-year intervals, removing two whorls of branches at each treatment. At fifteen years of age (*ca.* 12 m. mean height) the stands are thinned to 1,800 stems/ha. and, thereafter, thinning will be carried out at three-year intervals. There are few stands older than fifteen years, however, and the intensity of thinning has yet to be decided.

It is clear that foresters in Manchuria are thinking in terms of numerical low thinning, at fixed intervals rather than in accordance with height increment. With the great uniformity in height growth of *L. dahurica*, low thinning has obvious merits though it seems probable that thinning must become heavier than at present (and initial spacings wider). A combined spacing and thinning trial at Liang Sui forest, some 30 miles northeast of Tailing, in which initial densities ranged from 12,500/ha. to 2,500/ha., clearly demonstrates the merits of wider spacings; within the widest spacing, the heaviest experimental thinning (from 2,500 to 625 stems/ha. at age ten years) was also the most effective.

Pinus sylvestris var. *mongolica (Scots pine)*

This variety has a limited natural distribution on the stabilized sand dunes of the Hailar steppes in western Manchuria and on the western slopes of the Greater Khingan mountains bordering the Mongolian grasslands. The "parent" species, of course, has a much wider distribution in the northern coniferous forest region but, in view of the peculiar habitat restriction of *P. sylvestris* var. *mongolica*, varietal status is probably justified. Chen (1945) notes that the lowest temperatures ever observed in China were in the Hailar region (−50.1°C.). The growing season is short, with fewer than 110 frost-free days per year.

In its natural habitat, *P. sylvestris* var. *mongolica* grows to little more than 16 m. and is scattered over otherwise treeless grassland. Surprisingly, the tree form is said to be good, even under these conditions, and, from photographs, it resembles var. *horizontalis* Don, but with a broader crown and coarser branches. The stems have no hint of crook in them, however, and, consequently the tree does not fall into the Habit Type No. 2, of Steven and Carlisle (1959). No information on mature timber properties of the indigenous variety is available but it has been assumed to resemble *P. sylvestris*. In many areas where it is now being planted, however, it must be regarded as an exotic and, in view of its relatively rapid growth, wood quality must remain questionable.

P. sylvestris var. *mongolica* is generally planted on drier sites and at higher altitudes than either *P. koraiensis* or *Larix dahurica;* it is particularly useful on shallow soils, while it may be introduced into cut-over coniferous-broadleaved forest, in mixture with *L. dahurica.* Although clearly a light-demander, it has usually been close-planted (1 m.) in lines, though group-planting (in five-tree groups at 3-m. spacing between groups) is currently favored. It is claimed that group-planting with *Pinus sylvestris*, while it does not affect height increment markedly, increases mean diameter growth by 75 per cent over line-planted stock. (In view of the very close spacing in line-planted areas, this is perhaps scarcely surprising.) Heights of trees planted on a shallow, sandy soil in the Liang Sui forest are about 3 m. to 4 m. at six years of age; compared with planted *P. sylvestris* in Europe, tree form is outstanding.

Of the three major plantation species in Manchuria, *P. sylvestris* var. *mongolica* appeared to be the most sensitive to weed growth and to biotic damage (mainly voles and the aphis, *Adelges pini*). *Armillaria mellea* is also prevalent on trees planted in cut-over areas. As a result, stocking in plantations is sometimes inadequate.

No silvicultural schedules have yet been derived for *Pinus sylvestris* var. *mongolica* and practice follows that for *P. koraiensis.* There is a clear need for more careful pruning than is current, for branches appear to be more persistent than in the latter case. It will be of interest to see whether, as an exotic, the species achieves reasonable height growth.

Pinus tabulaeformis (Chinese pine; Horsetail pine)

The natural distribution of *P. tabulaeformis* is extremely wide, ranging throughout the deciduous-broadleaved forest formation and extending into the mixed coniferous and deciduous-broadleaved forests on the drier sites, the mixed deciduous and evergreen broadleaved forests at high altitudes (about 1,000 m.), and the evergreen broadleaved zone, also, above 1,000 m. As might be expected, it varies greatly in habit, from a stunted, flat-crowned specimen on the high ridges to an erect 20-m. to 30-m. forest tree on the lower hill slopes of the northern provinces. Ecologically, it may be a pioneer, colonizing burned-over mountain foothills in the northern provinces, a preclimax species forming a seral stage in a broadleaved association of *Quercus, Tilia,* and *Acer* spp., or a climax component (together with *Biota orientalis* and occasional *Juniperus rigida*) on the steepest and most arid slopes of the hills bordering the North China plain.

The timber of *Pinus tabulaeformis* is coarse-grained and resinous. It works well, however, is of medium durability, and also treats easily. The heartwood is reddish and the sapwood yellow; as a timber species it is not unlike the European *P. sylvestris* or the North American *P. resinosa* and it is used for much the same purpose as these species, i.e. construction, joinery, ties, case manufacture, etc., It is also tapped for resin and can be made into charcoal. Sawmill residue is pulped, though it does not yield a high-quality furnish.

In the northern provinces, *P. tabulaeformis* is extensively planted on dry, eroding, hill sites in areas of low rainfall (35 cm. to 75 cm. per year). Its site tolerance is wide, covering the slightly alkaline chestnut soils of the loess regions to high-altitude acid podsols; except for a sensitivity to late frosts, it is hardy. A problem with this species, however, is said to be a restriction in duration of root development; there are, apparently, two periods of root growth—early spring and late summer— and if the soil is excessively dry at either of these times, trees can be killed by drought. This is surprising in a species with a wide natural distribution over arid sites.

P. tabulaeformis may be pit-planted in lines (1 m. × 1 m. spacing) on gentle slopes or set out in a variety of patterns on eroding steep hillsides; these patterns range from simple troughs or platforms cut into the hillside to elaborate "fish-scale" terraces, sometimes inter-cropped with, for example, maize, wheat, millet, or even fruit trees. The fish-scales are semicircular platforms, 1 m. to 2 m. at the widest point, sloping in toward the hillside; they are spaced anywhere from 2 m. to 10 m. apart. Trees may be planted only on the shoulders of the fish-scale (at a spacing of 50 cm.) with crops on the terraces or, where inter-cropping is not practiced, over the whole terrace in groups, with 1-m. spacing within the groups. As far as this writer could judge, inter-cropping is not widely practiced by the State Forest Service, except for demonstration and extension purposes, and pit-planting into the bare hillside is usual.

Apart from ubiquitous pruning, no silviculture has been evolved for *P. tabulaeformis* plantations. Survival is generally poor (20 to 30 per cent) and, in most areas, it will be many years before thinning is needed. Growth is also poor (0.3 m. per year, height increment) and erratic. It is doubtful, too, whether many of these plantations will serve a useful purpose in erosion control. Performance of *P. tabulaeformis* has, therefore, been disappointing so far; with increased attention to planting practices and tending, however, it may be that the species will prove itself.

Cunninghamia lanceolata (=C. sinensis) (Chinese fir)

The "bread and butter" species of central and southern China, *Cunninghamia lanceolata* is the most useful general purpose timber outside Manchuria. Its natural distribution is throughout the provinces bordering the Yangtze, and south into Kweichow and Hunan. Under forest conditions it is an impressive tree, growing to 50 m. in height with a straight cylindrical bole up to 2 m. in diameter, and often clear of branches for 18 m. to 20 m. Even stands of coppice origin comprise trees of beautiful stem form. Though sensitive to early frosts, it grows well at high altitudes (up to 1,800 m.) in China and possesses the valuable attribute among conifers of being able to shed frost-killed branch tips and regenerate from an adventitious bud. It achieves its best development on deep, well-drained soils derived from sandstone, in a climate where the growing season temperatures and atmospheric humidity are fairly high.

The timber and its traditional uses have been extensively described (see e.g. Wilson, 1913). The wood is light (0.45 gm./ cu. cm.), easily worked, even- and fine-grained, and durable, closely resembling in appearance, *Agathis australis*. It is used for construction, joinery, shipbuilding, case-manufacturing, tea chests, furniture, and veneer. Because of its fragrance, it is still much in demand for coffins and ornamental chests. By-products include several essential oils and medicinal bases, while the bark is used as a roofing material. It is, in fact, used for almost as many purposes as bamboo.

South of the Yangtze, *Cunninghamia lanceolata* is grown on a twenty-five to thirty-year rotation (Afanasev, 1959) after establishment by sowing or with closely spaced (1 m. × 1 m.) rooted cuttings or suckers. The soil is cultivated before planting and the plantations are clean cultivated, except on steep slopes, for several years after establishment; they may be inter-cropped with maize or vegetables. Thinning must be carried out lightly and frequently owing to the ease with which cut stumps coppice, and stands are kept dense for the first fifteen years. In some areas, after a heavy thinning at fifteen to twenty years of age, plantations of *C. lanceolata* are maintained until rotation age in the form of coppice with standards. When the standards are felled, the coppice is thinned and the cycle repeated. Alternatively, the standards and coppice may be clear-felled at the same time, the young shoots being processed for oil extraction or used for craftwork and pulpwood.

In normal plantations, mean annual increments of up to 30 cu.m./ha. have been recorded; in Kweichow, for example, an experimental plot at age sixteen had a density of 1,180 stems/ha., a mean height of 18 m., mean diameter of 21.8 cm., and a standing volume of 400 cu. m./ha. (Afanasev, 1959).

Most of the veneer production of this species in China is still from natural stands, though plantation-grown material of exploitable size is becoming increasingly available and promises to yield large logs of excellent form and wood properties.

It is surprising that *C. lanceolata* has not been more widely planted outside China. It has been successfully established in Asiatic Russia as a plantation species and has, of course, been extensively planted as an ornamental tree, even as far north as Scotland. There is little doubt that it would do well in, for example, many Mediterranean countries and in subtropical and tropical regions of the world. The excellence of its timber, its growth rate and exceptional stem form make it a species well worth trying elsewhere.

Pinus massoniana (=P. rubra) (Masson's pine)

On inhospitable, frosty, or excessively dry sites, where *Cunninghamia lanceolata* fails, the common plantation species in southern China is Masson's pine. Naturally, it is very widely distributed. In Wu's "Forest Regions of China with Special Reference to the Natural Distribution of Pines" (1950), it appears as a type species in no fewer than five of his twelve zones (i.e. the Szechuan evergreen forest; the southern Yangtze mixed forest; the southern subtropical monsoon forest; the Hainan subtropical forest; and the Taiwan forest). Following the classification of Hou *et al.*, it is a major constituent of the mixed deciduous and evergreen broadleaved forest and the eastern region of the evergreen broadleaved type, a secondary species in the tropical monsoon rain forest, and a minor component of the southern extent of the deciduous broadleaved forest. *Pinus massoniana* is, thus, a common native species, particularly at low altitudes, throughout the Yangtze provinces and to the southeast. Ecologically, it is a pioneer and, as such, is much more light-demanding than its northern equivalent, *P. tabulaeformis*. However, it tolerates a wide range of soil types from the dry yellow podsols of the Tsinling foothills to the laterites of Hainan island. It is generally fast-growing, to a height of 35 m. to 45 m.

Commercially, another "red" pine, the timber of Masson's pine is not dissimilar to that of the Chinese pine or the red deal of Scandinavia. It is moderately dense (0.53 gm./cu.cm.), easily worked, finishes well, and takes a paint coat easily; seasoning presents no problem but it is not a durable timber and, in south China, it is also readily attacked by termites. It is used for construction, ship-building, flooring, and in the round. Unlike many of the Chinese pines, it is said to be a good pulpwood. As with Scots pine in Scandinavia, oil and resin are extracted from the roots, while the wood yields turpentines, tars, and other products.

P. *massoniana* has been grown extensively as a plantation tree and as a farm woodlot species, not only on the mainland of China but also on the islands of Hong Kong and Taiwan. In Kwangtung and Hong Kong it is normally established by sowing, but, further north, planting is more usual. Sowing is often in nests (eight to ten seeds per nest) with a first thinning of the resultant clumps at age six months and a second at age five years (to leave two to three seedlings). The clumps are reduced to a single plant at age seven years, when the trees are about 3 m. to 4 m. high.

Sowing is normally carried out in January; where planting is preferred, seedlings are lifted when three to five months old and planted out in May/June at the time of the typhoon rains. In state plantations, a first thinning at ten to twelve years aims at removing some 25 per cent of the crop for poles (planting density is around 3,500/ha.); no silvicultural schedules have been evolved beyond this stage.

Commune plantations receive more intensive treatment. Established at some 4,000 stems/ha. density, stands are thinned to less than 1,700 stems/ha. at age four to five years for poles and fuel. Thereafter they are thinned (and pruned) every two years.

The plantations of P. *massoniana* visited by the author in China do not provide a satisfactory basis for judging the potential of the species. Many of them have been ravaged by *Tortrix* and all of them show symptoms of chlorosis, probably associated with nitrogen deficiency. Tree form was generally poor and, except at the Kwangtung Forest Research Institute, growth rates were well behind the obvious potential. With a virtually continuous growing season, P. *massoniana* can produce two and a half to three growth flushes annually in southern China, yet stands established in 1950 are often of less than 7 m. mean height and no more than 10 cm. mean breast-height diameter. There are clearly problems associated with the growth of this species and it would be premature to pronounce judgment. In the Kwangtung Research Institute, however, the Chinese have a very ably led organization, well fitted to tackle and overcome these difficulties.

Eucalyptus globulus (Canton gum, Chinese blue gum)

Eucalyptus globulus is the blue gum of Victoria and Tasmania; it has been grown in southern China since about 1890 and, although not established in large-scale plantations, it is a most impressive tree, reaching heights of 50 m. at age thirty (with volumes/ha. of up to 1,200 cu.m.). In stands of coppice origin, it may grow as much as 4.5 m. to 5.5 m. per year for the first ten years. Plantations administered by the Forest Research Institute, Kwangtung, provided the statistics given in Table 8, which are said to be unexceptional.

Table 8. Statistics Relating to the Growth of *Eucalyptus globulus* in Plantations Administered by the Forest Research Institute, Kwangtung

Age	Initial Spacing (m.)	Present Mean Height (m.)	Present Mean Girth (cm.)	Volume/ha. (cu. m.)	Establishment
5	1.8 × 1.8	20	30	148	Coppice
8	1.8 × 1.8	24	42	427	Sown
11	1.8 × 1.8	17	53	242	Coppice
20	1.8 × 1.8	27	57	1,044	Coppice
25	2.4 × 2.4	26	62	639	Planted
30	1.8 × 1.8	88	102	520	Planted
30	1.8 × 1.8	49	157	1,180	Coppice
40	2.7 × 2.7	48	135	1,033	?
45	1.8 × 1.8	48	152	902	?

The wood properties of the *E. globulus* in Australia are well known and have been frequently described (see e.g. Dadswell, 1942); these descriptions will not be repeated here. In China, the species appears to resemble plantation-grown material in India (Troup, 1913). It does not have a good reputation as a timber tree (possibly in part because of poor conversion) but is extensively used for pulp, fuelwood, craftwork, oil production, and round produce (it is said to last about fifteen years in ground contact, if termites do not attack it). Its density (0.6 gm./cu. cm.) is markedly lower than in Australia.

The species is not exacting as to site, provided it is not subjected to severe frost or snow and has adequate rooting depth; the red earths of Kwangtung and Yunnan, even though deficient in nitrogen and phosphate, appear to be ideal, while the abundant rainfall and long frost-free season account for the high growth rates.

E. *globulus* in southern China is grown from seed or coppice. In the nursery, seed is broadcast-sown and seedlings are raised under shade; they are transplanted at intervals of about 15 cm. to 30 cm. height growth until they are *ca.* 2 m. high (nine to twelve months, usually). They are planted out, bare-rooted in pits, at the beginning of the wet season. In the recent past, the spacing has usually been 0.5 m. to 1.0 m. (within and between rows) but, as in other parts of China, wider spacings (2 m. × 2 m.) are becoming common. An initial thinning is carried out at age five years (mean height, 7.6 m.) for light building poles and fuelwood; plantations are then thinned at three- to five-year intervals until "about twenty to thirty" years old when they are clear-felled. Subsequent crops are raised from coppice, the first on a twenty-year rotation and the remainder on progressively shorter rotations, down to ten years, when new stock is introduced. The coppice shoots are thinned to two to three per stool at age five years and then left to rotation age. According to the Chinese, there is no mortality between the coppice thinning and maturity—from which it may be inferred that not every stump of the original crop coppices. Growth rates of coppice stands are, initially at any rate, greater than those of seedling stands.

The species seeds early (at age five years) and abundantly in both seedling and coppice stands, and germination capacity of the seed is said to be "more than 80 per cent." This is extremely high by standards elsewhere.

E. *globulus* is a proven exotic species in southern China, and although it does not produce a high-quality timber, its rapid growth rates amply justify plantation establishment if only for minor produce (oils, pulp, and fuelwood). It seems probable that its range could, with advantage, be extended further north, at any rate in the coastal provinces.

Eucalyptus citriodora (Lemon-scented gum)

Indigenous to central and northern areas of coastal Queensland, *Eucalyptus citriodora* has been widely planted in the drier tropics and has proved to be extremely adaptable. In China, it takes the place of *E. globulus* on nutrient-poor sands and severely eroded hills, though it is nowhere planted in areas of low rainfall. Nonetheless, it is said to survive a marked dry season. Initial growth rates in plantation are rapid but fall off abruptly when tree heights of about 30 m. to 35 m. have been reached; it does not attain the size of *E. globulus,* nor are volumes per unit area so great. Stem form is often poor, though timber quality is considered good. Certainly, the wood is denser than that of *E. globulus* and is used for construction, railway ties, short pilings, and tool handles as well as for pulp, craftwork, and fuel. In Australia, of course, the species is known for its fine saw timber. Because of the oil of citronella, extractable from the leaves of *E. citriodora*, it is commonly treated as an "economic" tree in southern China and serves as a basis for commune industry. It may be grown as a roadside tree in such cases or raised in small groves and inter-cropped with vegetables, etc. In both Yunnan and Kwangtung provinces (and, probably, elsewhere), it has also been used as an ornamental tree in the cities; even here, however, the foliage is harvested and citronella extracted.

Contrary to experience in other parts of the world (where *E. citriodora* has been grown as an ornamental tree), the Chinese appear to find little difficulty in raising the species from seed. In fact, it is often established on hillsides by direct sowing.

In the nursery, seed is broadcast-sown and the plants are raised under shade. Frequent transplanting appears to be necessary. After the first rotation, regeneration by coppicing is practiced, as for *E. globulus*.

Plantation growth of *E. citriodora* is a recent development in southern China and silvicultural schedules have yet to be generally adopted. While it has not shown great promise on the coastal sand dunes of Kwangtung (where, apart from a fluctuating dry season, there is an ever-present risk of typhoons), there seems to be considerable scope further inland where atmospheric humidity and soil drainage are adequate. The tolerance shown by the species to soils of low nutrient status is a distinct advantage.

Pinus yunnanensis (Yunnan pine)

This pine closely resembles *P. tabulaeformis*; in fact, some authorities regard it as a variety of the latter species. Ecologically, it is also the western equivalent of *P. massoniana* in the evergreen broadleaved forests of Yunnan, western Kweichow, and Kwangsi. Both species are secondary and frequently follow forest destruction by burning. *P. yunnanensis* is found (together with the closely allied *P. insularis* [*P. khasya*]) as far south as the mountains of Burma, Thailand, and Vietnam in similar situations. Since it is a pioneer species, it tends to be light-demanding and generally short-lived. In pure natural stands, the trees reach heights of no more than 25 m. to 30 m. with breast-height diameters (maximum) of around 40 cm. to 50 cm. Such forests tend to be open and poorly stocked, with an understory of scrub hard-woods and grasses. Tree form, however, is surprisingly good, with many straight stems and deep narrow crowns.

The timber of Yunnan pine is very similar to European red deal—coarse-grained, resinous, but nondurable, with a specific gravity of about 0.45 gm./cu.cm. It is used for the same purposes as red deal (construction, joinery, case manufacture, charcoal, and resin-tapping) and is a useful general purpose timber. Its good form gives it a marked advantage over *P. tabulaeformis* as a pole timber.

The site requirements of *P. yunnanensis* are not exacting, though it is less catholic than *P. massoniana* and does not grow well on lime-stones; neither will it thrive in very dry areas, though this is said to result from a high atmospheric humidity requirement rather than a big soil moisture demand.

The State Forest Service is not particularly active in afforestation in southwest China and the majority of *P. yunnanensis* plantings are being established by communes around the major cities. They are extensive (the species is only rarely seen as a roadside tree or in line plantings along irrigation ditches and railways, etc.) and are usually pure, though currently there is a trend toward planting the pine in mixture with evergreen oaks. Many of the earlier plantations have suffered from establishment on excessively dry sites and through over-grazing; the evergreen oaks are said to improve the soil moisture status and to protect the pines from animal damage (chiefly sheep and goats) by providing an alternative fodder supply.

P. yunnanensis is raised in temporary woodland nurseries or on small patches of free ground within the communes. After two years in seedbeds and a further year in transplant lines, stock is about 0.50 m. to 0.75 m. tall when out-planted. On the planting sites (invariably hill country) contour strips are precultivated and the trees are planted in them at 0.5-m. to 1-m. spacing.

Yunnan province was the only area in China where the author heard specific reference to plantation blanking prescriptions (elsewhere, the Chinese averred that initial establishment was such as to preclude the need for this practice!). In the southwest, however, all plantations are blanked for two consecutive years where the initial stocking falls below 70 per cent. Often this is done with wilding stock. Plantation forestry is, of course, a new pursuit for the southwestern Chinese and stands have not yet reached the thinning stage; in consequence, no other silvicultural prescriptions have yet been adopted.

P. yunnanensis will never achieve the impressive growth rates of the native poplar or the introduced *Eucalyptus* species. If overgrazing and burning can be controlled, however, it may eventually prove a useful plantation softwood in an area sadly lacking in native conifers for production forestry.

Populus yunnanensis (Yunnan poplar)

Most of the indigenous poplars of China are planted either as protection forestry species (north of the Yangtze river) or for special purposes (e.g. matchwood) on commune woodlots; in the latter case, they are usually inter-cropped with maize or vegetables and raised more in the fashion of arboretum specimens than forest trees. *P. yunnanensis* in southern China is a noteworthy exception. Indigenous to southern Yunnan and Kwangsi, it is a member of the Tacamahaca section of the genus (balsam poplars). It is not a common tree but, in nature, it is one of the most impressive of the poplars, reaching a height of 40 m. to 50 m., often with 30 m. clear bole. Although demanding climatically (it cannot tolerate frost and requires a long growing season), it is extremely adaptable edaphically and, as such, is well suited to plantation establishment.

In China, *P. yunnanensis* is being extensively planted south of the Yangtze river, both as a plantation tree and along roadsides, irrigation channels, and river banks. Initial growth is impressive, with plantation trees reaching 10-m. to 12-m. heights and 30-cm. to 40-cm. diameters in five years, at stocking densities of 350 stems/ha. (in Yunnan). There is little evidence of "rational close spacing" being applied to *P. yunnanensis* in southern China. Undoubtedly, however, in many plantations, stocking densities could with advantage be lower; trees, along irrigation ditches, spaced at 6 m., produce an equivalent C.A.I. per hectare of 25 cu.m. at age six years.

Little is known about the timber properties of plantation-grown trees, though it is already being used on a significant scale for building poles, mine props, light railway ties, box and pulp wood, etc. Sawn wood appears to dry rapidly and without distortion; it is not, however, a durable timber. The species is also used in China to make charcoal and the foliage is collected for animal fodder.

In spite of the ease with which the balsam poplars can be propagated vegetatively, *P. yunnanensis* in China is usually grown from seed (often in commune nurseries on drained paddy fields) and out-

planted in prepared pits at nine months to one year, when the seedlings are about 1.5 m. tall. In plantations the spacing is normally 3 m.
to 4 m. within and between rows while, for line-plantings along roadsides, etc., it ranges from 1 m. to 5 m. Typically, the stocking density
is reduced to about 500 stems/ha. in the third year, and thereafter,
thinning is carried out annually. The rotation age is not yet known,
but may be of the order of twenty to twenty-five years, when the stocking density has been reduced to less than 100 stems/ha.

Pruning, of course, is universally practiced in China but *P. yunnanensis* has so far remained free of canker infection. Indeed, apart
from rodent damage, all Chinese poplars appear to be free of the major
pests and diseases to which the genus is susceptible in temperate
regions. If this situation continues and, given satisfactory wood properties, there seems to be no reason why *P. yunnannsis* should not rival
the *Eucalyptus* species as a major broadleaved production afforestation species in southern China.

OTHER SPECIES

In addition to the above species, several others appear, on the evidence of growth in natural stands and on the results of experiments
currently under way in the research institutes, to hold promise as plantation species—not only in China but also as exotics in other parts of
the world. The most noteworthy are, of course, the bamboos native to
central and southern China. Most production plantations in China are
of the dumetose *Phyllostachys* and *Arundinaria* spp., and elaborate
thinning and felling schedules have been devised; the silviculture of
bamboos, however, is too large a subject to be treated here. Also worthy
of trial outside China are *Populus euphratica*, *P. cathayana*, *Fraxinus
chinensis*, and *F. mandshurica* from north-central China; *Cedrela sinensis*, *Cupressus funebris*, *Melia azedarach*, *Metasequoia glyptostroboides*,
and *Acacia confusa* from the central and southeastern provinces; and
Larix potanini, *Picea likiangensis*, *Abies delavayi*, *Tsuga chinensis*,
Populus rotundifolia var. *duclouxiana*, and *P. szechuanica* from east-
central China and the Tibetan plateau. In particular, *Melia azedarach*
should do well in tropical monsoon regions (in Kwangtung, experimental plots have reached a mean height of 8 m., a mean diameter at breast
height of 15 cm., three years from sowing), while the poplars would be
of interest in dry, continental-type climates. Many other Chinese
species have particular application to special "problem" sites, but the

complex nature of species-site interrelationships prevents generalization. China's flora is among the richest in the world and has yielded many species of horticultural and other economic importance to other parts of the globe. Yet as a source of plantation forestry species, it remains virtually unexploited. In view of the patent need for plantation establishment in many areas climatically and edaphically similar to parts of China, it is to be hoped that some of her tree species—together with the silvicultural experience which her foresters are rapidly accumulating—will become more freely available in the future.

THE MAJOR FOREST INDUSTRIES

In view of the limited opportunities afforded the author for visits to industrial operations in China, it is scarcely possible to appraise the level of technology in the forest-based industries. It is unlikely that the plants visited are representative of the whole country. Like all hosts, the Chinese try to show their visitors only the best, so it is safe to assume that the operations described here represent above-average conditions for the industries.

In spite of this caveat, the forest industries in China do not give the impression of thriving. With the exception of the more modern pulp and paper mills, machinery is old and in poor repair, and what remains in working order is often not used efficiently. It is doubtless in this field that the withdrawal of Russian technical assistance has had its biggest impact on forestry operations in China.

Exploitation

In the coniferous and mixed coniferous-deciduous forests, clear-felling followed in the same or the next year by replanting is general practice. In Manchuria, experiments were made in the 1950's with various natural regeneration systems, but none proved satisfactory because of the swamping of the conifers by secondary hardwoods; selection logging was also tried but, with the equipment available, was hopelessly uneconomic. In any event, in view of the overmature structure of these virgin forests, clear-felling is obviously the most suitable system to apply—in spite of its denigration by some foresters as being a primitive form of silviculture.

Each coupe is about 3 ha. to 4 ha. in extent and separated by a buffer strip about 20 m. wide (from which the biggest trees are removed). The strips are left to provide wind protection and to serve as a local wood supply while the second rotation crop is growing. Within the coupes every tree is felled, with the exception of a few broadleaved saplings left for soil improvement purposes and virtually every twig is removed from the forest in the subsequent logging operation. Logging operations, in fact, provide an object lesson in clean harvesting and close utilization. After clear-felling and saw log extraction, branch wood down to a 3-cm. diameter is harvested for mining timber, pulp-wood, handicrafts, charcoal, and, in the case of hardwoods, manufacture into blocks for tractor fuel; finally, twigs and foliage are collected and dried for fuel or the preparation of animal fodder.

Nowadays, some 60 per cent of the felling operations in stands of large-sized trees are said to be mechanized—gasoline driven chain saws of Russian manufacture (the "Druzhba") are the most usual tools, though the Chinese themselves now make a chain saw to the Russian pattern. It is 10 kg. in weight, has a 3-h.p. engine and a 60-cm. cut; a "stand-up" frame allows the feller to remain upright and to use his knee to exert pressure on the saw.

Where chain saws are not available, felling is done by extremely heavy and unwieldy one-man cross-cut saws; two-man saws are, apparently, not used in Manchuria, though they are said to be the standard felling tool in Szechuan. In Yunnan, axe felling is invariable.

Logging is a simple operation in the virgin forests of the northeast, now almost entirely mechanized. The power unit is a 5-ton, wood-burning tractor (again, Russian-designed and -built, or Chinese-built from the Russian blueprint). Closely resembling the Russian TDT-40 (apart from its adaptation for wood-burning), it is equipped with a tilting deck apron, a power winch behind the cab and a fair-lead mounted on the apron. The tracks are 40 cm. wide and some 4.5 m. long, with the front idler and driving sprockets raised from the ground, to enable the machine to traverse rough country. The deck apron, or back plate, can be used in the lowered position to lift the butts of the logs off the ground for hauling, or it can be fully raised above the tracks when carrying loads of small produce. With the tractor, tree-length logging is general practice, logs being cross-cut and loaded directly on to tramway wagons. Since there are few forest roads, extraction is mainly by narrow gauge, temporary tramway. In hill country, where tractors cannot operate, logging is left until winter, when ice chutes are used for extraction.

The Chinese are fully aware of the short-sightedness of tramway logging; at the present time, however, they have little alternative, since they lack both the roads and adequate motor transport heavy enough to haul timber. Road construction, nevertheless, has a high priority in forest areas and, since 1958, some 8,000 km. of forest roads have reportedly been built. These are used for winter logging by means of horse-drawn sleds.

In the broadleaved forests of the south and southwest, the terrain does not lend itself easily to mechanization. Where there are roads or tracks, teams of horses and donkeys (harnessed together) are used to haul, load, and transport logs, while in some areas (e.g. Fukien), waterways are available. In the more inaccessible areas, however, where there are no facilities for log-transport, a form of selection logging is practiced; the timber is pitsawn *in situ* and the lumber packed out by man or beast.

The "Wood Factories"

The main timber processing centers in China are Lungkiang and Harbin—serving the greater and lesser Khingan mountains—in Manchuria; Shenyang and Antung in Liaotung, drawing timber from the Changpaishan massif; Peking and Shanghai, based on logs imported from Manchuria and elsewhere; Foochow (Fukien), Kwangchow (Kwangtung), Ipin and Chengtu (Szechuan), using indigenous timbers. The majority of the bigger plants are integrated, though not in any obviously planned fashion, comprising one or several sawmills, a plywood mill, several fiberboard plants, and, often, a furniture factory. Each unit represents an addition to an original sawmill; where there is more than one sawmill in the complex, it is because the ancillary plants have become too big to be kept supplied by the original mill and there is insufficient space available to enlarge it. These collections of plants are known in China as "wood factories." The Peking wood factory, for example, consists of two sawmills, a plywood mill, a fiberboard plant, a furniture factory, a joinery plant, and a box factory. Run by the municipality, it began in 1952 with one sawmill and the furniture factory. The other components were added later and the whole complex now employs a labor force of 2,600 and utilizes some 100,000 cu. m. of roundwood annually. The Shanghai No. 1 wood factory, on the other hand, was built up from a British-owned sawmill established in 1932 and taken over in 1950. A plywood mill, two fiberboard plants, and a factory making sewing machine cases have been added; it now employs over 1,000 workers and has an annual log intake of around 30,000 cu. m. The wood factories buy their logs from the

State Forest Service at prices fixed by the government and they sell most of their products through state trading companies, also at decreed prices. During 1962 for example, two-thirds of the furniture output of the Peking wood factory was taken by state marketing organizations and only one-third could be sold on a free market, while the entire manufactured output of the Shanghai No. 1 wood factory in that year was absorbed by state enterprises; since the demand exceeded the supply, these enterprises were, in fact, rationed, with the allocations decided by the people's council of the muncipality.

The sawmills are invariably band mills (though some circular mills exist in country districts) and cut all species (softwoods and hardwoods) with the same saws, speeds, and settings. At the Peking factory, apart from the segregation of peeler logs, no sorting is carried out until the timber emerges from the sawmills. The hardwoods (for furniture) and softwoods (for joinery) are then separated and dispatched to the relevant plants either manually or by donkey cart. The sawmills are very simple, comprising a band head rig, two band re-saws, and a pendulum saw for end-trimming on the green chain. Slabs are carried from the head rig to the re-saws on manually operated rollers and virtually all handling beyond the re-saws is manual. Sawmill waste is sent to the fiberboard plant.

Plywood is manufactured from rotary-cut veneers of both softwoods and hardwoods. At the Peking factory, 330 workers are employed in the plywood mill, which turns out 240,000 sq. m. of $\frac{1}{16}$-inch veneer per month. Two 3-m. (10-ft.) peeling machines are in operation but, at the time of the writer's visit they were peeling only 1.2 m. bolts. The logs are de-barked manually and the bark goes to the fiberboard plant. The plywood is made up by hand, machine-pressed, and the glue cured by flat irons.

The Shanghai plywood mill appears to be much more efficient than that at the Peking wood factory. It has two 2.7-m. (9-ft.) peeling machines (one of which, however, was out of action when the writer visited the plant) and in 1962 produced 400,000 sq. m. of $\frac{1}{16}$-inch veneer per month (compared with a record production in 1961 of 500,000 sq. m.). Production per man amounts to 1,295 sq. m. compared with 727 sq. m. at the Peking mill. The Shanghai factory produces a greater range of plywoods than that at Peking, including exterior and structural grades, and hardwood-faced (birch and oak) panels. Glues are of the usual types, with soya bean powder replacing casein for interior use. The product is of high quality, in spite of the primitive techniques employed. In terms of manpower usage and costs, however, it could scarcely be claimed that veneer production in China is efficient by modern industrial standards.

Fiberboard plants are extremely variable. The first plant to be built in China was at the Shanghai wood factory and it is still in operation. It employs forty-seven men and produces 900 tons per year of 1.2-m. × 0.6-m. sheets. Alongside it is a semiautomatic plant, built in 1962, employing only twenty-three men to produce 3,000 tons per year in 2.4-m. × 1.0-m. sheets. In neither case is the product of a high quality. All species (including barks) are mixed and sometimes straw is put in as well; particle size varies enormously, as does the texture and density of the finished product. Oil tempering appears to be unknown in China.

The furniture and joinery factories also show little evidence of efficient mass production, though the quality of individual workmanship is high. Factory layout is haphazard with much wasted space and even converging assembly lines carrying different products. The Peking wood factory, for example, produces cupboard units, chairs, tables, and a variety of miscellaneous items; any or all of these may arrive at the finishing shop at one time, giving an impression of utter confusion. Lack of "good housekeeping" on the shop floors creates a high fire hazard. Mechanization is primitive and is usually limited to devices designed and built by the factory employees. One cannot help but admire the ingenuity of some of these precarious pieces of equipment and the enthusiasm of their designers—but they scarcely represent realistic examples of modern industrialization and mass-production techniques, which is what the Chinese often claim for them. In general, apart from the initial cutting and planing, all joinery operations are manual, including assembly, painting, and polishing. Again, the Shanghai factory (which produces only sewing machine cases) appears to be more efficient though here, also, most of the operations are manual and factory hygiene leaves a lot to be desired. The same criticisms can be levelled at the box factories.

Critical comments on the lack of mechanization in the wood factories would not be justified, were it not for Chinese insistence on the need for mechanization and even, on occasions, claims of labor shortages. If there is one thing the Chinese have in abundant supply, it is labor, even though much of it is unskilled; and this writer confessed to being utterly baffled by such claims, made (as they sometimes were) in the presence of obvious underemployment.

The wood factories are more than simply places of employment; they provide housing and all social facilities for all their workers; they are, in fact, completely self-contained communities and may house several thousand individuals. That at Peking, for example, has a number of day nurseries, several schools, and even a museum (containing furnished rooms representative of the Chinese dynasties since 1,000 A.D.).

Seasoning and Wood Preservation

It is to be expected that both timber-drying and wood preservation in China will make rapid progress during the next decade or so, since research in these fields is well ahead of practice. At the present time, however, techniques are primitive. Air seasoning in uncovered stacks is the norm and the author saw drying kilns only at the Forest Products Research Institute. In Peking, stack weighting is practiced and stack construction is generally good; elsewhere, seasoning leaves much to be desired.

Wood preservation is virtually limited to surface treatments, though pressure-plants for the impregnation of railway ties are said to be in operation. The lack of treatment appears to be due more to a shortage of preservatives than to deficiencies in technical knowledge. Creosote and tung oil are the principal components used and treatment is limited to timber in ground contact. Thus, transmission poles are either treated only at the base or are left untreated and joined to a treated section in ground contact; railway ties are often treated on the undersurface only. There is no doubt that the development of timber preservation in China could help considerably in the conservation of scarce timber resources.

The Pulp and Paper Industry

In the field of pulp and paper manufacture, the technical competence of the Chinese is much greater than it appears to be in the other forest-based industries. The Chinese were, of course, the inventors of paper-making and they have not lost their skill. The fact that much of the paper currently used in China is of very poor quality is symptomatic not of any lack of technical ability, but of the atrocious raw materials that perforce go into its manufacture (see Appendix I). Over 120 types of paper are now made in China and an export trade in newsprint and certain speciality papers to several countries has been developed. According to Russian sources (Solecki, 1964), paper output rose from 108,000 tons in 1949 to more than 1,700,000 tons in 1959. At least a dozen major paper mills have been built since 1958 (some with Russian or German assistance), including a number with capacities of more than 100 tons per day. The fact that the Chinese are themselves supplying technical assistance in this field to other countries is an indication that these mills function successfully.

LOCAL INDUSTRY AND COMMUNE PLANTS

Apart from the large enterprises, small sawmills, fiberboard plants, box factories, etc. are found within some of the communes. The vegetable-growing communes, for example, need substantial supplies of boxing while the tea communes similarly require tea chests. These are usually made within the commune. Fiberboard plants were set up in large numbers during 1958 in an attempt to mitigate the effects of the timber shortage. There were said to be more than 2,000 in operation (NCNA, 4/5/60) though this is scarcely credible. In 1958, too, some communes built and operated paper mills, and an aggregate production of three to five million tons of paper was planned for them; needless to say, this plan did not materialize and only a few of the back-yard paper mills remain. Many of the communes operate small chemical extraction plants, however, and they also produce manufactured wood products.

China is extremely rich in oil-bearing and aromatic tree species, which yield medicinal bases, edible oils, oils and fats suitable for soap manufacture, tallow, perfumes, etc. They are extracted and the products made in the communes. These operations, together with wood hydrolysis plants (producing ethyl alcohol), units producing animal fodder from dried and ground conifer needles, bamboo utilization plants, and woodcraft work (cooperage shooks, agricultural implements, tool handles, cabinet work, furniture, ornaments, fiberboard, etc.), are more than just "cottage industries." There are some 480,000 production brigades, averaging 250 households (500 workers), in the rural communes and their industrial contribution must be considerable. An indication of their importance in the forest industries is gained from the fact that, since 1958, government policy has been to assign 50 per cent of the annual tree planting program (currently, some five million ha.) to so-called "economic" or "industrial" trees.

LABOR ORGANIZATION AND WORK CONDITIONS

A problem that inevitably arises in any discussion of conditions in a foreign country is that, while administrative structures and politico-social concepts may have terminological counterparts in one's own

country, their significance and implications lie outside the traditions
and experience of the non-national; in consequence, the barrier to communication is not simply one of language. This difficulty is well exem-
plified in the consideration of industrial organization in present-day
China. For example, although the Chinese have trade unions, they are
not the industrially powerful but politically impotent organizations of
the U.S.A., neither do they have much in common with the politically
conscious labor unions of western Europe.

Membership of trade unions in China is limited to "manual and non-
manual workers living entirely or mainly on their wages" and does not
extend to the members of the rural communes, shopkeepers, craftsmen,
or government servants. In 1958, there were only 16 million trade
unionists out of a work force of perhaps 300 million. The functions of
the unions are to "strengthen the unity of the working class, to consolidate the alliance of workers and peasants, to educate the workers
to observe conscientiously the laws and decrees of the state and labor
discipline, to strive for the development of production, for the constant
increase of labor productivity, for the fulfillment and overfulfillment of
the production plans of the state . . ." and to improve "the material and
cultural life of the workers." They are, in fact, administrative organizations of the industrial proletariat, run by members of the Communist
party and providing, in the tradition of Marxist-Leninism, a "transmission belt" for the implementation of party policy—they have no right
to call strikes, nor do they play any part in wage negotiation. Strikes
("industrial sabotage"), of course, are illegal and fall into the category
of "economic offences," punishable by decree of the so-called "comrade
tribunals" (see e.g. Hughes and Luard, 1959), while wages are determined according to a "wage-point"—a consumer goods price index—
which is laid down by the government and is not subject to discussion.
The unions, too, have been warned off political activity. According to
Lai Jo-yu, until 1958 the head of the All-China Federation of Trade
Unions, "It is not permissible to express dissatisfaction with the Party
either openly among the members or at trade union meetings. . . .
Trade unions must accept the leadership of the Party. This is the first
rule of heaven" (Lai, 1953).

In spite of their restrictions, the unions do provide some services for
their members; at the wood factories, for example, the union organizers
supervise the recreational and welfare facilities, including housing and
schools; they organize savings campaigns and three-year training ap-
prenticeships for the timber industry; and they oversee such safety
regulations as operate in the mills. Of more dubious value to their

members, they organize production competitions, notice-board publicity for outstanding workers ("industrial heroes") etc., and they have been active in the current campaign to persuade white-collar workers (including factory managers and cadres) to work part-time at manual jobs. (During the author's visit to the Shanghai No. 1 wood factory, the Vice-Director was operating a peeling machine in the veneer mill; all the administrative personnel, including the Director, were said to work for forty-five days a year at the factory bench).

Perhaps the most important function of the trade unions is to administer social security. Established by the Trade Union Law of June, 1950, and expanded by Regulations on Labor Social Insurance promulgated in March, 1952, impressive benefits are available to industrial workers (see For. Lang. Press, 1956). Sickness benefits of between 60 and 100 per cent of wages are awarded to victims of industrial accidents, while all medical and surgical costs (including hospitalization, doctors' fees, and drug charges) are payable by the employer. Retirement pensions at age sixty for men and fifty for women range from 50 to 70 per cent of the average wage, depending on length of service, while a death benefit of two to three months' wages and a maternity benefit (full wages for fifty-six to seventy days) are also mandatory.

Although wages are pitifully small by the standards of developed countries, the industrial worker is undoubtedly better off (in terms of purchasing power and fringe benefits) than his predecessors under the Nationalist regime. In the timber industry, wages are said to range from 50 yuan per month for a logger to 75 yuan per month for a skilled operator of a head rig saw; factory managers may earn up to 200 yuan per month. The minimum wage rate at the Peking wood factory is 33 yuan and the average 62. At the current exchange rate, via sterling, 100 yuan represents about $36 U.S.; the translation is meaningless, however, because of enormous differences in both the cost and the standard of living between China and the U.S. Thus, the factory worker in China has virtually free housing and welfare benefits, food and clothing are rationed and very cheap, such entertainment as is available is well within his means (a circus or theater performance costs the equivalent of a few cents), and the opportunities for spending money on other than basic necessities are extremely restricted. A six-day working week is standard, with no vacations other than seven "legal holidays" in the year.

Until 1958, the industrial worker in China was paid almost entirely on piecework (Hughes and Luard, 1959); recently, however, there has been a shift toward time-rates and currently there appears to be no standard pattern. At the time of this writer's visit, logging crews and sawmill workers, for example, were on piece-rates, while workers in the ancillary plant of the wood factories were paid fixed monthly rates. The Chinese do not recognize any incompatibility between a piece-rate system and communist theory; eight grades of skill are recognized in industry—irrespective of job content—and the piecework rates vary according to the grade of the worker. A complicated incentive system of reward bonuses also operates.

In forestry practice, the Chinese are faced with three major challenges: firstly, they must solve the many problems associated with the establishment of young trees on very inhospitable sites; secondly, they have to develop silvicultural schedules and management methods for their major species; and, finally, they must increase the efficiency of their industrial operations and achieve maximum output from scarce industrial machinery. There is no reason to doubt that they will be able, given time, to achieve the first and the second of these objects, but whether they can accept the third challenge must remain in question.

CHAPTER VI.

WATER CONSERVANCY AND PROTECTION FORESTRY

WATER CONSERVANCY and forestry are the Siamese twins of land use; attempts to separate them involve dire risks. Most countries of the world have learned this truth through bitter experience and communist China is no exception. The fact that she has learned it more quickly than many countries reflects, perhaps, the spectacular nature of soil erosion in China and the accumulated evidence of decades of neglect.

Problems of water conservancy have several distinct, but interrelated aspects, and in all of them protection afforestation plays an important role. The propensity of China's major rivers for disastrous flooding is legendary; and flood control, together with hydroelectric power development, provided an early focus for communist endeavors in the field of river control. The need to increase agricultural productivity demanded extensive reclamation of marginal land and major increases in irrigation, while the provision of shelter and the control of soil erosion are essential components of land development policy. Although the objectives vary, the methods of protective afforestation associated with all these aspects have much in common.

WATER CONSERVANCY ADMINISTRATION

As with production forestry, water conservancy in China is organized at several administrative levels. A Ministry of Water Conservancy, established in 1950 and combined with the Ministry of Electric Power Industry in 1958, has a primary responsibility for carrying out the

107

policies of the State Council. It comprises some twenty-three departments and bureaus, etc., including executive control commissions for the Yellow, Yangtze, Hwai, and Ching Chiang rivers. Numerous planning commissions (e.g. Yellow river, hydrology investigation, sand control, etc.) also operate, but these are staff departments and report directly to the State Council. Composed of members from several ministries and, usually, scientists of the *Academia Sinica*, they study economic potentials of specific regions, make recommendations, and prepare detailed development plans (see e.g. JPRS, 1963). Often, they establish specialist investigation teams which, until 1960, included Soviet scientists.

At the regional level, local planning commissions (including a soil conservation committee) work through the provincial people's councils but, again, for executive purposes, the provinces are divided into control areas under the ministry and into water conservancy districts. The latter cut across other administrative subdivisions and are demarcated by natural features such as catchments or river valleys. As in forestry administration, the limits of responsibilities of the various national and local bodies are obscure but, in general, the ministries are concerned with large-scale, multipurpose programs, the provincial councils with medium-sized, co-operative projects carried out with state aid, while small-scale improvements are left to the production units of the communes. At all regional levels, however, national policies are directed and enforced by technical cadres sent out by the Communist party organization.

The organizational structure for water conservancy is further complicated by the fact that other land-management ministries are closely involved at both national and regional levels. The Ministry of Agriculture is concerned with crop and animal production, while large-scale land development is the responsibility of the Ministry for State Farms and Virgin Land Reclamation. Major protection forestry projects, such as catchment afforestation programs, sand-dune fixation, etc., are the financial responsibility of the Ministry of Forestry, working through the production teams of the communes, and with the local people's councils responsible for the allocation of manpower and physical resources. Small-scale plantations associated with localized erosion control and irrigation canals, on the other hand, are left to the communes, though the State Forest Service may provide planting stock and technical advice. With responsibilities divided between several ministries and the people's councils, it is inevitable that the demands of agriculture, water conservancy, and forestry sometimes conflict (see e.g. *Far East. Econ. Rev.,* 1958; Chao, 1961); in theory, the people's councils can resolve these issues but, in fact, it is often the party cadres who attempt to do so—not always with conspicuous success.

POLICY DEVELOPMENTS 1949–63

River Control and Irrigation

Since 1949, water conservancy developments in China have been considerable, though progress has not been smooth. Initially, priority was assigned to flood control, land drainage, and the rehabilitation of irrigation works destroyed or damaged during the war. The reconstruction and strengthening of dikes along the major rivers (and their consolidation through tree-planting) were reportedly accomplished by 1952 (NCNA, 9/13/52) and attention then turned to the further development of irrigation facilities. A State Council resolution setting up local organizations for "drought prevention" and the introduction of the so-called "lower stage" co-operatives provided a framework for local irrigation campaigns and at the same time gave a boost to large, multipurpose works designed to control the flow of the bigger rivers. Between 1952 and 1957, some 9,000 small or medium-sized* reservoirs and storage ponds for irrigation were reportedly constructed (NCNA, 11/1/59), together with some six million wells (NCNA, 6/13/54); *People's China*, 5/16/56; *Chung-kuo shui-li*, 5/14/57; *Shui-li hsueh-pao*, 12/29/57). At the same time, nine major reservoirs for flood control, irrigation and hydroelectric power generation—with a total capacity of 7,300,000 million cu. m.—were completed (SSB, 9/1/59). In total, an increase in irrigated area of 17.21 million ha. was claimed, much of it resulting from a second irrigation drive in 1956.

At this time, the water conservancy program was further decentralized and "small projects" were emphasized at the expense of large-scale works (JPRS, 8/15/60). The Ministry of Water Conservancy also became concerned about inadequacies of technical control of many local operations and began to advocate a few standard projects,

---

* Chinese sources invariably refer to water conservancy projects as "small," "medium," or "large" but, until 1958, no criteria for the definition of size were issued except "the scale of work, the technical questions involved, and the results expected. . . ." In 1958, standards were defined for reservoirs: with a capacity exceeding 100 million cu. m. they were "large"; from 10 million to 100 million cu. m., "medium"; and below 10 million cu. m. capacity, "small" (NCNA, 8/30/59).

rather than a multiplicity of locally designed schemes. Thus, in 1956 emphasis was placed on sinking new wells; in 1958, it shifted to storage ponds and reservoirs; and in 1959, to canals and larger reservoirs. Handbooks and reports on soil and water conservation, compiled under the auspices of the *Academia Sinica*, were issued (see e.g. Lin Jung *et al.*, 1959; *Acad. Sin.*, 1958; JPRS, 1963), in which recommended designs and methods are described in considerable detail. Some of them were clearly intended for the inexperienced cadres and so-called "peasant technicians." The latter, often without any schooling and trained on the premise that "the construction site is the school and work the textbook" (U.K., BBC, 12/4/58), were sometimes called upon to supervise major projects (NCNA, 11/1/59).

A third water conservancy drive began in 1958 and was so successful that on January 20, 1959, the editors of the *People's Daily* warned against overenthusiasm and the undue proliferation of small-scale projects. After the formation of the communes (and the amalgamation of the Ministries of Water Conservancy and Electric Power), official policy again switched the emphasis to major developments (particularly in the arid north and northwest) with mass improvement of existing small irrigation works advocated rather than the construction of new facilities at the local level. Although this policy continued through 1960 and 1961, some 3.1 million small and medium-sized projects were allegedly under construction in 1960 (NCNA, 12/22/59; *Peking Review*, 2/23/60).

Since 1961, further changes in the approach to water conservancy have become apparent, though no policy directives have been formally announced. Official sources still advocate decentralization ("Rely on the people rather than the government" [*China Reconstructs*, 1959]), but it is clear that state control of all projects, irrespective of size, is tightening. The commune production units can no longer initiate projects without ministerial approval and the poorly trained "peasant technicians" have lost much of their authority. Deficiencies in planning and direction were recognized by the administration as early as 1957. According to one source (*Chi-hua Ching-chi*, 1957), "We have learned three lessons. First, in the absence of over-all plans for the river valley, important water conservancy projects must not be hurriedly started. Second, before the start of important conservancy projects, we must have sufficient time to collect data, draw up several plans, and repeatedly compare and select them. Third, the standard of important conservancy projects must not be set too low." In spite of such recognition, these deficiencies were perpetuated for another four years (in 1958, indeed, they were augmented) before practical measures were taken to remove them. Thus, the communal tail continued to wag the state dog and, doubtless, this fact accounts for the increasing centralized control apparent in 1963, despite an avowed policy of administrative decentralization.

It is significant that major changes in water conservancy policy have more or less coincided with changes in social organization of the rural communities. Thus, the first irrigation campaigns in 1952 accompanied the introduction of "lower-stage" co-operatives; the second drive in 1956 was associated with the development of the "higher-stage" co-operatives; and the third increase in tempo (and the policy shift to emphasis on large-scale projects) paralleled the formation of the communes in 1958. The grass roots origin of the commune system (which was truly born in the countryside and not, as some authorities allege, imposed on a reluctant populace by arbitrary edict) perhaps explains why the central government was slow to contain the mismanaged enthusiasm for water conservancy apparent immediately after 1958, and why current policy declarations do not always closely coincide with practice.

Land Reclamation

According to Kapelinsky *et al.* (1959), state farms, following the Russian pattern, were set up in China in 1947—two years before the Communists obtained complete control of the country. They were established on virgin land (mainly grasslands) with a view to the postwar settlement of demobilized Red Army men. It was not until 1952, however, that the Ministry of State Farms and Virgin Land Reclamation (together with the usual provincial satellites) came into being and large-scale developments were set in motion. Even at this time, land reclamation was not promulgated as an official policy and it was not until the adoption of the first National Agricultural Development Program in January, 1956, that it became a formal part of the charter for agriculture.

China claims over 100 million ha. of cultivable virgin land (*Current Events Handbook*, 9/10/55), much of it in the provinces of Heilungkiang, Sinkiang, Tsinghai, Inner Mongolia, and the Uighur autonomous region. Smaller areas occur in the southern provinces (Yunnan, Kwangsi, and Kwangtung), Szechuan, and the northeast seaboard. The communist administrators rightly argued that since the development of "waste" land is a labor-intensive operation, demanding little in the way of advanced technology, it was eminently suited to conditions existing in China during the early years of the regime. From a modest figure of 112,000 ha. during 1949–52, the area developed annually rose to 2,000,000 ha. in 1956 (Chao, 1961), mostly in the predominantly pastoral northern provinces. For example, from 1949 to 1958, the cultivated area in the Uighur autonomous region doubled (to 2.3 million hectares [Sai, 1959]), while developments in Sinkiang (where seventeen state farms were established by the pioneer corps of the Red Army), Kansu and Inner Mongolia have also been publicized (Buchanan, 1960).

The location of land reclamation projects in the sparsely populated pastoral areas of China is not surprising. The river valleys and flood plains of the southeast have been intensively farmed for generations and in these densely populated regions, every square meter of ground that could be cultivated was being tilled long before the Communists gained control. Only in the areas of marginal settlement, remote from economic improvement before 1949, was there land available in sufficient amount to justify the scale of operation envisaged by the land developers. It must be realized, too, that the land reclamation projects were only a part of comprehensive economic development programs planned for the remote areas and based primarily on the exploitation of mineral resources. Agricultural development was needed to service the increased population.

During the period of the first five-year plan, land reclamation appears to have been virtually restricted to state-controlled projects. Inevitably, many of them were ill conceived, badly planned, and poorly co-ordinated. In some areas, newly planted forests were burned and ploughed up; all too frequently, alternative grazing for the dispossessed pastoralists (many of whom were members of "minority nations") was not provided, which led to stocking densities exceeding the carrying capacity of their now restricted holdings; and pressure on the scarce resources of natural forests (to provide animal fodder and fuelwood for the increasing labor forces) became too great to be resisted. Accelerated soil erosion, silting up of many newly constructed reservoirs, and reduced water yields resulted. Nevertheless, in spite of these deficiencies, even as late as 1955, the administrators firmly believed that China's cultivated area could be doubled and that the only limitations were lack of capital, suitable machinery, and adequate communications (*Current Events Handbook*, 9/10/55). It is of interest that, as has happened in many countries of the world, the first warnings that indiscriminate land reclamation was posing more problems than it solved were sounded by foresters (Liang, 1956), who led the demands for a national and integrated land utilization policy. As discussed already (p. 8), these demands prompted a policy shift in 1957, when large areas of developed pastoral land were taken out of cultivation and mass afforestation of "waste" land got under way.

Land reclamation is one field in which the Communists seem to have applied the lessons learned from past mistakes relatively rapidly. Since 1959, at any rate, foresters have been closely associated with land development schemes, which have been based on comprehensive catchment surveys by scientists rather than on the dreams of political administrators and economists.

PROTECTION FORESTRY PRACTICES

Protective afforestation in China can conveniently be treated under three heads: erosion control (including plantations associated with flood prevention and irrigation schemes); sand fixation, which is, of course, a form of erosion control but which is sufficiently specialized to justify a distinction; and shelter planting. Many of the large-scale projects in China incorporate aspects of all three categories, so their separation is primarily one of convenience.

Erosion Control

Without doubt, the most dramatic soil erosion problems in China arise in the vast north and northwestern provinces—wind-swept, arid, and continental areas of loess, and sand desert—and it is here that Chinese foresters, drawing upon techniques developed in many parts of the world (including Asiatic Russia) have devised elaborate preventive measures. Species and methods employed vary according to the objectives of protection (watershed improvement, gulley control, stabilization of stopbanks and reservoir banks, etc.), the conditions of the environment, and the extent to which protection afforestation is combined with economic crop cultivation. In most regions, priority is given to soil and water conservation, but in populated areas species may be selected with a view to the production of timber, fruits, fuelwood, charcoal, animal fodder, and organic manure.

Sheet Erosion. In the afforestation of major catchments in China, four types of country are delineated and separately treated—hilltops, steep slopes, gentle slopes, and terraced fields. In the loess areas, the hill crowns tend to be half-domed in the cross-section, some 30 m. to

100 m. across, wind-swept, and generally intractable. The important tree species planted are *Ulmus pumila, Populus cathayana,* and *P. simonii;* but, where soil conditions are suitable, *Salix matsudana, Pinus tabulaeformis, Biota orientalis,* and *Quercus serrata* may also be used. The trees are pit-planted in circular, 45-cm. diameter × 45-cm. deep holes, spaced at 1 m. × 2 m. Tree rows run the length of the hill crown and are flanked by lines of secondary tree species (e.g. *Tamarix juniperina*) and shrubs spaced at 0.5 m. × 0.5 m.

On the steeper hill slopes (e.g. >25° gradient), in addition to the three major species cited above, *Robinia pseudoacacia, Ailanthus altissima, Elaegnus angustifolia, Morus alba,* and various other fruit trees are widely used, together with the more demanding *Populus nigra* and *Pinus tabulaeformis.* Several establishment patterns are employed, depending on the steepness of the slope and the degree of exposure. Some of these are illustrated in Figure 4. They include:

Fish-scales: semicircular pits, 80 cm. to 120 cm. long, 40 cm. to 60 cm. wide, and 25 cm. to 35 cm. deep, breasted by a 20 cm. to 25-cm. high embankment, and spaced 1.5 m. to 2.5 m. apart. Two seedlings may be planted in each pit, unless fruit trees are used.

Double furrows: double surface-furrows, along the contours, with a ploughed furrow (30 cm. to 40 cm. wide) superimposed and a 20 cm. to 25-cm. embankment below. Trees are planted singly in pits 0.5 m. to 1.0 m. apart and 20 cm. below the last furrow. Furrow lines are 1.5 m. to 2.5 m. apart.

Level-grade steps: a narrow step, 4 m. to 8 m. long and 60 cm. to 80 cm. deep, is dug along the contours, the spoil forming a shoulder. Living willow branches (2 cm. to 3 cm. diameter) just protruding beyond the shoulder, are tamped into the step surface and covered with 10 cm. of soil from the upper side of the step. Willows are spaced at 20 cm. to 25 cm. within the steps, while the latter are some 1.5 m. to 2.5 m. apart. Legumes may be sown on the exposed soil surface of the steps.

Level ditches: discontinuous contour ditches, 4 m. to 6 m. long, 80 cm. wide at the top, and 30 cm. at the bottom, 30 cm. to 40 cm. deep, and with a breasting embankment 20 cm. to 30 cm. wide. The ditches are 0.5 m. to 1.0 m. apart along the contour with 3.0 m. to 3.5 m. between contours. Trees are planted 0.5 m. to 1.0 m. apart at the junction of the embankment and the slope surface.

Level ditch-pit combinations: rows of discontinuous contour ditches, 10 m. to 20 m. between rows, with 40 cm. to 50 cm. square pits, 1 m. to 1.5 m. apart, between them.

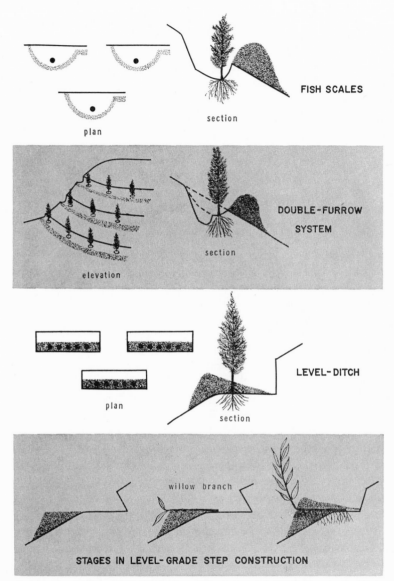

Figure 4: Various Establishment Patterns and Techniques for Protective Afforestation on Loess Slopes

Level grade step and fish-scale combinations: same as the previous method but combining contour rows of steps, with fish-scales between the rows.

The above establishment patterns aim to combine moisture conservation and soil stability. Since they are labor-intensive operations and require careful maintenance, they are not appropriate to the more sparsely populated pastoral regions. Here, where slopes are fairly gradual and where terracing for cultivation is irrelevant, tree belts of varying degrees of sophistication may be established. The simplest type comprises contour belts, 50 m. to 150 m. apart and 20 m. to 30 m. wide, of intimately mixed trees and shrubs, notch- or pit-planted. Others may consist of fruit trees established in fish-scale pits about 5 m. apart, interspersed with shrubs; or, where grazing is important, pasture grasses may be sown or planted along with shrubs and tree species. Timber trees often grown in such belts include *Populus cathayana, Quercus liaotungensis, Pinus tabulaeformis,* and various species of *Acer, Tilia,* and *Betula.* The fruit trees *Malus pumila, Pyrus bretschneideri, Prunus davidiana, P. ensu, Juglans* spp., and *Zizyphus jujuba* are frequently raised in this way while the shrubs include *Amorpha fruticosa, Sambucus racemosa, Neillia sinensis,* and *Cerasus tomentosa.* The principal pasture grasses are *Medicago sativa* and *Melilotus dentatus.*

The lower slopes of the loess hills along the waterways are invariably terraced and cultivated; indeed, this has been the case for many hundreds of years. In an attempt to achieve maximum use of scarce land in populous areas, the Chinese have recently advocated tree-planting on the earth-retaining walls of the terraces and in the ditches immediately below the walls. Shrubs and fruit trees are proposed for the tops of the embankments and timber trees on ledges cut into the sides (or planted during the construction of the earth walls).

Indiscriminate cultivation of grazing land during the earlier reclamation projects has already been stressed. Since 1957, a more enlightened approach has developed and the Chinese now claim that contour ploughing, strip-cropping, and other farming methods aimed at reducing soil loss are standard practices on all state farms concerned with land development. One such practice widely publicized is that of alternating 20 m. to 30 m. wide belts of pasture grasses with similar crop belts separated by 1.5-m. wide plantings of *Amorpha fruticosa.*

In other than loess or sand country, sheet erosion results from the action of water rather than wind; the need to conserve moisture is less important and a wider range of tree species can be used in protective plantations (see Table 7, Chapter V). Ground preparation may be deemed unnecessary and, following rudimentary contour draining, trees may be pit-planted without any obvious pattern being used.

Elsewhere, simple benches, 1 m. to 2 m. wide × 50 cm. deep are cut into the hillside and the trees sown or planted in lines along them. In Kwangtung province, broadcast-sowing of seed, followed by trampling by the local populace, has been practiced.

China has experienced soil erosion for several thousand years, and there are regions so badly depleted that only barren subsoil is available for plant growth. Since the success of revegetation in soil and water conservation usually depends on the speed of strike of the plants (and, in particular, the rapidity of initial root development), it may be necessary to aid establishment through the use of fertilizers or fertile soil brought in from elsewhere. It is not possible to judge the scale on which these practices are employed in protective afforestation—they are not used in production forestry—but certainly in the loess areas, in the highly saline soils of the far northwest, and in the depleted yellow earths of the southern provinces they are not unknown. Imported soil is normally introduced in pits or as a shell over subsoil embankments. The fertilizers used are many and varied, though almost entirely organic. The following examples of prescriptions in common use in Shensi province are taken from a conservation handbook for the middle Yellow river loess region:

a) Fresh urine plus 10 per cent limestone and wood ash, boiled.

b) Urine, set aside three days, closely sealed for the first two days, boiled with 10 per cent grass and wood ash.

c) Yu-lin Chao-shih kiln coal dust.

d) Wu kung urine, 28 per cent; grass and wood ash, 12 per cent; soil from the base of a latrine wall, 10 per cent.

e) Nitric saline water, 5 chin; gypsum, 1 chin; human urine, 8 chin; grass and wood ashes, 8 chin; limestone, 20 chin; rubber, 1 chin; miscellaneous grasses, 8 chin.

f) Water, 50 chin; superphosphate of lime, 8 liang; horse manure, 1 chin; human urine, 1 chin; the whole, closely sealed for fifteen days ("artificial urine").

g) Soil baked for sixty days.

h) Soil burned for two hours over a wood and grass fire.

These brews—some of which read more like potions from a witch's cauldron than plant nutrients—are particularly low in available nitrogen and phosphate; and it is doubtful whether their usefulness justifies the time and effort involved in preparation. There is, however, a desperate shortage of inorganic fertilizers throughout China and it is likely that local recipes of this sort—together with night soil and tree foliage—will form the only fertilizers available to forestry for many years.

Gully Erosion. The protection afforestation methods described so far have been concerned with the prevention of sheet erosion in large catchments. Less widely destructive, but infinitely more spectacular (again, particularly in the loess regions) are examples of gully erosion. Tree-planting techniques employed to heal and stop the development of gullies and ravines are rather different from those used in the prevention of sheet erosion, and are usually combined with some form of simple engineering works.

To prevent cutting back of the gully head a contour embankment is built some 2 m. to 3 m. beyond it; then come one or more (depending on the size of the gully head and the severity of erosion) contour lines of discontinuous ditches interspersing small fish-scale pits, spaced at 1 m. × 1 m. The tree species planted are chosen for their ability to develop an extensive, spreading root system. *Populus cathayana, P. simonii, Robinia pseudoacacia, Salix matsudana, Ulmus pumila, Tamarix juniperina,* and *Hippophae rhamnoides* have been used successfully.

On gully slopes trees may be established in level-grade steps, in fish-scale pits, or in simply prepared 40-cm. diameter × 30 cm. to 40-cm. deep, circular holes, spaced 1 m. apart, and with the excess soil forming a protective rim around the lower edge. These techniques vary little from those employed to counter sheet erosion. Planting to inhibit deepening in gully bottoms, on the other hand, almost invariably requires extensive preparation. Aprons running the full width of the gully may be constructed from soil, cement, dry stone-walling, or willow stakes used with woven wattle, boulders, etc., the distance between adjacent aprons determined by the slope and the apron height. There is nothing new in these methods and constructional details are available in any textbook dealing with erosion control; the objects are to reduce the force of flood waters, to cause silting behind the aprons, and to alter the profile of the gully to the point where revegetation becomes possible. The structures range from rudimentary aprons formed by scattered debris to complex engineer-designed, alluvium-retaining dams. Trees are planted in dibble holes, 1 m. apart over the floor of the ravine between the aprons; and if willows are available, 3-cm. branches are cut and buried in shallow prepared holes with just the apical sections visible above ground.

In very wide ravines, where the movement of water is slow and sporadic, "patch afforestation" may be carried out. Strips of trees some 30 m. to 50 m. wide run the entire width of the ravine, at intervals of about 50 m. Shrubs at 0.5-m. × 0.5-m. spacing provide an upstream border for the trees. Somewhat similar are the so-called "cha" strips, which comprise five to ten rows of trees (usually willows) grown in dibble holes, at 10 m. to 20-m. intervals down the gullies.

Stopbank Protection. Apart from catchment maintenance and the control of gully erosion, tree-planting plays an important part in stabilizing the banks of rivers, irrigation channels, and reservoirs, etc. Since there is normally adequate moisture on such sites, more exacting tree species can be utilized and criteria other than drought resistance determine the choice. In particular, shade trees—which will reduce evaporation from the water surface—and species that yield high-value products other than timber (e.g. fodder, fruits, extractives, medicinal compounds, etc.) are sought.

On river beaches, unsuitable for agriculture but which provide some protection for the stopbanks when vegetated, willows or high-yielding poplars are planted in 50-cm. × 50-cm. square pits, 50 cm. deep, and spaced at 1 m., with a tree in each corner. The pits are filled only to within 10 cm. of the beach surface, thus providing space for silt deposition during flooding. A low stone dike is usually built between the river bed and the beach, to prevent outwash and to trap the silt. This principle reaches a higher level of sophistication in the so-called goose-wing and willow-fence dam patterns of silt retention. In the former, tree belts, 3 m. to 6 m. apart, are established on mud or sand embankments breasting the river at an angle of about 35° to the direction of flow; not only is the force of the water reduced during flooding, but silting occurs between the embankments and, in time, adds to the cultivable land area. The willow-fence system consists of a flood-lead dam built out into the river, forcing the silt-laden water into elaborate sedimentation grounds, outlined by densely planted willows to slow down the water flow and to act as filters. These sedimentation grounds are reminiscent of those bordering the lower Rhine in Europe and associated with brick-making plants. Since Holland has no clay deposits suitable for brick-making, she harvests silt, brought down the Rhine from Germany and Switzerland and continuously deposited in specially constructed holding grounds. In China, of course, the silt is deposited only during floods. When the beds are sufficiently deep, they are cultivated and used as rice paddies.

To protect the banks of rivers, irrigation channels, and drainage ditches, various patterns of planting may be adopted. If a large channel runs across the slope of a hill, four or five rows of shrubs may be planted on the upper side, with mixed trees and shrubs on the lower, and such species as *Strobilanthes flaccidifolius* or *Hemerocallis flava* on the drain sides. On flat land, the tree-shrub mixture is often more intimate, as it is in plantations bordering reservoirs. In the latter case, willows are usually grown in the area between the lowest and the highest water level and production species in a 25-m. to 50-m. belt around the reservoir above the high water mark; at inlets, grass and shrub belts supplement the tree plantations.

As a general principle in the selection of tree species for stopbank protection, willows are used wherever there is a danger of periodic inundation. The common species include *Salix matsudana*, *S. babylonica*, *S. purpurea*, *S. capraea*, *S. cheilophila*, and *S. angustifolia*; shade and timber trees include many poplars, elms, and the ubiquitous black locust, while the wide range of fruit and "economic" trees employed makes generalization impossible (see e.g. Table 7, Chapter V). North of the Yangtze, land bordering water channels is highly prized for fruit tree and vine cultivation, often inter-cropped with vegetables. Further south, in the higher rainfall areas, fruit trees appear to be planted along roadsides and in walled orchards, rather than along the waterways.

Sand Stabilization and Afforestation

The sands of China are of two types—the coastal dunes of the eastern and southern provinces, and the desert sands of the north and northwestern interior. The former present no major problems with respect to stabilization and afforestation; where a littoral vegetation exists, planting with salt-spray resistant species such as *Casuarina equisetifolia* and *Pandanus odoratissimus* is carried out directly, while unstable dunes are first fixed by means of a seaward belt of sand plants (e.g. *Spinifex littoreus* and *Ricinus communis*) and then planted or sown with trees. If the inland extension of the dunes is substantial (and the prevailing wind is on-shore), timber species such as *Pinus tabulaeformis* and *P. massoniana* may be grown behind a 50-m. to 100-m. belt of salt-resistant trees; the methods employed are essentially similar to those in other regions of the world where coastal dune afforestation is carried out. The desert sands of the interior, however, present much greater problems.

Areas of aeolian sands and sand deserts in the Chinese interior are, by any standards, enormous (they cover some 10 per cent of the land surface area); furthermore, they occur in regions of very low precipitation, high winds, and excessive salinity. Chinese endeavors in the field of sand control can be divided into two categories: efforts to halt the advance of the deserts on a broad front, and attempts to fix and utilize sands in the immediate vicinity of oases and other settlements. The former involve the establishment of shelter belts of Herculean proportions and will be discussed later; the latter can be appropriately considered here.

Local sand-stabilization projects may be concerned with the protection of villages, roads, and railways; with the prevention of sand influx into reservoirs or the burial of arable land; or with increasing the productive capacity of land for crops, grass, or timber. Whatever the objective, the principles involved are the same: the moving sand is fixed temporarily and then stabilized by woody vegetation.

The Chinese employ several methods of sand fixation. Along lines of communication, temporary palisades have been used, though this is considered "not a good basic method of preventing shifting sands" (Lin *et al.*, 1959). If the sand movement is slow and sporadic, and where there is adequate moisture, belts of *Salix mongolica* or *Tamarix juniperina* are established without pretreatment along the contours of the dunes and are effective in preventing movement. More usually, however, the sand must be fixed with brushwood and sand species before trees can be planted. Brushwood and straw are laid in strips or squares across the path of the sand and either pegged or weighted down with stones; drought-resistant trees or shrubs are then planted. The strips are spaced 1 m. apart while the squares are 1 m. × 1 m. Where possible, *Artemisia* spp. are established by sowing, using about 500 gm. seed/ha., and trees are introduced two or three years later.

Other methods of sand fixation have been used on a small scale, including laborious practices such as covering the dunes with layers of clay, loess mixed with chopped grass and water, or "Kang-mien"—bricks made of clay and chopped tree branches—but they are not widespread.

A frequently used pattern in the protection of oases or farmland from moving sand is to isolate the area with a 50-m. wide belt of trees (using irrigation water to get the trees established), and then to form a so-called "sand-sealing" area in a zone several kilometers wide surrounding the tree belt. The sand-sealing area consists of trees planted in the dune hollows, with shrubs and grasses on the sides and tops of the dunes. If the sand-sealing is effective, the protected area is gradually enlarged until the soil moisture resource becomes limiting.

This practice of working *against* the face of the moving sand runs counter to one of the cardinal principles of sand dune afforestation

established in Europe and elsewhere; it is unavoidable in most parts
of China, however, because the origins of the sands are the remote
central Asian deserts—for the most part quite barren and lacking any
water resource. It is this fact, too, that has led to attempts to seal off
large sections of desert by shelter belts.

The choice of plant species for sand areas is usually empirical,
though the characteristics required are fairly obvious. Drought resistance and the ability to grow on highly saline sites are important
criteria. The Sand Control Team of the *Academia Sinica* (organized
in 1957 and comprising both Chinese and Russian scientists) has
drawn up a list of 116 species native to northern China which can be
grown in the sand areas; in its first report (1958) it lists them in order
of effectiveness in sand fixation and describes their relevant characteristics, methods of establishment, and economic uses. The complete
list is given in Appendix IV. The more common tree species employed
in sand dune forests are included in Table 7.

Not all the species listed in Appendix IV are notably drought resistant; some, indeed (such as *Phragmites communis*) are swamp species.
These, however, are useful in sand fixation where there is high ground
water and when they are planted immediately after rain. Others have
a particular tolerance to high salinity, a feature of major importance
in the great basins of the far northwest, where there is no external
drainage and where irrigation offers little hope of solving the problems
of revegetation. It is significant that all of them have in common the
possession of some economic value—many have medicinal properties,
others yield animal fodder, raw materials for craftwork, fuel, charcoal,
or edible fruits.

Shelter Belts

China's "great green wall" is undoubtedly the most ambitious pro-
tection-afforestation project ever undertaken. As already mentioned,
it consists of a series of massive shelter-belt systems which, although
planned as individual entities, will ultimately form a more or less complete ring around the northern deserts. One section extends from the
Greater Khingan mountains in Manchuria, along the borders of Heilungkiang and Kirin provinces with Inner Mongolia, to the Liaotung
peninsula—a distance of 1,200 km. (NCNA, 6/1/61). Another section
runs through the northern parts of Hopeh and Shansi and southern
Inner Mongolia (NCNA, 12/1/61); a third extends for some 600 km.
from Yulinhsien in Shensi, across Ninghsia and into Kansu (*SCMP*,

1961); another, some 1,600 km. long, is intended to border the Tengri desert (Hsu, 1959), while further extensive plantings have been reported in northern Sinkiang (NCNA, 11/21/62) and the Dzungaria basin (NCNA, 8/8/62). Edaphically and climatically, the over-all project covers a wide range of conditions and it might be expected that many diverse tree species would be involved. Surprisingly, this is not so—possibly because the limiting factor for tree growth, whether in Manchuria or Sinkiang, is lack of moisture. The principal species are the hardy *Populus simonii*, *Ulmus pumila*, *Salix matsudana*, and *Elaeagnus angustifolia*, with, as secondary species, *Populus ussuriensis* in Manchuria, *P. diversifolia* and *P. pseudosimonii* in the north-central provinces, and *Tamarix chinensis* and *Hippophae rhamnoides* on the highly saline soils of Sinkiang.

There is, however, some variation in the patterns employed in the shelter systems. In Manchuria, the main network consists of belts, 50 m. wide, at roughly 90° to the prevailing wind direction and spaced at 10 km.; they are cut obliquely by narrower (30 m.) belts also spaced at 10 km., thus giving a series of diamond-shaped enclosures, each about 100 sq. km. in area. Within these major enclosures, the pattern is repeated with 20-m. to 25-m. wide belts at varying intensity to provide diamond-shaped fields of 24, 48, or 96 ha., depending on the need for protection. In more exposed and sandy areas, where the shelter belt has an additional function of preventing sand movement, a simple checker pattern of 50-m × 50-m. squares is employed, while in parts of northern Shensi and Kansu a solid barrier some 1.5 km. to 2.5 km. wide abuts onto the desert. Elsewhere in Kansu, the great green wall comprises five to ten forest belts, 50 m. wide and 200 m. apart, running generally east-west. Subsidiary belts in Kansu are composed of four sections—a frontal zone of erosion-resistant clover, then a belt of timber trees, followed by several rows of fruit trees and a fourth zone of perennial herbs and medicinal plants. In Sinkiang, where the primary objective is to protect oases and farms, 50-m. wide tree belts abut onto sand-sealing areas, as described already.

Apart from the great green wall, shelter belts have been established on the Manchurian and North China plains and in many of the southern provinces. In general, the patterns used are less regular and greater use can be made of features such as waterways, roads, and administrative limits in determining the layout. According to a recently published soil conservation handbook (Lin *et al.*, 1959), primary "field protection belts" (i.e., belts at 90° to the prevailing wind direction) should be spaced at a distance equal to twenty times the height of the trees at age twenty to thirty years; secondary belts, running with the prevailing wind, can be spaced rather more widely. Within the belts, wide spacing to avoid turbulence is advocated, and the use of timber trees and fruit trees is recommended.

Methods of ground preparation and planting practices also vary through the country. In Manchuria, on soils which were once cultivated, the ground is first ploughed, then harrowed and sown to grass; in the following years, the grass is turned in as a green manure and the shelter-belt trees planted at 1.5-m × 0.75-m. spacing. Elsewhere, if there is a ground cover, mattock-planting without ground preparation is common; but where soils are actively eroding, pit-planting, sometimes in the lee of temporary protective barriers, is more usual. In general, the Manchurian steppe country is amenable to treatment and, if properly managed, there is no reason why the shelter plantations should not prove successful. The steppes of Inner Mongolia and the desert fringes of the north and northwest, however, present a different picture, and success is far from being assured. Many devices have been tried in attempts to establish trees in the arid zones: aerial sowing of seed pelleted with organic matter; the placement of ice blocks alongside planted trees to provide moisture early in the growing season; the scattering of coal dust and charcoal onto glacier snouts and snow fields in order to achieve an earlier melt for irrigation; and the use of loam and clay in prepared spots to provide a more favorable environment for root development than is offered by the coarse desert sands. It is not possible to judge the extent of these practices, or their success. But there can be no doubts about the scale on which China's shelter projects have been conceived, or about the enthusiasm and energy of her foresters in their determination to stay the advance of the deserts.

Forest Rehabilitation

To complete the picture of China's endeavors in the field of protection forestry, mention should be made of her attempts to preserve and enrich natural forest remnants. In the critical loess and sand regions, natural forest has little significance; but in the south (particularly the southwest), where the forest holdings formerly belonging to the Buddhist temples are extensive, the current forest policy undoubtedly contributes to soil conservation. In Yunnan, for instance, where the forest area relative to population is comparatively high, the temple forests were taken over in 1951 and rigid control of tree-felling, fuel-gathering, and forest-grazing was imposed immediately. Throughout the country, large areas of derelict woodland have been closed to grazing and reportedly regenerated. According to one claim (Wen, 1958), during the period of the first five-year plan 5,910,000 ha. of forest land were closed to grazing.

National drives to stimulate hog production at the expense of free-ranging cattle and goats have also helped to protect the forests. The writer visited one commune in Yunnan where goat herds totaling 10,000 animals had allegedly been replaced by hogs and, as a result, annual "burning-off" had stopped, forest fires were eliminated, and the hill forests were being regenerated.

In many of the commune forests, as well as in cut-over state forest, enrichment planting with timber or "economic crop" species is being fostered. Timber trees are usually close-planted in groups and given no subsequent treatment, other than pruning for fuelwood; "economic" trees, however, are carefully nurtured.

As with other forms of protective afforestation it is not possible to make an accurate assessment of the extent of natural forest rehabilitation. However, the closure of forests to grazing is undoubtedly widespread—it is a method of increasing the forest area which requires little investment of capital and can yield spectacular results—and abundant evidence can be seen throughout China of forest-fire consciousness. Certainly, the policies of protection and rehabilitation are enlightened from the viewpoints of both forest productivity and soil conservation; and with a closely regimented population, there is no reason to suppose that they are not widely enforced.

CURRENT PROBLEMS IN WATER CONSERVANCY AND PROTECTION FORESTRY

During the past fifteen years the Chinese claim to have put into effect more than thirty million water conservancy projects and to have planted over thirty million hectares of protective forests. It would be surprising indeed if developments on this scale had taken place without formidable problems arising. Undoubtedly, a goodly number of the water conservancy projects—conceived in haste, supervised by poorly trained technicians, and misleadingly reported as successful by over-optimistic and zealous cadres—and many of the mass afforestation schemes have failed to achieve their objectives. The Chinese have recognized these shortcomings and an extensive catalogue of "mistakes" could be compiled using communist sources.

Many of the smaller irrigation facilities were badly planned and were inadequate to meet requirements. For example, 82 per cent of the 14 million small and medium-size reservoirs and ponds in Hupeh province dried up during 1959 (NCNA, 11/22/59), and half the 500,000 reservoirs in the hilly regions of Kiangsu ceased to be of any use by August, 1959 (*People's Daily*, 9/9/59). Some projects were started, but never completed; others were ineffective because essential ancillary equipment was not available. In 1959 it was reported that the land area under irrigation amounted to 71.3 million ha. but that only two-thirds of the facilities had been completed and that "much work still remains to be done to increase the efficiency of the completed works" (NCNA, 10/28/59). "In some cases, wells have been sunk, but water-carrying tools are lacking" (*Red Flag*, 12/16/60). "In irrigation, the building of reservoirs itself does not mean that the irrigated area indicated in the construction figures has all actually received the benefits of irrigation. These benefits can only be obtained when the reservoirs are filled, canals and ditches are dug, the land is levelled off, and lifting equipment is at hand" (Tan, 1960). "Through several years of practice, our country has gained much experience in selecting dam types . . . such experience, however, was only obtained by learning through errors" (JPRS, 3/30/60). This awareness of deficiencies could be extensively documented.

As mentioned already, criticism of the larger water-conservancy projects centers on inadequate preparation and poor co-ordination between the various government departments involved. The minister for Water Conservancy in 1957 admitted that the Hwai river projects were begun with inadequate hydrological data. Several large reservoirs have had to be rebuilt; others have failed to meet their design standards (*Chi-hua Ching-chi*, 1957). Even the Yellow River Commission had to announce in 1957 that only one-fifth of the preliminary soil-conservation work planned (which would control the rate of sedimentation behind the Sanmen dam, and so determine its life span) had been completed; delays were ascribed to clashes of authority between the commission and the ministries of Agriculture and Forestry (*Far East. Econ. Rev.*, 1958).

In view of the Olympian scale on which water conservancy has been conceived in China, it is only to be expected that problems of co-ordination will be manifest. The size and scope of some of the proposed schemes, in view of the limited capital available and the lack of an industrial base, give them a heroic—if somewhat quixotic—flavor. The Yellow river project itself provides a good illustration.

It is a vast multipurpose operation not dissimilar to that of the Tennessee Valley Authority, except that its problems of soil erosion, population density, and inaccessibility are much more formidable. The plan calls for the construction of forty-six dams on the main river itself and twenty-four reservoirs along the larger tributaries, together with major soil-conservation schemes on the upper and middle reaches. On completion, the Yellow river will allegedly be entirely free from flooding and the irrigated area will be increased sevenfold (to 8 million ha.). Hydroelectricity produced by the dams on the main river will reach 110,000 million kw.-h. and will support industry, agriculture, and transportation throughout the basin. Power dams far upstream in the arid regions of Ninghsia, Kansu, and Tsinghai—where the rainfall is less than 25 cm.—will provide a development base for the hitherto backward and isolated indigenous communities now being supplemented by Chinese from the overpopulated eastern seaboard.

Perhaps even more ambitious are proposals for the development of the Yangtze (see e.g. Chu, 1959a; Chen, 1959). One such has already been mentioned—a scheme to divert some 142,000 million cu. m. of water from the Upper Yangtze (which has an annual flow of 9.34 billion cu. m.) to supplement that of the Yellow river (with an annual flow of only 0.47 billion cu. m.). Five possible routes have been surveyed, ranging in length from 1,660 km. to 6,800 km., the most feasible requiring a series of canals from the Tungtien river (a tributary of the Yangtze) in central Tsinghai through the Bayenkara mountain range. Downstream, grandiose schemes are planned for hydroelectric development of the Yangtze, to provide 18.25 million kilowatts and including a dam, 4 km. long and 200 m. high, with a reservoir capacity of 60 million cu. m. Investigations of development potentials on the Yangtze are involving more than eighty professional research units (Wiens, 1961).

The water-conservancy projects, then, call for resource development on an unprecedented scale in China and with unskilled labor the only readily available input factor. Despite inadequacies in planning and execution, however, it ill behooves the Western World to scorn the efforts of the Chinese visionaries who have initiated them, or to deride their administrative difficulties. After all, conflicts in land use are not unheard of in the West and it would be a foolhardy man who would claim that our own governments had never made mistakes in the management of public lands. That the Chinese are taking steps to improve co-ordination between land-management agencies and to achieve a rational balance between conflicting land uses is apparent from several recent publications (e.g. Pai *et al.*, 1961; *People's Daily*, 8/6/64). Nonetheless, the programs are so ambitious that difficulties of co-ordination and in the allocation of scarce capital and technical resources are likely to constitute a major problem for many years to come.

Turning now more specifically to the protective afforestation schemes, the major problems here are technical and biological. The widespread failure in new plantations has already been discussed in Chapter IV. Deficiencies in technical supervision and in plantation maintenance have been stressed and need not be treated further; the Chinese are fully aware of past inadequacies and there is no reason why, given time, they should not repair them. The biological problems, however, are much less simple and their successful solution is far from assured. Essentially, they relate to the growth of trees in excessively dry, highly saline, or unstable soils, often outside their natural climatic range. And since an objective is to vegetate the deserts to the point where literally nothing can survive, there can be, at best, only a partial solution to these difficulties. The selection of species for arid sands and saline conditions is well advanced in China and the next phase of this particular problem will doubtless involve refinements of ecotypic selection and breeding for drought resistance and salt tolerance. In this, as in many areas, Chinese scientists would undoubtedly benefit from closer contact with biologists working in other arid regions of the world—as, for instance, Israel—and they could also contribute significantly to work currently under way in other countries, particularly in the field of drought physiology.

A rather different problem, and one that may be restricted to China, relates to the use of poplars in the northwest. Because of their rapid growth, even on dry sites, and their ability to tiller, such species as *Populus simonii, P. pseudosimonii,* and *P. hopeiensis* have been used extensively in desert afforestation—often at markedly higher latitudes or altitudes than within their natural distributional range. Since the species are extremely sensitive to photoperiod (daylength), they tend to come into leaf in the spring earlier than is normal in their natural habitat; and, since soil temperatures in early spring are low, the trees may flush before root development is possible. Consequently, although there may be adequate soil moisture available, they die of drought. This problem is a serious one and crossbreeding with a more northerly species offers the best hope of a solution. Again, the Chinese could profit from acquaintance at first hand with the work being done on poplars in other parts of the world. Participation in the work of the

International Poplar Commission, for example, would be of considerable benefit. (To Chinese scientists it is a matter for regret that they are unable to take part in the programs of such organizations. As long as Taiwan purports to represent China at the United Nations, however, attendance at conferences held under the auspices of UNESCO, FAO, and similar bodies is denied them. And there are very few of the major international scientific conferences that nowadays do not obtain at least a part of their funds from UN sources.) In spite of their inability to join in co-operative projects, however, the Chinese seem well aware of overseas work. It was a matter of some interest (and, it must be confessed, some pride) to this writer to find that papers of his in the field of tree physiology—and dealing specifically with the problem of root development in relation to shoot dormancy—had been translated into Chinese.

The water-conservancy and protection-forestry programs of the Chinese Communists have been drawn up on a veritably Gargantuan scale and prosecuted with feverish energy. Many mistakes have been made and many projects have been misdirected; but the Chinese recognize these deficiencies and appear to be making creditable attempts, within the limits of the politico-social structure, to avoid them in the future. Doubtless, they will commit new errors and they still face massive problems of finance, organization, technology, and biology. Any prognosis, of course, needs to be hedged around with qualifications but, on present evidence, it is the biological problems that may prove to be the most intractable.

CHAPTER VII.

EDUCATION AND RESEARCH

THE CHINESE COMMUNISTS have from the start shown an avid respect for education, particularly in scientific and technological fields. In forestry, faced with formidable problems in bringing millions of hectares under protective management and launching an enormous afforestation campaign, the lack of trained personnel was all too apparent from the earliest days of the regime.

The Chinese tackled the issue with vigor, and during the first five-year plan concentrated their energies on providing forestry education. The development of research facilities did not take place on any scale until the period of the second five-year plan. As a result, education and research tend to be divided and, except for a few senior scientists at the Academy of Forest Science at Peking, who are also honorary university teachers, the members of the forestry faculties do very little research.

EDUCATION

There are, at present, twenty forestry colleges and departments in China: nine university colleges and eleven forestry departments in university agricultural faculties. They are said to have trained over 11,000 students since 1952. In addition, intermediate-level training is carried out at various technical schools (to provide subordinate staff and "forestry cadres"), while most of the university schools also run correspondence schools.

The forestry college of the University of Peking can serve to illustrate the level of training provided at a specialist college. It was founded in 1953 (to supplement two others, at Nanking and Harbin), with 29 teachers and 300 students, as a general "forestry" department. In 1958, the department was divided into four sections (silviculture, pathology and entomology, soil conservation, and economics) and two further departments were added—engineering (comprising "technology," wood chemistry, and forest machinery) and landscape gardening (a single section only). In 1963, there were 2,134 students and 378 staff, of whom 120 were in the forestry department, 100 in engineering, and 60 in landscape gardening; the remainder teach basic sciences common to all departments. Of the total staff, there are 20 full professors and associate professors and 80 lecturers. The others comprise assistant lecturers and 38 graduate students. (In China, graduate students are essentially instructors; even before the revolution, higher degrees were not awarded at Chinese universities and, while graduate students do some research, they are primarily teaching assistants.)

In all departments the course is divided into three parts. Every student takes one to two years of pure science subjects (depending on his educational standards); these include mathematics, physics, chemistry, a language (usually Russian or English), botany, and mathematical statistics. Specialization in science basic to forestry follows for two to three years (e.g., dendrology, soil science, meteorology) and, then, applied science for four to five years. The subjects taught (and number of hours of formal teaching per year) during the third stage of the forestry department courses are set out in Table 9.

The students take some twenty-six hours of lectures and laboratory work per week and work for about eight weeks of the year at practical tasks; these may range from participating in the national forest inventory to laboring on the construction of field stations. Some 10 per cent of the total time is spent on laboratory work. About one-third of the students in all departments are female.

As far as could be judged from a one-day visit, students appear to be given a thorough grounding of factual knowledge. As in most forestry faculties throughout the world, however, insufficient time is available for tutorial work. No complaints can be levelled at the physical facilities available—the buildings (five stories) were constructed in 1962 and are very well equipped and much better furnished than the students' hostels—and the enthusiasm of the teachers is evident. Two features were surprising: firstly the prominence given to tree physiology in the curriculum, and secondly, the fact that the examination system follows the European rather than the American

Table 9.   Subjects of Instruction and Hours of Formal Teaching
at the Peking Forestry College

Subject	Hours Taught/Year
Mathematics	110–130
Physics	120–130
Chemistry (inorganic)	140
Chemistry (organic)	90
Botany	140
Tree physiology	130–140
Surveying	120–140
Genetics	60– 70 (in the 3rd year)
Meteorology	70
Soil science	140–150
Statistics	60– 70
Dendrology	140
Applied silviculture	60– 70
Mensuration	80
Entomology	60– 70
Pathology	70– 80
Wood technology	60
Utilization	90
Management	120
Aerial survey	60
Economics	80
Soil conservation	60
Gymnastics	2 hours/week
Political theory	360 hours in 5 years

pattern.   Owing to staff shortages and the cumbersome nature of written examinations in Chinese, the examination standard is said to be "not very high." What they lack in quality, however, the Chinese certainly provide in quantity and by 1972 they expect to be training some 5,000 students per annum.

Intermediate-level training (six months to three years) is said to be tailored to meet the requirements of the individual students; essentially, it provides "on-job" instruction in forestry techniques with some training in labor control. A training school at Tailing, for example, provides experience in logging methods; students spend most of their time on operational work and in manual tasks around the school. (At the time of the author's visit they were building an extension to the dormitory facilities; all the work, from construction to the provision of plumbing and electrical facilities, was being done by the students.) The correspondence courses, on the other hand, are designed to supplement practical work and to give it a theoretical framework.

In the field of general education, China's policy is to use all possible means at her disposal—whether efficient or not—to provide the rudiments of a schooling for a large proportion of the population. This approach is epitomized in the widely quoted slogan, "walking on two legs": the traditional and the new, the theoretical and the empirical, are all pressed into the service of the regime. "Presently we are setting up, in great number, agricultural middle schools, and also elementary schools and spare-time middle and elementary schools administered by the people. The main purpose of these schools is universalization, and not too much is expected of them. . . . First we must energetically complete the universalization process and, immediately afterwards, seek to consolidate and elevate" (*People's Education*, 5/1/58). At the present time in China, therefore, there are basically two educational streams: the framework as it existed in pre-revolutionary China, comprising six years of primary school, followed by six years at either a general secondary school (leading to university entrance), a teacher-training school, or a vocational secondary school; and, in addition, a large number of facilities of varying standards, ranging from commune schools (which aim to teach little more than the ability to read and write) and the so-called "red and expert universities"—institutions staffed by unlettered peasants and workers—to part-time college-standard establishments. In 1958, there were some 40 million attendants at the "anti-illiteracy schools" and 26 million in spare-time primary schools; in the traditional schools, there were 86 million enrolled in primary departments, 8.5 million in the general secondary schools, and 1.5 million attending the vocational institutions (SSB, 1960). At the other end of the scale, university-level training is being vigorously fostered—enrollments have risen from 137,000 in 1950 (SSB, 1960) to 810,000 in 1959 (NCNA, 1/22/60). "Our present policy is to push the middle by emphasizing the two ends. In other words we should wipe out illiteracy on the one hand, and vigorously promote the development of technical secondary and higher education on the other hand. By emphasizing the two ends, the middle part—the primary and secondary schools—would be automatically stimulated" (*People's Daily*, 6/4/60). Orleans (1961) has commented on this policy as follows: "It is not the most efficient system; many qualified students do not have the opportunity to pursue their studies and are, in effect, wasted; but despite the limited facilities, teaching personnel, and funds, it manages to provide a large number of people with an appreciation for education, which will perhaps be passed on to their children, while providing a relatively small number of people with the knowledge necessary to lead the drive toward industrialization and world status."

One effect of "walking on two legs" is that the educational standards of students presenting themselves for university admission are
extremely varied; this was said to be particularly true of aspiring
foresters. Forestry as a vocation in China, as in several other countries, is neither fish nor fowl: it does not have the professional status
of medicine or engineering, but, at the same time, it is not simply a
pursuit for artisans. Consequently, the wastage rate at the universities is high and there is considerable transferring of students from
the forestry colleges to the intermediate training schools.

One major criticism may be levelled at the Chinese system of forestry education. In field forestry, the trained forester seldom has any
executive control—he is, in effect, an advisor to a nontechnical administrator, who has the widest powers. It is surprising, therefore, that no
facilities are available to provide some minimal technical training for
these administrators; it is true that they can take a correspondence
course, but there is no compulsion for them to do so and, since their
careers lie in political administration, and not forestry, it is scarcely
surprising that few of them do so.

RESEARCH

Organization

Recently, some far-reaching changes took place in the organization
of forestry and forest products research in China. Formerly, "national" research was carried out by two institutes in Peking (the
Forest Research Institute, founded in 1953, and the Forest Products
Research Institute, founded in 1956, both part of the Academy of
Forest Science, operating under the Ministry of Forestry). In addition, each province had its own research organization, while the Institute for Forest and Soil Research at Shenyang came under the control of the *Academia Sinica*. The standards of the provincial institutes
varied considerably and co-ordination between them was poor. The
changes which are now taking place are designed both to improve
research co-ordination and to increase control of provincial research
by Peking.

In 1962, Cheng Wan-chun became Vice-President (research) of the
Academy of Forest Science, working to the deputy-minister for research (the other vice-president is responsible for recruitment and
training, so Cheng is *de facto* research director). Four more institutes have been established in Peking (for wood chemistry, engineer-

ing, economics, and shellac) and six "forestry research centers" (for northeast China, north China, the Yangtze river provinces, northwest China, southwest China, and the tropical zone) are being set up under the academy. Of these, that for the northeast has been established at Tailing (Heilungkiang); that for the north at Peking; that for the Yangtze provinces, in Hunan; and that for the tropical region, on the island of Hainan. Centers for the northwest and southeast have yet to be established. The function of the research center is to carry out research and, also, to train young scientists. Control from Peking is fairly close, with a member of the academy spending several months at the research center every year both directing and integrating the programs with those of other centers and of the provincial institutes.

The institutes at Peking are, not surprisingly, the best equipped and staffed, with an annual budget of 1,800,000 yuan for salaries and travel and 2,500,000 yuan for buildings and equipment. This is sufficient to support a graduate staff of 700, of whom about 150 are employed by the Forest Research Institute and rather more than 100 at the Forest Products Institute. In addition the institutes have staffed field stations in all provinces.

The Forest Research Institute, Peking

The Forest Research Institute has ten departments—silviculture, management, genetics, "economic crops," entomology, pathology, ecology and soils, tree physiology and biochemistry, wood anatomy, and fire protection. Of these, tree physiology is the latest to be formed and consists of eleven graduates and twenty-four technicians.

Work being carried out at the institute is difficult to assess; when compared with that at some of the botanical institutes it is not impressive. The author came away with the impression that some of the staff were working on rather abstruse, academic subjects, having little relation to any practical problems, and others lacked any over-all direction. For example, some interesting work was being done on the identification of poplar clones by means of dehydrogenase activity and by chlorophyll absorption phenomena—but this is a problem that bears little relation to matters of great moment in Chinese forestry. In the fields of soils, dendrology, and insect taxonomy, however, the work is first-class and of obvious practical value. The institute is engaged in a mammoth survey of forest soils and in extensive physicochemical analyses of soils derived from loess; also, soils from the southern provinces supporting bamboos and other short rotation crops are being sampled annually and attempts are being made to relate nutrient deficiencies to visual symptoms and foliar diagnoses. Dendrology, of course, is a traditional pursuit of Chinese botanists which requires little in the way of facilities and equipment; in Peking— doubtless due partly to the interests of Cheng Wan-chun—the conifers receive particular attention. Other features of the research program include photogrammetry in relation to surveys, autecological studies of the major production forest species and "economic" crop trees, salt tolerance of tree species in relation to land reclamation, studies of the population dynamics of the field vole (an important pest to young trees in Manchuria), and the biology of *Armillaria mellea* and *Fomes annosus*. In genetics (which would be more correctly designated tree improvement), the program is concerned with the selection of desirable phenotypes among the pines and poplars and with attempts to hybridize *Pinus koraiensis* and *P. sylvestris* var. *mongolica*.

Forest Products Research

The Forest Products Research Institute consists of four departments: wood properties; seasoning, preservation, and wood-working; adhesives and improved woods; plywood and composite wood. The "wood properties" department, with a graduate staff of thirty-five, includes timber mechanics and timber physics; it has a big strength-testing program for native timbers and claims to be covering about twenty-five species annually. Methods are routine and follow European, rather than American, standards. The only unusual feature is the effort being put into studies of the dielectric properties of wood, as an aid to the selection of suitable species for the manufacture of musical instruments. The test machinery is modern and of French, German, and Swiss manufacture. A very recent acquisition is a Japanese electron microscope.

The "seasoning, preservation, and wood-working" department provides some mixed impressions. The section head of timber-seasoning is an able and enthusiastic chemical engineer, interested primarily in kiln-drying. He operates four laboratory kilns and has worked out drying schedules for about thirteen Chinese species. Paradoxically, in spite of an almost complete lack of kilns in the timber industry in China, no work is being done on air-drying. Similarly, the preservation section's program has an air of unreality about it. It appears to be concentrating on the development of new preservatives while doing very little on treatment methods, yet in no field could the results of research have more immediate application in practice. Some preservation research is also being carried out by the Academy of Railway Research in Peking and it may be that, here, methods of treatment are given more prominence.

In the "adhesives and improved wood" department, research appears to be concentrated on the application of overseas developments to Chinese raw materials. Routine testing of plywoods bonded with urea, phenol, and soya bean glues, laboratory scale production of a densified wood veneer impregnated with phenolic resin (following a Russian process), the gluing of bamboos and bamboo veneers, and routine exposure tests of joints and plywoods incorporating various species appear to make up much of the program. Similarly, work in the "plywood and composite wood" department is of a routine nature: it includes strength-testing of veneers, fiberboard, chipboard, and strawboard; veneer-drying tests; experimental production of a board made out of bark, sawdust, and straw; and sample testing of overseas (including American) chipboards.

An over-all impression of the work of the Forest Products Research Institute is that, in general, it is unexciting and limited in scope. Apart from the fields of seasoning and preservation, however, it seems to be related to the practical needs of wood users in China. Nevertheless, the amount of modern equipment and the extent of the library facilities available are impressive.

The Provincial Research Institutes

In the provincial research institutes, work is allegedly limited to problems of local significance and to empirical research. Judging by the Kwangtung Forest Research Institute, however, this is not always true. This institute is doing first-class work in a variety of fields that go well beyond the immediate environment. The institute was set up as a demonstration and extension forestry unit in 1952 but, much to the relief of the director, became a research institute in 1959. It has a staff of forty, and ten sections: silviculture, management, soils and microbiology, genetics and exotic introduction, minor products, pathology and entomology, protection forestry, ecology, utilization, wood structure and properties. In addition, it has six substations, one in each of the local administrative districts. The substations specialize on particular species or fields of research; there is one devoted to *Eucalyptus* species, for example, and another to bamboos. The budget of the Kwangtung institute amounts to 190,000 yuan.

The provincial research program is drawn up by the local bureau and submitted to the ministry. At this point it may be amended by the Peking academy which "guides" the provincial institute. In fact, however, the academy can call for research to be carried out at any time by a provincial institute and relations can become considerably strained. Excessive direction from Peking would be particularly galling to Kwangtung, where the program is well planned and executed.

Investigations being carried out at Kwangtung include a study of root-grafting in nest-sown trees, biological control of *Tortrix* by *Bacillus thuringiensis* and *Beauveria bassiana,* investigations into the use of various legumes established with *Pinus massoniana,* spacing and thinning trials and the construction of volume and yield tables, paper manufacture from local woods, and the screening of locally grown species for minor products.

The Director of the Kwangtung institute, Dr. Zhu Zhi-song, is a dynamic, able scientist who can clearly inspire his staff to give their best. The atmosphere of the institute is exceptionally good, and it is unlikely that many provincial research institutes are of this standard. Indeed, judging by the budgets of some of those in the more remote provinces, they are little more than field stations. From work reported in the forestry journals, the only provincial research institutes which compare with Kwangtung in productivity are Heilungkiang, Liaotung, and Hunan.

It is, of course, too early to comment on the work of the research "centers." That for the northeast at Tailing, however, is based on an existing experimental forest and, to that extent, its program is partly predetermined. Long-term experiments already under way include trials of various planting methods and patterns of group establishment, spacing trials and thinning plots in *Pinus koraiensis* and *Larix dahurica,* a study of the influence of microclimate on the growth of *Pinus koraiensis,* and a survey of wildlife in the region (bears, wolves, Manchurian deer, and the almost extinct Manchurian tiger). The forestry experiments are, in general, well laid out and replicated; recording is less satisfactory, with, according to the local research forester, frequent changes in the methods of measurement.

Other Research Organizations

In addition to the research activities of the Ministry of Forestry, numerous other organizations carry out research of direct interest to the forest service in China. There is, for instance, a water-engineering research institute in Peking and fourteen provincial research stations for water-engineering—these are closely concerned with soil conservation. Also, the *Academia Sinica* operates a number of commissions concerned with research requirements for the development of the remoter areas of China. Thus, there is a sand-control team (which operates jointly with a team from the Soviet Academy of Science), a Sinkiang Survey Team, and an Inner Mongolian Development Commission. They have done much to discover new forest resources and to analyze the problems of vegetating the dry zones.

The botanical institutes of the *Academia Sinica*, too, contribute much to forestry research. That at Kunming (Yunnan), for example, has a strong wood anatomy section with a timber collection of more than 1,000 genera. The staff comprises two senior research scientists and some fifteen graduates. Their principal work is the compilation of an atlas of Yunnan timbers and their chemical products. The South China Institute of Botany at Canton is carrying out a vegetation survey of South China, screening all oil-bearing and aromatic species, to produce a map of "economic" trees; it also has plans for establishing a tree physiology unit. The Botanical Institute at Peking is working *inter alia* on the bio-assay of simazine and atrazine in soils and on the physiological role of zinc in trees. Finally, the Institute for Plant Physiology and the Institute for Biochemistry, both at Shanghai and both headed by Western-trained scientists of international reputation, are doing excellent fundamental work into some problems associated with the growth of poplars on excessively dry sites and at low temperatures.

Apart from the *Academia Sinica*, whose work is of a very high standard but largely fundamental, routine "screening" of species (mainly trees) for by-products is done by several organizations such as botanic gardens. The Hangchow Botanic Garden, run by the city of Hangchow, has 10 ha. devoted to introductions of aromatic and possibly oil-bearing trees and 16 ha. under experiments on the breeding and cultivation of bamboos. Again, economic botany is a "traditional" field in Chinese science and it has been estimated that some two to three thousand native species are of economic value; many of them are trees.

Problems of Research Administration

Scientific research in China is faced with three major problems, none of them unique. Firstly, there is a desperate shortage of trained personnel, the effects of which are aggravated by the teaching and administrative duties imposed on the senior scientists in the research institutes. Lack of facilities for post-graduate research training at their own universities has prompted the Chinese to send relatively large contingents of students abroad for study. Under the first five-year plan, some 10,000 were to go overseas; by May, 1957, there were 7,075 students in fourteen countries and, of these 1,331 were doing postgraduate work, most of them in Russia (Lindbeck, 1961). The foreign orientation of these students—together with the fact that most of the senior research scientists in China were trained overseas—has repercussions that constitute the second major problem facing the scientific administrators: the fact that research interests developed by scientists abroad may have little relevance to the urgent practical problems facing the Chinese at home. Having specialized in a field selected by his supervisor because of its relevance (directly or indirectly) to conditions in a relatively advanced country—and, furthermore, nurtured on the current credo that no academic researcher should be subject to any direction but his own—the scientist returning to China may be inclined to follow a path that leads to an ivory tower as far as his own country is concerned. This fact may explain the rarefied atmosphere of academe that pervades some sections of the research institutes. It may also explain in part why, from time to time, the Communist party attempts to increase its control over scientists (see Chen, 1961) and urges them to learn from the "rich-experienced peasants." According to Yu (1957, quoted by Chen, 1961), "In order to carry out the research work needed by the nation, it is necessary to pool together a group of scientists or even require some scientists to change their lines of research. . . . The research work may suffer to some extent for some time when it has to be carried out in a new environment, but in the long run this is beneficial to scientific development in the country."

The judgment that some research programs may be insufficiently related to practical requirements is a subjective one and is in sharp contrast to assessments made by American scientists of published research in China. In 1961, the American Association for the Advancement of Science helped to sponsor a symposium on the "Sciences in Communist China" at which scientists (only one of whom had visited China since 1950) analyzed and evaluated recent scientific and other material published in China. Recurrent criticisms (expressed or implied) were that the Chinese overemphasize applied technology at the expense of fundamental research and that scientists suffer undue political control. Obviously, judgments of this nature are conditioned largely by the background and experience of the assessor and, while research in China may strike the modern American scientist as overly applied and restricted, it is doubtful whether this reaction would have been evinced a few decades ago in the United States. Certainly, to a present-day resident of New Zealand (and head of a governmental research organization), a science policy that stresses applied technology seems only realistic in the light of China's national needs. Even the advocacy of closely directed research—provided the control is exercised by men with an understanding of science—does not have the savor of heresy and academic servitude that it doubtless would to the university scientist in America.

The third difficulty facing the scientific administrators in China has particular application to forestry: with many widely scattered organizations having at least a fringe interest in forestry matters, the problem of research co-ordination becomes a major one. There is no evidence that the Chinese have yet solved it. Duplication of research certainly occurs and, perhaps even more frequently, very similar projects but with dissimilar objectives are carried out by different organizations. For example, an ecological survey undertaken by the South China Botanical Institute overlaps the forest inventory being made by the Forest Service in the area. Although the objectives and methods of each differ, the survey parties cover the same ground and those of both organizations measure tree heights and diameters. Such duplication could readily be avoided by integration of the two surveys, but this has not been done. Even within the Forest Service, the only positive attempt in the past to co-ordinate the research programs of the provincial institutes was a biennial meeting between the institute directors of the south China provinces and, even then, they had no knowledge of work being done in other provinces.

To a minor extent, the Chinese Forestry Association (which publishes *Silvae Scientia*, a quarterly journal of forestry science) plays a co-ordinating role by the organization of meetings and symposia, but it could never hope to do more than inform its members about research already carried out. This situation is undoubtedly a primary reason why research within the State Forest Service has been reorganized and closer control over the provincial institutes is being exercised by the Academy of Forest Science. Through Cheng Wan-chun, who is a member of the *Academia Sinica*, it should also be possible to ensure that work carried out by the botanical and other institutes of the *Academia* becomes known to the forestry research workers.

In conclusion, mention may be made of the conditions under which scientists work in China. From the limited observations of the author, there appear to be at least three levels of scientists. At the top, with a salary of 300 to 400 yuan per month, is the Western-trained scientist or the very bright indigenous product; he is usually engaged in fundamental research, with virtually no restriction as to his program and excellent equipment, but with a heavy commitment to training junior workers. At the next level is the good, but unimaginative, research man, doing applied research—often closely patterned on previous work—under fairly close direction. Most forestry research workers fall into this category; their salaries range from 150 to 300 yuan per month. Finally there is the routine investigator, working under strict supervision and with virtually no equipment, employed on tasks such as plant-screening; he is not really a research worker but, nevertheless, does a useful, if humdrum, job. His salary is about 100 yuan per month. To put these salaries into perspective, the wages of a laboratory technician average 40 yuan per month, while a private soldier earns 10 yuan per month. The scientist of course is provided with accommodation free of charge. He also gets extra food and clothes rations and a bonus for any papers he publishes.

The scientist in China, then, is a much-favored citizen; in view of the tasks which lie ahead of him, this is, perhaps, not unfitting.

CHAPTER VIII.

THE IMPACT OF MICHURINIST
BIOLOGY ON FORESTRY

THERE IS NOW a formidable literature in both Russian and English on the so-called Michurinist biology of Soviet Russia and its application to forestry (see e.g. Lanner, 1963; Frei, 1959; Yablokov, 1960; Lysenko, 1957; Nesterov, 1956a, 1956b; Nikitin, 1941). Historically, its divergence from classical biological theory lies in the field of genetics, but in recent years differences have extended into many areas, in particular, those of plant competition and ecology. I. V. Michurin was a Russian horticulturist and plant breeder who, until his death in 1935, achieved considerable success in the introduction and improvement of varieties of horticultural species, principally fruit trees. He was largely self-taught, a forceful personality, and a sufficiently successful empiricist to be suspicious and highly critical of professional botanists and geneticists. The basic tenets of his faith were that the mechanism of heredity lies not merely in chromosomes but in every part of an organism, and that all parts of the organism can assimilate the influence of environment, transmitting this influence to subsequent generations. In effect, he revived the Lamarckian concept of the inheritance of acquired characteristics. Michurin's standing in early Soviet science was undoubtedly due in part to the similarity between his biological theory and the social concepts of communism (see Lanner, 1963); nevertheless, that he was a successful applied scientist in his own right is indicated by his work on frost-hardiness and his discovery of the "pollen mixture" technique of facilitating "difficult" crosses (see Michurin, 1949; Huxley, 1949).

In the late 1930's another successful empiricist, T. D. Lysenko, further developed the theories of environmentalism, renamed the old La-

143

marckian doctrine "Michurinism," and identified it with the Marxist philosophy of dialectical materialism, denouncing traditional Mendelian genetics as "metaphysical, formalist, idealist, reactionary, mystical, bourgeois, and pseudo-scientific." "Experiments in vegetable hybridization provide unmistakable proof that any particle of a living body, even the plastic substances, even the sap exchanged between scion and stock possess hereditary qualities." At the same time, Lysenko did not ignore the role of the chromosomes in the transmission of inheritance: "Is heredity transmitted through the chromosomes in the sexual process? Of course it is. We recognize the chromosomes. We do not deny their existence. But we do not recognize the chromosome theory of heredity. We do not recognize Mendelism-Morganism" (Lysenko, 1954).

The arguments for and against Lamarckism cannot be treated here. It is a complex subject, characterized by oversimplification on the part of many Mendelists and by a naive dialectical pragmatism on the part of the Michurinists. Of more relevance in the present context are the implications of Michurinist thinking in other, though related, fields. The Darwinian theory of natural selection implies competition between individuals of a population and "survival of the fittest." To a Marxist, the notion of intraclass competition is anathema in both social philosophy and in science. Thus, Lysenko (1954) avers that "intraspecific competition does not exist in nature and there is no reason for fabricating it in science." This rejection has led to some unusual silvicultural and ecological concepts and practices in the Soviet Union and China. For example, nest-sowing of seed (Lysenko, 1949), group-planting, and very close spacing of seedlings have been widely advocated and pronounced successful. The occurrence of natural thinning in such cases is explained not by intraspecific competition but on the grounds that it improves the competitive ability of the species against other species: "The property of self-thinning consists in the ability of dense sprouts of a particular species by reason of their mass to successfully withstand other species and at the same time not to interfere, to compete, with each other. . . . The more densely the species in question is sown, the greater the probability of its favorable development in the particular area" (Lysenko, 1954). Similarly, deliberate thinning is regarded by Michurinists not as a means of regulating intraspecific competition, but as recognizing "the existence of struggle and co-operation between different forest species and the absence of internal struggle within the species" (Nesterov, 1952).

In other fields, Lysenko has developed the Lamarckian notion of the inheritance of acquired characteristics by claiming that nutrition can alter the hereditary potential of an organism (Lysenko, 1946); and, in extending the original concept of acclimatization (see Lanner, 1963), he, and others, have instanced several examples of a supposed new species arising from the plant body of another species (e.g. Karapetjan, 1952; Abotin-Pavlov, 1952; Lysenko, 1953) through altered environmental conditions. It would also follow that characters could be transmitted from one genotype to another by means of grafting and, again, several claims to this effect have been made (Bogdanov, 1946; Nikitin, 1958), thus reviving earlier beliefs (e.g. Daniel, 1927). Nikitin (1941), in fact, has advocated close spacing of trees in order to encourage root-grafting, thereby inducing vegetative hybridization, greater "plasticity" of the genotype and, hence, greater susceptibility to heritable modification by the environment. Needless to say, claims of drastic species change have not been widely accepted by geneticists, even in Russia (see USDA, 1961).

Michurinist thinking has also influenced the classification and evaluation of plant communities (see Lanner, 1963). On grounds that the classical systems of tree classification based on crown dominance reflect "the degree of domination or exploitation observable among men in a capitalist society," Nesterov (1956b) developed a system derived from Lysenko's theory of phasic development in which five "growth classes" are recognized, each containing two "development phases"; essentially, the growth classes are dominance classes and the development subclasses are distinguished by tree form and seeding characteristics. While it is questionable whether Nesterov's system has any practical advantages over other systems, there can be no doubt that the distinction between growth and development is a useful biological concept, particularly in the physiological field (see e.g. Went, 1948). Equally, there can be no doubt that it is a concept not limited to Michurinist biology.

Of more practical interest is the controversy which has developed in the field of plant ecology between the Michurinists, championed by Nesterov, and the school led by the academician Sukachev. Sukachev has embraced the idea of "biogeocenosis," in which all factors of an environment—be they climatic, edaphic, or biotic—interact to determine the nature of the plant community. This concept clearly involves the acceptance of intraspecific competition as a significant ecological factor and, as such, it has attracted strong criticism from Nesterov

(1956a). The crux of the argument appears to devolve around the extent to which the vegetation type is regarded as in harmony with its environment or in "contradiction" with it (and, in consequence, amenable to relatively short-term change). The distinction is not merely academic; Sukachev has evolved a system of forest type mapping based on the evaluation of interacting environmental factors. The interpretation of vegetation patterns is a *sine qua non* of extensive management of natural forests; since the principles underlying the two viewpoints are diametrically opposed, they lead to very different management systems.

In spite of the ramifications of Michurinism, however, there is little evidence that forestry *practice* in the U.S.S.R. has been significantly affected by the "new biology." So far, it has remained almost entirely within the realms of experimentation and argument. According to a recent American forestry delegation to the U.S.S.R. (USDA, 1961), even in the field of tree improvement—in which Michurinist tenets might be expected to hold strongest sway, and in which extensive experimentation along Michurinist lines has been carried out—forestry practice (as distinct from research) continues to follow pre-Michurinist lines.

Turning now to the impact of Michurinist canons on science and forestry in China, it would appear that, somewhat paradoxically, while geneticists have maintained a more open-minded attitude than their Russian counterparts, practical foresters have been strongly influenced by the successes claimed for Michurinist practices; and it may well be that forestry practice has been more affected by the "new biology" than in Russia.

Michurinism was formally promulgated in the Soviet Union at a meeting of the Lenin All-Union Academy of Agricultural Sciences in 1948 and, although there are many references to the new biology which pre-date 1948, it was this meeting which so startled the scientific laity of the Western world. In China, too, controversy soon arose between Mendelists and the followers of Lysenko (see Li, 1961) though it was not until 1956 that the debate became public. In August of that year, the *Academia Sinica* and the Ministry of Higher Education sponsored a conference at Tsingtao which was attended by a large number of biologists. According to Li (1961) the object of the conference was to remedy a situation in which the talents of the "trained geneticists" (i.e. Mendelists) were wasted because of their dominance by Michurinists. In view of the free discussion which occurred during and after the conference, however, it is questionable whether Li's evaluation is correct. Following this conference, Fong (1956) wrote an account of it in which he stressed the need for a critical examination of current genetical thought. He argued that the controversy between Mendelists and Michurinists is a scientific one and not philosophical or political; as such, the respective claims should be evaluated experimentally, not dialectically. Fong accepted as a working hypothesis the Darwinian theory of natural selection and rejected as unproven Lysenko's contention that intraspecific competition does not exist. At the same time he recognized the possibility that environmental factors may induce mutation and that, in this way, evidence for the inheritance of acquired characteristics may be reconciled with Mendelian theory. In his plea for experimentation, Fong was strongly supported by Tan in a review of the gene theory (Tan, 1957) as a result of which Mendel's *Versuche über Pflanzen Hybriden* was translated into Chinese and published in 1957. A further result of the Tsingtao conference was the publication by Li (1957–58) of thirteen articles outlining the principles of Mendelian genetics, while several authors discussed the need for a statistical approach to genetics (Wu, 1956) and properly designed experiments (Wu, 1957; Dzei and Cheng, 1957).

Since 1957 the Chinese Michurinists, ably led by Mi (1960), have counterattacked. It is significant, however, that with some exceptions the debate has been conducted on a scientific rather than an ideological plane and, as a result, the prospects for objective analysis are markedly better than in Russia, in spite of a recently reported swing toward classical biological concepts in the U.S.S.R. (Nekrasov, 1958) and Lysenko's fall from grace. It is perhaps scarcely surprising that this is so. Traditionally in China empirical discovery and technical improvement based on experiment has developed to a much higher level than scientific theory (but see Needham, 1964). Furthermore, there is a predominance among Chinese geneticists of Western-trained scientists (and, in the botanical field, of taxonomists), and, because of the relative scarcity of well-trained scientists in all fields, their status in the community is high. Such men have a great degree of scientific and political freedom. There is evidence, too, of increasing interest in biochemical genetics and it seems unlikely that ideology will stifle investigation.

From the foregoing, it will be apparent that in Chinese genetical science, Michurinist influences are not overpowering. In forestry genetics, the impact is virtually limited to research; and, because of the wide range of native species available for use in afforestation and the consequent lack of interest in the introduction of exotic species, forest tree improvement is not a prominent feature of forestry research programs. Some work is proceeding on basic aspects of hybridization of forest trees and on ecotypic selection for special "problem" sites, but its priority is not high. With few exceptions (e.g. Lee, 1959; Li, 1960) tree-breeding research now follows classical lines.

The situation with respect to afforestation techniques, however, is rather different, in that Chinese foresters have here readily accepted the implications of Michurinist thinking, though without necessarily accepting Michurinist arguments. While it is impossible to gauge the extent to which China's vast areas of young forests have been established by methods such as cluster-sowing and close planting, it is clear that these techniques have been used in many parts of China on much more than an experimental scale; almost certainly this is not due to the deliberate application of Michurinism, however. The early Russian claims of success, particularly in afforestation of the steppe regions (Lysenko, 1950), led to *ad hoc* trials in many parts of China as early as 1949 and their translation into large-scale operations by 1958. There is evidence, in fact, that the adoption of what Chinese foresters term "rational close spacing" in forestry preceded its extensive application in agriculture. In 1958, Mao Tse-tung promulgated Ma Yin-Ch'u's "eight-point charter for agriculture," which included "close-planting" as one of its principles (see Buchanan, 1960); rice, for example, was to be planted to give a density of up to twenty-eight million ears per ha. As in forestry, while the method was not new, its widespread application was only feasible through the intensive labor use brought about by the formation of the communes. Since 1961, in both agriculture and forestry, the technique has been largely abandoned, though lip-service may still be paid to its value, and individual land administrators continue to advocate and practice it. Nest-sowing and group-planting in forestry, on the other hand, are still practiced on "problem" sites and, as far as could be judged by this writer, with some success. Again, however, the rationale is not that of Lysenko and Nesterov; the primary objective in nest-sowing is to induce early root-grafting—not in order to effect vegetative hybridization, but, rather, to provide an extensive root system (following an early thinning) and, thus, facilitate establishment and rapid initial growth. Group-planting, as in European trials with this method, has an additional aim: to establish a cover of well-grown trees of good form, with a minimum input of labor and materials and with minimal tending requirements. These objectives, though perhaps not very relevant to the Chinese forestry scene, are far-distant from Michurinist tenets.

In forest ecology, too, the proponents of Michurinism are making little headway in China. Forest type mapping is an active project in many research organizations and in all those visited by the author (Peking, Yunnan, Heilungkiang, Shanghai, and Kwangtung), methodology follows that of Sukachev.

In summary, therefore, any marked continuing influence of Soviet biology on Chinese forestry seems improbable. While there is abundant evidence that afforestation practices in the 1950's followed methods developed from Michurinist concepts, few attempts are now made to justify them on ideological grounds; and the criterion for acceptance appears to be performance only (at any rate, by foresters). In other fields, the impact has been imperceptible. In view of China's current preoccupation with ideology and her pedagogic attitude toward alleged "deviationists," this is, perhaps, an unexpected conclusion. If the evaluation is sound, however, the explanation of the enigma probably lies in the traditions, training, and status of her scientists.

CHAPTER IX.

ARBORICULTURE

A STRIKING (and pleasing) feature of modern China is the extent to which the Communists foster traditional arts and crafts among the forty-odd races that make up the polyglot nation which is the People's Republic. Music, painting, wood-carving, and the theater are, perhaps, more popular (in both senses of the word) than they have ever been; and, in spite of a recently reported move to purge Peking opera of its alleged "reactionary ideology," it is unlikely that the classical themes and imagery of Chinese art forms will change substantially in the near future. They provide flashes of color which appear all the more brilliant in contrast to the otherwise unmitigated drabness of cultural and social life.

In some of its aspects, traditional arboriculture in China may be described as an art form; the ancient practice of P'an-tsai (the creation of miniature landscapes dominated by dwarf trees), with its highly stylized regional forms and strict rules of practice, is an obvious example. Others include the formal landscaping of temple grounds and gardens and the training of ornamental trees to provide motifs for artists and calligraphers. In other respects, the close association of trees with the Taoist and Buddhist religions, and with the subtle (though rigid) distinctions of rank in the feudal hierarchy, formerly afforded them an importance virtually unique in ancient civilizations. These associations, of course, no longer hold, and emphases are changing from the cultivation of "landscape" and ornamental trees to the decoration of city streets and parks, and from the ornamentation of temples and graveyards to the establishment of botanic gardens and groves of "economic" trees. P'an-tsai is more limited than formerly and provincial variations in technique are becoming less clear-cut.

Nonetheless, the ancient skills involved in the propagation and cultivation of individual trees are still taught and practiced extensively. As mentioned in Chapter IV, training is provided at nurseries devoted to ornamental tree culture and at those associated with botanic gardens. Since these nurseries also train cadres for the State Forest Service and since, furthermore, research carried out at the botanic gardens may be at the behest of the forest service, arboriculture is a subject that has some relevance in a book on forestry. This chapter, therefore, illustrates some features of Chinese arboriculture in relation to roadside trees, city parks, and botanic gardens.

ROADSIDE AND CITY TREES

The earliest recorded reference to roadside tree-planting in China dates from the Chou dynasty (1122–240 B.C.) while, slightly later during the Ch'in dynasty (221–206 B.C.), the first emperor of a unified China constructed thousands of miles of military highways and lined them with trees. The most common species used were pines (especially, *Pinus tabulaeformis*), willows (*Salix babylonica* and *S. matsudana*), chestnut (*Aesculus chinensis*), elm (*Ulmus parvifolia*), and the Chinese scholar tree (*Sophora japonica*). Of these, the pine and the scholar tree form two of the five official memorial trees of ancient China—the pine for kings and *Sophora* for high officials (the others were arborvitae [*Biota orientalis*] for princes, *Koelreuteria* for scholars, and the poplar for commoners). *Aesculus chinensis*, a religious tree of Taoism ("Chestnut of the Heavenly Teacher") was later adopted by Chinese Buddhists to take the place of the Indian *Shorea robusta* which, of course, is not hardy in northern China, while the weeping willows are perhaps the most famous of all ornamental trees originating in China. They have long played an important part in Chinese folklore, literature, and painting, and must have been one of the earliest exports from China to the west via the old "silk road." Other species used in early roadside plantings were the poplars (notably *Populus maximowiczii* and *P. simonii*) and the linden (*Tilia mandshurica*), another tree adopted by Chinese Buddhists, in this case to replace the tropical *Ficus religiosa*.

China's afforestation projects include extensive roadside plantings along the main highways. Of the "traditional" trees, the poplars are frequently used, but outside the cities the choice of species is clearly aimed primarily at timber production rather than ornamentation. The principal species are: in the southwest, *Populus yunnanensis, Eucalyptus globulus, Robinia pseudoacacia, Pinus yunnanensis, P. armandi,* and *Keteleeria davidiana;* in the south, *Eucalyptus citriodora, E. exserta, Populus robusta, P. canadensis, Cunninghamia lanceolata,* and *Pinus massoniana;* in central China, *Cunninghamia lanceolata, Cedrela sinensis, Cupressus funebris, Pinus massoniana, P. tabulaeformis, Melia azedarach,* and *Metasequoia glyptostroboides;* in the north, *Robinia pseudoacacia, Pinus tabulaeformis, Populus simonii, P. suaveolens, P. canadensis, Ulmus parvifolia, U. davidiana, Fraxinus chinensis,* and *Acer negundo;* and in the northeast, *Larix dahurica, Fraxinus mandshurica, Salix matsudana, Pinus sylvestris* var. *mongolica,* and *P. koraiensis.*

Methods of establishment naturally vary but, with the exception of poplars and willows, all species are usually planted at least three rows deep and close-spaced (0.5 m. to 1.0 m. within and between rows). Planting stock is older than for plantation establishment and clean cultivation is general but, otherwise, methods closely follow the local afforestation practices. In south China, willows and poplars are raised in the nursery to between 2 m. and 3 m., and before planting their stems are wrapped in grass or matting to prevent sun scorch; they are normally planted in single rows. Maintenance is intensive and pruning is carried out meticulously; in coastal Kwangtung, for example, the broadleaved trees may even be manually defoliated in May/June to minimize damage during the typhoon season. As a result of the care lavished upon them, China's roadside plantations appear in much better condition than those of the large-scale afforestation schemes.

Within the cities, the range of species is extended to include ornamental and fruit trees, as well as speciality timber trees. In the subtropical south and southwest, *Cupressus torulosa, Grevillia* sp., *Magnolia* spp., *Albizzia julibrissin,* and *Davidia involucrata* are among the ornamentals, while "economic" trees include *Gleditschia sinensis* (the famous soap-pod tree), *Ficus* spp., *Litchi chinensis, Catalpa* spp., *Cinnamomum camphora, Morus alba, Hovenia dulcis,* and *Sapium sebiferum.* Further north (in Peking, for example), *Tilia mandshurica* (which yields wood suitable for carving and bark from which rope and fiber-matting are made), *Diospyros kaki* (the persimmon), *Juglans mandshurica* (Manchurian walnut), *Citrus* spp., *Zizyphus jujuba,* and *Pistacia chinensis* are common.

It is, of course, impossible to list all the urban trees of China; suffice it to say that their variety, the extent of the plantings and the flowering shrubs which are often grown with them are serving to put new developments in China's city suburbs among the most attractive in the world. The millions of trees which have been planted in Peking make a memorable sight, while the avenue plantings of Kunming, Sian, Hangchow, and Kwangchow are almost as impressive; even the industrial slums of Harbin and Shanghai are being systematically blotted out by greenery.

TEMPLE TREES

In beautifying the older cities and towns the Chinese have been materially helped by their traditional reverence for ancestry and by the Buddhist religion. In the grounds of the ubiquitous temples, graveyards, and memorial shrines, and in the gardens of the former palaces, Chinese arboricultural arts reached their highest developments; and in spite of the years of natural calamity, and incessant wars and banditry which preceded 1949, these beautiful monuments have survived, remarkably unscathed. Despite land nationalization and the confiscation of private property, most of the ancient buildings and their gardens have been preserved intact and turned into nurseries, tea gardens, public parks, and the like. A few of the temples still serve primarily a religious function, but, in the majority, religious observance is perfunctory only. Many of the monks remain as caretakers (supported in part by the local populace and in part by the government) and are responsible for the upkeep of the building fabric, while the gardens are beautifully maintained. To a Western visitor, many of the temples now have the atmosphere of a particularly exotic (and garish) *al fresco* restaurant; a bowl of joss sticks smouldering pathetically in a corner provides the only evidence that the *maître d'hôtel* also ministers to the faithful.

In spite of the timber shortage in China, the patches of natural forest which invariably surround the temples remain relatively little exploited, while the preservation and propagation of the ancient memorial trees, artificial landscaping, experiments with natural grafting, and P'an tsai continue as before. An idea of the range of species currently propagated can be gained from the list of trees (far from comprehensive) recorded by the writer during visits to temple gardens in Yunnan, Kansu, Chekiang, and Kwangtung provinces and in Peking. This is presented in Table 10.

Of considerable botanical interest are the relict conifers, *Ginkgo, Metasequoia,* and *Taiwania,* and the rare *Larix leptolepis* var. *louchanensis,* all of which occur naturally in the mixed deciduous and evergreen broadleaved forest zone. Two of them (*Metasequoia* and *Taiwania*) are recent discoveries, while *Gingko* is one of the most

Table 10. Tree Species Recorded in Temple Gardens in Yunnan,
Kansu, Chekiang, Kwangtung, and Peking

Abies delavayi	*P. likiangensis* var. *purpurea*
A. chensiensis	*Pinus armandi*
A. fargesii	*P. bungeana*
A. faxoniana	*P. densiflora*
Acer buergianum	*P. kwangtungensis*
A. truncatum	*P. massoniana*
A. mono	*P. parvifolia*
A. mandshurica	*P. tabulaeformis*
A. tegmentosum	*P. thunbergii*
A. ginnala	*P. yunnanensis*
A. griseum	*Pistacia chinensis*
Aesculus chinensis	*Podocarpus macrophylla*
Betula alba var. *chinensis*	*P. forestii*
Biota orientalis	*P. nagi*
Calocedrus (*Libocedrus*) *macrolepis*	*P. neriifolia*
Caryota ochlandre	*Populus adenopoda*
Catalpa duclouxii	*P. laurifolia*
C. ovata	*P. simonii*
Cedrus deodara	*P. tomentosa*
Cleistocalyx operculata	*P. wilsonii*
Cryptomeria japonica	*P. yunnanensis*
Cunninghamia lanceolata	*Prunus buergeriana*
Cupressus duclouxiana	*P. mume*
C. funebris	*P. padus* var. *pubescens*
Diospyros kaki	*P. wilsonii*
D. lotus	*Pseudolarix amabilis*
Eucommia ulmoides	*Pseudotsuga forrestii*
Ginkgo biloba	*P. sinensis*
Hovenia dulcis	*P. wilsoniana*
Juniperus chinensis (*several varieties*)	*Punica granatum*
J. formosana	*Quercus acutissima*
Larix leptolepis var. *louchanensis*	*Q. densifolia*
Liquidambar formosana	*Q. dentata*
Liriodendron sinensis	*Q. glauca*
Maackia amurensis	*Salix* spp.
Magnolia delavayi	*Taiwania cryptomerioides*
M. liliflora	*Taxus chinensis*
M. officinalis	*Tilia* spp. (*several*)
M. parviflora	*Torreya grandis*
Melia azedarach	*Tsuga chinensis*
Metasequoia glyptostroboides	*T. longibracteata*
Paulownia tomentosa	*T. yunnanensis*
Picea glauca	*Ulmus* spp. (*many varieties*)
P. likiangensis var. *balfouriana*	*Vitex quinata*

famous of all Chinese trees. Surprisingly, however, it was unknown
in ancient China and was first recorded in the eleventh century when
it was described as a "rare fruit" and sent to Kaifeng (then, the capital
of China) as tribute from Anhwei. It was later cultivated and so cele-
brated in literature and art that it became a tree to be worshipped—
though it has no formal associations with Buddhism.

P'AN TSAI

The peak of arboricultural technique in China is, of course, reached in P'an tsai. Well established in China by the tenth century, it has, as its object, the representation of an idealized landscape in miniature; in its highest art form, a tree provides the central feature while a single piece of stone recreates the landscape. In traditional Chinese art, certain natural features—for instance, the characteristic precipitous rocky peaks and gnarled pine trees of Kiangsu province—are greatly accentuated but are nonetheless portrayals of actual landscapes. And the shapes into which P'an tsai trees are trained to grow, though uncommon, are designed to represent the same features. In view of the great scenic variety in China it is scarcely surprising that there are more than sixty characteristic regional forms of P'an tsai, each one readily distinguishable to the eye of an expert.

Originally, only four tree species were grown in P'an tsai, but currently many more are used. Pines, cypresses, *Ilex* spp., and *Gingko* are the most common, with elms and maples providing some of the very few deciduous species acceptable. Suitable species must be small-leaved, very slow growing and, of course, able to tolerate considerable mutilation by pruning of root and shoot, cutting and hollowing of stems and roots, wire-training, strangling, etc.

Training in the art of P'an tsai is both long and arduous. At the Lon Wha nursery, near Shanghai, for example, student-gardeners spend up to ten years learning the theory and practice. In order to reproduce regional styles they need to be able to read classical literature and must therefore study language and calligraphy; they must learn to draw and to paint (Lon Wha has the services of several visiting artists as well as its own resident teacher of painting); and they must, of course, acquire the techniques of tree-breeding, grafting, and propagation, in addition to the specialized practices of manipulation.

Landscaping, too, has become highly specialized and is taught at the universities. As mentioned previously, Peking University Forestry College, for example, established a Landscape Gardening Department in 1958. In 1963 there were 400 students (one-third girls) and 60 full-time staff, together with numerous part-time teachers in the basic sciences. Students study pure science subjects for one to two years (depending on their educational standards); these include mathematics, physics, chemistry, a language (usually Russian or English), botany, and mathematical statistics. Specialization in selected sciences basic to landscape-gardening follows for two to three years (e.g. dendrology, soil science, surveying, meteorology), and then applied subjects (art, architecture, tree-breeding and propagation, etc.) for four to five years.

BOTANIC GARDENS

Before 1949, there were only two important botanic gardens in China—one at Nanking, established in 1929, and one at Lushan, set up in 1934. They were largely destroyed during the Japanese war, but have since been restored, while major new gardens have been located in Peking, Kunming, Wuhan, Kwangchow, Hangchow, Shanghai, Chungking, Kweilin, Sian, and Harbin. In addition, arboreta and gardens limited to certain plant groups have been formed at many centers.

The new gardens are of two types, those attached to botanical research institutes of the Chinese Academy of Sciences and those sponsored by the people's councils of the provinces and major cities. The former are financed directly from Peking and are primarily servicing units for the research institutes; the Institute of Botany near Kunming in Yunnan province, for example, controls three gardens—one devoted to subtropical plants (and covering 150 acres) at the parent institute, a tropical garden at Sishuan Bana in the south of the province, and an alpine garden in Likiang in the north. They provide regional banks of native plant species and specialist facilities for the propagation and screening of potential "economic" trees; the institute is particularly strong in research into the alkaloids and essential oils of woody plants and has isolated several compounds of medicinal or other economic value. The botanic garden at Hangchow (Chekiang province), on the other hand, is financed and run by the city and serves both as a field testing ground for plants known to yield useful by-products and as an ornamental garden. Nevertheless, the provincial gardens also tend to specialize in raising particular groups of plants (e.g. ornamentals, perfume-yielding species, medicinal plants, bamboos, etc.) and they support some applied research.

The Hangchow Botanic Garden illustrates the scope of a new provincial garden and gives an idea of the speed with which new developments are taking place. Planning for the garden began in 1956 and an area of 250 ha. was set aside. Half of it was hill country (ranging in altitude from 20 m. to 200 m.) and all of it covered in secondary scrub growth of *Pinus, Liquidambar, Pteroceltis, Castanea, Castanopsis, Quercus, Lisocarpus, Phoebe, Ilex, Phyllostachys,* and other genera of the mixed deciduous and evergreen broadleaved forest zone. By 1963, almost half the area had been developed and divided into the following sections a taxonomic garden of 1,500 species in 202 families (10 ha.), "economic" plants (11 ha.), ornamental trees (20 ha.), bamboos (15 ha.), fruit trees (20 ha.), and a plant introduction field (28 ha.). Sections devoted to local trees and to trees of eastern China had been delineated, but not developed. The staff of the garden totals 195, of whom 21 are graduates and 9 administrative. The graduate staff is concerned mainly with the collection and propagation of economic species and its strength may well be exceptional—the chairman of the Hangchow People's Council is himself a biologist and is doubtless more sympathetic to experimental work than would be the case in many cities. Nonetheless, progress has been remarkable and the presence of bamboos 25 m. tall and up to 30 cm. in diameter and of magnolias 10 m. in height (and transplanted at this stage!) gives a semblance of maturity that belies the short time the project has been under way.

In general, the botanic gardens are strongly oriented toward economic botany. This is, perhaps, scarcely surprising in view of China's traditional interest in this field. Chinese literature is the richest in the world as source material for the history of the utilization and domestication of wild plants. Some 2,000–3,000 native species are thought to have an economic potential and, of 400 species regularly used in Chinese medicine, about 300 grow wild. The botanic garden at Nanking specializes in medicinal plants, while virtually every center for plant science is actively engaged in screening plants for oils, fats, starch, fiber, and drug materials, and in compiling handbooks and atlases of economic species.

The design and layout of the botanic gardens are excellent and their informality is in startling contrast to the symmetry of palace and temple gardens. The visitor is constantly being surprised by tiny landscapes and vistas, often centered around miniature artificial lakes, streams, or waterfalls and decorated with natural stone in the form of a bridge or a rock garden. They leave no doubt that, despite their utilitarian aims, good taste and an acute appreciation of harmony are still dominant characteristics of Chinese gardeners. If some of their expertise and meticulousness could be applied to the mass afforestation schemes, the prognosis for forestry in communist China would be markedly brighter than it is at present.

ILLUSTRATIONS

Virgin forest of the mixed coniferous and deciduous broadleaved type, in Manchuria. The large tree in the foreground is *Pinus koraiensis*. *Pinus densiflora* and *Abies holophylla* also occur, together with the broadleaved *Tilia amurensis, Corylus heterophylla, Acer* and *Quercus* spp. The standing volume approximates 200 cu. m./ha. Forests of this type supply some 30 per cent of China's timber needs.

These forests were ''creamed'' during the Japanese occupation of Manchuria. The prominent conifers are *Abies nephrolepis*, *Picea jezoensis*, and *Pinus koraiensis*. The utilizable volume of industrial wood amounts to no more than 50 cu. m./ha.

Pinus koraiensis and *Larix dahurica* notch-planted in 1954 on an area selectively logged in 1952. Liang Sui forest in Heilungkiang province.

Secondary forest of the evergreen-broadleaved type comprising, mainly, *Keteleeria evelyniana* and *Pinus armandi* in Yunnan province. The regeneration in this commune forest was said to have resulted from the replacement of goats by hogs in the local farm economy, and consequent protection of the forest from grazing and browsing.

Evergreen-broadleaved forest dominated by *Castanopsis delavayi*, *Quercus schottkyana*, and *Pasania* spp. primarily of coppice origin, near Kunming (Yunnan province). This is a commune forest, exploited for furniture wood, fuel, charcoal, and other small produce. It was formerly associated with a Buddhist temple.

A large-scale forest nursery, in Kirin province, devoted entirely to the production of *Pinus koraiensis* seedlings for planting by the State Forest Service. This is the principal afforestation species in northeast China. (Courtesy Ministry of Forestry, Peking.)

One-year seedlings of *Larix dahurica* in Tailing nursery in beds previously green-cropped with soya beans. The sowing density was 0.35 kg. seed/sq. m., yielding 200–300 seedlings/sq.m. These seedlings would be out-planted after a further season's growth. *L. dahurica* is the second most important plantation species in Manchuria.

Seedbed covers made from reeds at Tailing nursery. Seedlings are regularly covered during the first growing season to protect them from sun scorch.

Girls spraying seedlings of *Pinus sylvestris* var. *mongolica* with benzene hexa-chloride ("'666'") at Tailing nursery. These beds were drill-sown in 1961 and were considerably more weedy than any broadcast-sown beds. The knapsack sprayers were made in the U.S.S.R.

Pinus massoniana four months after sowing at the Dragon's Eye district nursery in Kwangtung province. The seed was sown in prepared "nests" (eight seeds per nest) and clean-cultivated. When photographed, the trees were almost 1 m. tall and very healthy. They had root-grafted and would be out-planted in their clumps as soon as the typhoon rains came. Nest sowing is a practice advocated by Michurinist biologists.

Miscellaneous ornamental species at the Lon Wha nursery near Shanghai. A variety of *Prunus* is in the left foreground and several bougainvilleas in front of the glasshouses. The latter are covered with water-soaked reed matting during the hot summer season.

A rare example of *Gingko biloba* used in P'an tsai. It is a style from Szechuan and the specimen is some 250 years old. Behind it are several dwarf conifers being grown for P'an tsai.

A recently transplanted specimen of *Magnolia grandiflora* in the Hangchow Botanic Gardens. The tree is 10 m. tall and the trunk has been carefully bound with rope to prevent sun scorch and excessive drying. Successful transplanting of large trees gives an air of maturity to newly-formed gardens and landscapes in China.

A specimen tree of *Cryptomeria japonica,* some 500 years old, in a courtyard of the Chang Tsu temple, Yunnan province. Dr. Wu Cheng-yih, a graduate of Duke University and currently Director of the Kunming Botanical Institute is standing in front of the huge bole. The careful maintenance of temple grounds—though the temples are no longer used for religious purposes—is a striking feature of modern China.

Specimen of *Pinus bungeana* in the grounds of the "Temple of the Azure Clouds," Peking. This is a three-needled pine, intermediate between soft and hard pines, and a component of the northern coniferous forest type. It has a very smooth, white, bark which is highly decorative. The species is endemic to the northern and northeastern provinces of China.

Salix babylonica and other species around one of the "Three Pools Reflecting the Moon" at Hangchow, Chekiang province. This famous beauty spot owes much to the effective use of willows.

The Botanic Gardens at Hangchow (Chekiang). On the left is a specimen of *Pinus koraiensis* showing a very different habit from the same species in Manchuria. The pavilion and landscape were designed in 1959.

A shrine at the "Gate of the Dragon" on West mountain, Kunming, with a recently planted specimen of *Metasequoia glyptostroboides.*

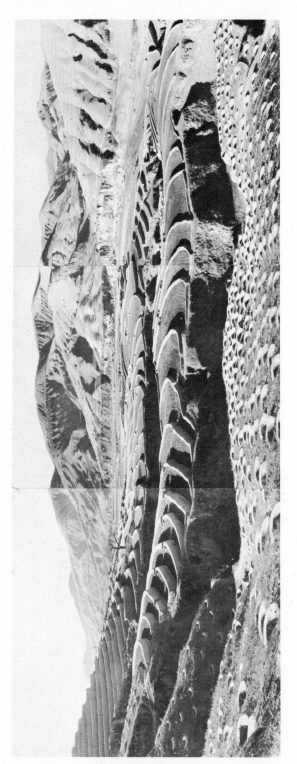

Land use and soil conservancy in eroding loess country in Shensi province, within the great loop of the Yellow river. The occasional trees in the left background indicate that the lower hill slopes were once forested. Now, the larger terraces are cultivated for crop production while the "fish-scales" in the foreground have been prepared for tree-planting (see Figure 4). China has millions of hectares of this kind of country. (Courtesy Ministry of Forestry, Peking.)

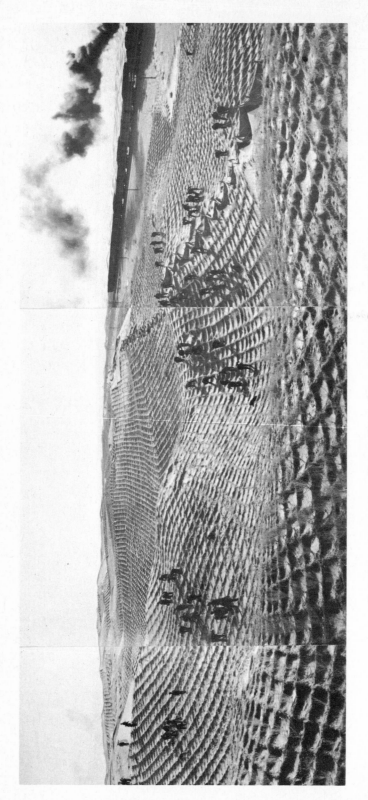

Part of a vast protective afforestation scheme designed to stabilize sand threatening to engulf a stretch of railway bordering the Tengri desert. Brushwood has been laid to form 1-m. × 1-m. squares and *Populus diversifolia* is being planted in them. On the right of the photo is a zig-zag palisade built in order to raise the height of the frontal dune before fixation. (Courtesy Ministry of Forestry, Peking.)

Reclamation of steep loess hills in the Hwang Tu highlands of Kansu province. *Populus simonii* is being planted in "level ditches" (see Figure 4). More usually, the trees are planted just behind the breasting embankment. To the right of the photo, trees are being planted on the breast works of terraces cultivated for crop production. (Courtesy Ministry of Forestry, Peking.)

A combined production and protective plantation of *Pinus massoniana* in Kwangtung province, established by a commune in 1958 and showing typical poor survival. The planting density would have been 1 m. × 1 m. and the over-all survival is less than 10 per cent. The drastic pruning of the trees (for fuelwood) is universal in China.

A successful shelter belt of *Fraxinus mandshurica* established in 1952 on a state farm in Kirin province. This belt is part of the "great green wall"—a project which, when completed, will provide a more-or-less complete ring around the northern deserts. (Courtesy Ministry of Forestry, Peking.)

Pinus koraiensis, eleven years from planting in a state forest bordering agricultural land in Heilungkiang province. A fire-prevention notice is being erected. The use of female labor is a common feature of the Chinese forestry scene, both in the communes and in State Forest Service projects. (Courtesy Ministry of Forestry, Peking.)

Planting by machine after the Russian pattern in a shelter belt project on a state farm in Kirin province. The tractor is Russian, but the ancillary equipment was built in China, including the spray boom mounted ahead of the tractor. Two-year seedlings of *Pinus koraiensis* are being planted, following a leguminous green crop. (Courtesy Ministry of Forestry, Peking.)

Pinus sylvestris var. *mongolica* planted in nine-tree groups on cut-over forest in Heilungkiang. The trees are eight years old and 3 m. tall. The spacing within groups is 25 cm., and 4 m. between them. Since the site is swampy, growth is reasonable for these conditions though survival is poor. The tree form of *P. sylvestris* var. *mongolica* in Manchuria is impressive.

Mixed coniferous and deciduous broadleaved forest cut-over in 1954 and line-planted at 1-m. × 1-m. spacing with *Pinus sylvestris* var. *mongolica* in 1958. Hardwood regrowth is encouraged for soil improvement and to provide intermediate yields of small-sized produce. On the left of the photo is Dr. Cheng Wan-chun, the *de facto* Director of Research of the Chinese Forest Service and a dendrologist of international repute. In 1948 he discovered and named *Metasequoia glyptostroboides*, a species previously known only from fossil records.

Larix dahurica, age seven years, line-planted at 1 m. × 2 m. into forest cut-over in 1950 in Manchuria. The trees are about 4 m. in height and extremely uniform. The *Betula* regrowth in the foreground will shortly be harvested for turnery and fuel.

Comparatively successful plantations of *Larix dahurica* and *Pinus koraiensis* established one year after logging in the mixed coniferous and deciduous broad-leaved forests of Manchuria.

Larix dahurica, age six years, group-planted in five-tree groups at 1-m. spacing within the groups. This species is second only in importance to *Pinus koraiensis* in production forestry in Manchuria and probably has considerable potential as a plantation species in other parts of the world.

Pinus massoniana, twelve years from planting on an arid and depleted soil on a Kwangtung commune. The mean height is 8 m. and the average diameter at breast height, 13 cm. It is not an impressive stand.

Twenty-year-old *Eucalyptus globulus* in a roadside plantation in central Yunnan. These trees are nearly 30 m. tall and 40 cm. in diameter. The eucalypts provide the only introduced production species being used in China on any scale.

The Chinese use ornamental trees for propaganda purposes. The slogan depicted by this juniper planting at Harbin (Heilungkiang) reads "Long live the people's commune." The primitive dwellings in the foreground were claimed by the Chinese to be the worst slums in this big industrial city.

A plantation of *Larix dahurica* bordering a railway track in Manchuria and photographed from the train. The uniformity of height growth is a striking feature of most plantations of this species.

A view of Peking illustrating the extensive city tree-plantings (mainly *Robinia pseudoacacia, Fraxinus* spp., *Pinus* spp., and *Prunus* spp.). The avenue leads to the famous Tien An Men, with the Great Hall of the People, the Museum of History, and the Museum of the Revolution in the right background. Buses moving in tandem are common in Peking.

An example of modern Chinese brick construction—the Forest Research Institute built in 1956 in the grounds of the former Summer Palace.

P. massoniana, six years from sowing and nearly 6 m. tall, established to enrich secondary forest in Chekiang. The broadleaved genera include *Liquidambar, Pteroceltis, Castanea, Quercus, Phoebe, Lisocarpus,* and *Fraxinus.* The conifers have been drastically and badly pruned for fuelwood.

A close-up of *Pinus massoniana* showing typically poor form and mutilation under the guise of pruning. This specimen is in Kwangtung province. Peasants have the right to remove dead branches for domestic fuel and can take two whorls of branches every second year. Many millions of trees are disfigured and probably killed by this practice.

A species of *Phyllostachys*, three months after regeneration in Chekiang. The stems are some 6 m. high and will be grown for three to four years, with annual thinning before clear-cutting. The cultivation of bamboos is, of course, highly developed in China.

An avenue of *Populus tomentosa*, age twenty-five years, at the Restaurant of the Fragrant Hill, some 30 km. west of Peking. Cheng Wan-chun and Wu Pao-lo (interpreter) are in the picture. This poplar is used in production forestry as well as for ornamental purposes.

Pinus massoniana planted as four-month-old seedlings in 1955 on a nitrogen-deficient site in Kwangtung. In 1962 the plantation suffered severe *Tortrix* attacks.

Melia azedarach, a species with a phenomenal growth potential in southern China (and probably elsewhere), growing near Kwangchow. The stand was established by sowing in 1960, thinned in 1962, and photographed in June, 1963. Mean height is over 8 m. and the mean diameter (breast height), 15 cm. Dr. Zhu Zhi-song, the able and enthusiastic Director of the Kwangtung provincial Forest Research Institute, is in the picture.

The main street of Tailing, a town of 25,000 population in Manchuria, based entirely on the logging industry.

A logging train, moving through forest exploited during the Japanese occupation of Manchuria. The author is in the center of the group, holding a white mosquito hat, provided by a Chinese forester.

Replanted felling coupes in virgin forest in Manchuria. The felled areas were cut over in 1950 and are separated by strips from which only the biggest trees were removed and which were intended to provide shelter and a seed-source for the next crop. The growth of broadleaved species swamped the conifers and the felled areas were cleared and planted with *Pinus koraiensis* and *Larix dahurica* in 1955.

Felling a large *Pinus koraiensis* tree in virgin forest of the mixed coniferous and deciduous broadleaved type in Manchuria. The power saw is gasoline driven, of Russian manufacture (the ''Druzhba''), and with a 60-cm. cut. It is guided by pressure exerted by the right knee on the stand-up type frame. The hard hat worn by the feller is made of woven bamboo.

A Chinese-built 5-ton tractor patterned on a Russian model (TDT-40) but modified to operate on wood fuel. It is shown here with the deck apron raised and fully loaded. The gas generator is mounted directly behind the cab. The produce from this phase of logging will be used for mining timbers, pulpwood, craftwork, and tractor fuel.

The fuel store for the logging tractor, containing small hardwood blocks (mainly *Betula*, *Quercus*, and *Fraxinus*).

Chinese laborers, with their heads protected from mosquitoes, gathering brushwood and foliage during the third phase of a logging operation. This material will form pulpwood, charcoal, animal fodder, and fuel. The removal of virtually every twig from the forest floor reflects the acute wood shortage in China.

The log pond at the Shanghai No. 1 wood factory. Hardwoods and softwoods are mixed indiscriminately (together with peeler logs imported from Vietnam and Malaysia) and, after segregation of veneer bolts, are milled together using the same saw speeds and settings.

A drying-stack in the log-yard at the Shanghai No. 1 wood factory. The large logs in the background are lauan from Malaysia and will be man-handled to the plywood mill.

A belt sander in operation at a plant manufacturing sewing machine cases in the Shanghai No. 1 wood factory. Mechanization in the Chinese timber industry is, by western standards, primitive.

Hand varnishing at a furniture factory. Layout and organization of industrial operations is somewhat haphazard.

A mechanical polisher invented and built by the operator at the Peking wood factory. Mass production techniques in timber industrial operations appear to be limited to relatively unsophisticated—albeit ingenious—devices of this sort.

A primitive jig-cutter in the sewing machine case plant of the Shanghai No. 1 wood factory. Factory hygiene and safety precautions leave much to be desired. The waste material will be collected and dispatched to one of the fiberboard mills.

A jointed transmission pole showing a short section treated with the preservative tung oil in ground contact and the untreated pole alongside. Preservatives (and long lengths of timber) are very scarce in China and such jointed poles are a common feature of the landscape, even in forested regions.

Pony transport in an autonomous minority region of Yunnan. The water wheel in the background is used to raise water to an irrigation ditch. The roadside trees are three-year old *Populus yunnanensis*, an important production species.

APPENDIX I.

The Production and Consumption of Forest Products; Future Requirements and Trade Prospects

THE Peoples' Republic of China covers an area of nearly 10 million square kilometers and supports nearly one-quarter of the world's population. That population, which almost certainly exceeds 700 million, is currently increasing at a net rate of 2 per cent (UN, 1964) or, expressed more graphically, by 26.6 bodies every minute. Global forest resource assessments, forecasts of regional wood requirements, and the evaluation of timber trade prospects are virtually meaningless unless they pay some regard to the implications of population growth and social-economic development in this vast section of the Eurasian land mass. The derivation of statistics relating to forest production and wood consumption in China, however, is fraught with difficulties. Official Chinese sources are apparently conflicting and terminology is seldom sufficiently defined to enable cross-checking. Since 1959, no official statistics relating to production and utilization of forest produce have been published. In this appendix, selected data are presented and their validity assessed. Until such time as the Chinese publish formal statistics, they may be of some value; they should, however, be treated with the greatest reserve and regarded only as giving an indication of probable orders of magnitude.

NATURAL FOREST RESOURCES

In Table A–1, data relating to forest areas and timber volumes, taken from selected sources, are presented. The area covered by forest has been variously estimated at from 5 per cent (Premezov, 1955) to 10 per cent (Kuo et al., 1959) of the total land surface area, and from 46.5 million ha. (Premezov, 1955) to 100 million ha. (NCNA, 4/7/58). The lower values were compiled by the Nationalist government before the war and provisionally accepted (in 1955) by Russian and Chinese writers (see Solecki, 1964). FAO has published areas of 76.6 million ha. (FAO, 1960, from Messines, 1958) and 66.8 million ha. (FAO, 1961, based on data quoted by Deng, 1959, and relating to

1955). Several sources cite an area of about 10 per cent (Lin, 1956; NCNA, 4/7/48; *Red Flag*, 12/16/58; Kuo *et al.*, 1959), and of the order of 100 million ha. In June, 1963, the Ministry of Forestry informed this writer that China's forest area was 96 million ha. (representing 9.9 per cent of the land surface area), of which some 46 million ha. was said to be secondary forest, following partial or complete exploitation and therefore of low productivity. Seventy-five per cent of this forest area was held to be potentially accessible.

Statistics relating to the volumetric timber resource are equally variable, ranging from 4,615 million m.^{3}* (Deng, 1959) to 7,460 million m.^{3} (Ministry of Forestry, 1963). The afforestation program set out in the National Plan for Agriculture, 1956–67, was based on an assumed resource of 5,400 million m.^{3} (Wang and Chi, 1957; NCNA, 2/5/58), though, shortly afterward, the official estimate was revised (NCNA, 4/7/58) and a figure of 6,300 million m.^{3} has since been widely quoted (Kuo *et al.*, 1959; *ECMM*, 1959; Hsu, 1959; *Red Flag*, 12/16/58).

The higher estimates of forest area and volume post-date extensive surveys, carried out jointly by Russian and Chinese technicians, of resources in the more remote parts of China (see e.g. Kuo *et al.*, 1959; Pobedinsky, 1961; Murzayev *et al.*, 1960). They also follow preliminary results from the national forest inventory begun in 1954 and still under way. Apart from the remote and inaccessible areas of Tibet, Yunnan, Sinkiang, etc., area survey appears to be complete in

Table A–1.   Forest Resource Statistics for China from Various Sources

National Forest Area (ha.)	% of Total Land Surface	Volumetric Timber Resource (million m.^{3})	Source
46,500,000	5.0	5,150	Premezov, 1955; Solecki, 1964
66,800,000	6.8	6,540	FAO, 1961
66,830,000	—	4,615	Deng, 1959
76,600,000	7.9	5,000	Messines, 1958; FAO, 1960
97,000,000	10.1	6,300	Kuo *et al.*, 1959
100,000,000	10.0	—	NCNA, 4/7/58
96,000,000	9.9	7,460	Ministry of Forestry, 1963
—	7.0	—	*ECMM*, 1956
—	8.0	4,900	*Foreign Trade Pub.*, 1959 (cited by Solecki, 1964)
—	10.0	—	Lin, 1956; *Red Flag*, 12/16/58
—	7.9	4,900	Wen, 1958
—	—	5,400	Wang and Chi, 1957
—	—	6,300	*ECMM*, 1959; Hsu, 1959; *Red Flag*, 12/16/58
—	—	6,000	NCNA, 4/7/58; Carter, 1958

* In this appendix, "cubic meters" is abbreviated to m³.

most provinces; volumetric assessments, however, are likely to continue for several years, and an accurate knowledge of the country's resources will be available only when the inventory has been completed.

Revision of the volumetric statistics has also resulted from recent advances in closer utilization of forest produce. As is discussed elsewhere (Richardson, 1964a) logging operations in China provide an object lesson in complete harvesting; in Manchuria, after clear-felling and saw log extraction, branch wood down to a 3-cm. diameter is harvested for mining timber, pulpwood, handicrafts, charcoal, and, in the case of hardwoods, manufacture into blocks for tractor fuel; twigs and foliage are collected and dried for domestic fuel and the preparation of animal fodder. A recent article (*People's Daily*, 6/9/63) claims an increase in utilization of 10 m.^{3} per ha. as a result of such practices, which are undoubtedly widespread, even in forest-rich areas. Under these circumstances, conventional volumetric assessments are likely to underestimate the resources significantly.

In the light of these factors, the statistics given by the Ministry of Forestry to the author in June, 1963, are not unreasonable and it is suggested that a total forest area of 96 million ha., with a volumetric resource of 7,500 million m.^{3}, can safely be used for purposes of global resource development planning. It is not possible to evaluate the Chinese claim that 75 per cent of the forest area will ultimately prove to be accessible. The fact that the Ministry of Forestry has used a figure of this order in forecasting the available timber supply (see p. 171), however, gives it some weight. If these statistics are accepted, and the population of China is taken to be 700 million, the forest area *per capita* amounts to 0.137 ha. and the available timber resource to 8 m.^{3}. These data are shown in Table A–2 in relation to reported values from other selected Asian countries.

The majority of China's natural forest resource is located in the northeast—in the horseshoe of mountains formed by the Greater and Lesser Khingan range and the Changpaishan massif. Elsewhere, significant reserves occur in Fukien, Szechuan, Kiangsi, Kweichow, Yunnan, and Kwangtung; in the Tsinling mountains; and on the eastern edge of the Tibetan plateau. The densely populated provinces of Kiangsu (533 inhabitants per sq. km. in 1953), Shantung (407 inhabitants per sq. km.), and Hopeh (192 inhabitants per sq. km.) have less than 0.5 per cent of their land surface area under forest (Deng, 1959) while those provinces where the most active industrial development is occurring (Shansi, Western-Inner Mongolia, Shensi, Kansu, Tsinghai, and Sinkiang) are also virtually devoid of a forest resource.

Table A–2.   Summary Forest Statistics for Selected Asian Countries

Country	Population	Forest Area (total ha.)	Accessible Area (ha.)	Total Land^a Area (ha.)	Forest as % of Land (all accessible)		Forest Area per Capita (accessible)	Accessible Growing Stock	Growing Stock per Capita (m.³)	Over-all Vol./ha. (accessible m.³)
China	700,000,000	96,000,000	72,000,000	973,000,000	9.9	7.4	0.13	5,625,000,000	8.03	78
Japan	91,540,000	23,040,000	21,650,000	36,968,000	63.0	59.0	0.20	725,000,000	7.92	33
India	410,686,000	75,752,000	59,557,000^b	326,287,000	22.0	18.0	0.16	n.a.	n.a.	n.a.
Pakistan	88,762,000	2,552,000	2,469,000	94,482,000	3.0	2.6	0.03	146,000,000	1.65	63
Nepal	8,910,000	4,533,000	4,333,000	14,504,000	31.0	30.0	0.50	287,000,000	32.21	69
Burma	20,255,000	45,274,000	25,643,000	67,795,000	67.0	38.0	1.30	1,015,000,000	50.11	39
S. Korea	23,303,000	6,472,000	5,895,000	9,070,000	72.0	65.0	0.26	53,000,000	2.27	90
U.S.S.R.	206,800,000	1,131,116,000	n.a.	2,240,300,000	51.0	—	5.50	69,847,000,000	337.94	62
China	700,000,000	76,600,000	28,100,000	976,101,000	8.0	3.0	0.04	3,850,000,000	5.50	137

Source: Data other than those for China in the first line of this table are derived from FAO, 1960. Population data are from UN (1964) for 1958, except for China, which is for 1962.
^a Including water.
^b Accessible productive forests only.
n.a. — not available.

TIMBER PRODUCTION, 1957–62

As with forest resource estimates, there is a variety of statistics available from Chinese and other sources, relating to industrial wood production during 1957 and 1958. Since 1958, however, no official statistics have been released through the press; the problem of interpreting such data as are available is not easy. Table A–3 presents various total production statistics for 1957 and 1958 together with their sources.

There are reasons, which cannot be detailed here, for accepting figures of 28,000,000 for 1957, and 35,000,000 for 1958, as reasonable approximations to actual industrial wood (i.e. excluding fuel) removals. For 1959, a volume of 41,200,000 m.³ has been claimed (see *Peking Review*, 1/26/60; Solecki, 1964) while FAO (*FAO Yearbook*, 1961) accepts a figure of 35,000,000 m.³, as for 1958. Actual production was probably about 40,000,000 m.³. For 1960, unofficial estimates range from 35,000,000 m.³ to 48,000,000 m.³ (Tass, 11/23/60); Solecki (1964) accepts 47,000,000 m.³ and FAO (*FAO Yearbook*, 1961, 1962), 39,000,000 m.³. A spokesman of the Ministry of Forestry informed the author in June, 1963, that timber production had fallen since 1959; numerous references were made in the Chinese press during 1960 to timber shortages, and exhortations to use wood substitutes for industrial purposes were frequent. FAO's estimate (39,000,000 m.³) seems, therefore, reasonable. The FAO figure for 1961—45,000,000 m.³ (*FAO Yearbook*, 1963)—is, however, almost certainly an overestimate. Reduced production continued during 1961 and 1962; if a figure of about 29,000,000 m.³ is accepted for 1962 production (see Table A–4) and

Table A–3. Timber Production Statistics for 1957 and 1958

	Total Industrial Wood Production (m.³)	Source
1957	12,800,000	FAO, 1958
	20,000,000	Carter, 1958
	26,000,000	Tass, 11/23/60
	26,500,000	NCNA, No. 111242, 1958
	26,580,000	NCNA, 1/2/58; Radio Peking, 1957; FAO, 1959
	26,700,000	*Biki*, 4/2/59
	27,870,000	SSB, 1960
		Solecki, 1964
	31,000,000	FAO, 1960
1958	26,630,000 (to 3rd week of October)	NCNA, 11/12/58
	27,400,000	*Red Flag*, 1958
	31,000,000	*Biki*, 4/2/59; FAO, 1959
	34,910,000	*Peking Review*, 1/26/60
	35,000,000	Tass, 11/23/60; NCNA, 1958; SSB, 1960; Solecki, 1964

a more or less steady decline from 1960 is assumed, 1961 production would be of the order of 34,000,000 m.³.

Derivation of a total production figure for 1962 demands some consideration of the national use pattern. In Table A–4 estimates of production by end-use categories are presented, to give a total roundwood volume figure of rather less than 30,000,000 m.³. The basis of this table will be discussed below.

Currently, some 50 per cent of total timber production is used for construction purposes (*Economic Research*, 5/12/62), while mines consume about 25 per cent of the total output (*Kuang Ming Jih Pao*, 5/9/63). Starting with the latter figure, it can be assumed that 75 per cent of the mining requirement is for pit props and that 25 per cent goes to produce sawn mining timber. According to the *People's Daily* (2/12/61), the pit prop requirement in China amounts to 0.023 m.³ per ton of coal mined. This is extremely low, by Asian standards (e.g. in Japan the requirement is 0.049 m.³/ton [FAO, 1961]), and may well be an unreal figure published in order to provide an incentive to timber savings and the use of substitutes; for the purposes of the present exercise, therefore, a figure of 0.027 m.³/ton has been taken. The sawn timber requirement (25 per cent) increases this amount to 0.036 m.³/ton. Coal production during 1962 in China was approximately 200,000,000 tons and ferrous mine production about 14,000,000 tons. On this basis, the mining timber requirement would be 7,704,000 m.³.

Turning now to railway tie requirements, there is an aggregate track-length of 33,000 km. in China (not including forest or temporary railways). New track construction amounts to about 2,000 km./year. According to a NCNA release (Nanking) on 8/11/62, the timber re-

Table A–4.   Estimates of 1962 Timber Production by End-Use Categories

Use	Roundwood Volume (m.³)		% of Total
Construction	14,745,000		50
Mines (coal)	7,200,000		24
Pit props (5,400,000)		18	
Sawn (1,800,000)		6	
Mines (ferrous)	504,000		1.7
Ties	2,451,000		8.3
Transmission poles	650,000		2.2
Boxwood (sawn)	1,000,000		3.4
Furniture	500,000		1.7
Plywood	200,000		0.7
Fiberboard	140,000		0.5
Pulp and paper	1,100,000		3.7
Miscellaneous	1,000,000		3.4
Total	29,490,000		99.6

quirement for ties is 200 m.³/km. of new track. This is, presumably, the sawnwood volume which, at 70 per cent conversion, translates to a roundwood equivalent of 285 m.³ (this statistic is confirmed by Kuo *et al.*, 1959, who cite a roundwood requirement of 280 m.³/km. construction). The service life of ties in China may be taken as five years; according to the Wood Preservation Officer at the Forest Products Research Institute of the Academy of Forest Sciences in Peking, timber, surface-treated with tung-oil (the only readily available preservative), has a service life in ground contact of six years, and less than 60 per cent of the railway ties in use in China are treated. Since, particularly in southern China, termites abound, a tie service life of five years is not unduly pessimistic. Making these assumptions (i.e. 2,000 km. of new track plus a replacement equivalent of 6,600 km.) the annual timber requirement amounts to 2,451,000 m.³. This is a high demand but not unreasonably so under present-day conditions in China, where the development of rail communications is more appropriate than road-building, and where problems of track maintenance (particularly in the loess and sand desert country of the northwest and the termite-ridden south) are formidable. And it is in precisely these areas that major railway development is taking place.

The quantity of wood allocated to paper manufacture during 1962 was allegedly 1,100,000 m.³ (*Ta Kung Pao*, 8/22/62). That this figure is of the correct order is confirmed by statistics given the writer in the Tailing forest district of Heilungkiang province. It was claimed there that during 1962 4.6 per cent of total production was allocated to pulp and fiber production. If this statistic is applied to the whole of China, and a total production of 29,490,000 m.³ is accepted (see Table A–4), pulp and paper and fiberboard would account for 1,356,540 m.³; this compares with a value of 1,240,000 m.³ used in Table A–4.

To this utilization chart have been added statistics for transmission poles and boxwood, given to the author by the Ministry of Forestry, and figures for furniture, plywood, and fiberboard, volunteered by the manager of Shanghai No. 1 wood factory. Fiberboard is calculated at 2 m.³/ton. In these statistics, there may be some overlap between fiberboard and plywood, since ply-log residues are usually sent to fiberboard plants; however, it is unlikely to affect their validity greatly. The figure for plywood incidentally, was said to be 75 per cent of 1961's "record output."

There still remain several items for which no data are available (e.g. piling, fenceposts, scaffolding, boats, wagons, tool handles, etc.) and it is suggested that a "miscellaneous" category of 1,000,000 m.³

is not unreasonable. This is slightly more than half the annual consumption (average 1953–55) of wood for "rural uses" and "other uses" (i.e. other than housing, construction, packaging, mining, transport, communications, and furniture-making) in South Asia (FAO, 1961).

An editorial in the *People's Daily* (4/10/63) implied that the forest area felled in 1962 amounted to 200,000 ha. Taking a volumetric figure of 29,000,000 m.^{3} as the yield, a mean volume/ha. of 145 m.^{3} can be derived, which compares with an over-all volume per unit area for China's forests of 78 m.^{3}/ha. (see Table A–2). From this difference, it may be inferred that the bulk of the industrial wood produced at the present time comes from primary forests or, in south China, from fast-grown plantation softwoods.

Timber production, in 1957–62, can now be set out as follows (rounding figures to the nearest 1 million m.^{3}):

1957	28,000,000	1960	39,000,000
1958	35,000,000	1961	34,000,000
1959	40,000,000	1962	29,000,000

Several factors undoubtedly contribute to the drop in production from 1959 onward. Firstly, retrenchment in heavy industry from 1957 (see Hughes and Luard, 1959; Richardson, 1964a) probably did not affect the logging and sawmilling industries until 1959 and not seriously before 1961. Coinciding with the withdrawal of Russian technical and financial aid (evidence of which can be seen in major utilization plants), it has undoubtedly influenced every sector of the economy and markedly reduced the rate of industrialization. In 1963, equipment lying idle for lack of repair facilities was not an uncommon feature of the sawmilling industry (Richardson, 1964b). Apart from production difficulties, however, there is evidence of deliberate restriction in timber production as part of the national forest policy. As is discussed later, the estimated industrial wood demand for 1962 was expected in 1958 to be 47,000,000 m.^{3} and the planned output, 40,000,000 m.^{3}; by 1967, demand would rise to 75,000,000 m.^{3} and output to 60,000,000 m.^{3} and, by 1972, to 118,500,000 m.^{3} and 80,000,000 m.^{3} respectively (*People's Daily*, 1/24/58). The deficit of 38,500,000 m.^{3} by 1972 might be partly made up by produce from afforestation schemes; by 1990, it was expected that a large proportion of the estimated annual requirement of 300,000,000 m.^{3} would come from such plantations. Since there is evidence of widespread failure in these plantations (Richardson, 1964a) and it is realized they cannot be relied upon to supplement production from the natural forests in the near future, Chinese foresters have been made uncomfortably aware of the dangers of over-cutting their limited resources. Exhortations and legislation (see e.g. Resolution of the State Council for May 27, 1963 [Appendix II]) designed to conserve forests and timber, and an almost desperate use of timber substitutes for many purposes (e.g. concrete-filled bamboo for pit props, bamboo railway ties, the use of concrete and steel in construction, etc.), reflect this awareness; it seems probable that it is also reflected in a gradual, if temporary, reduction in planned output.

THE NATIONAL USE PATTERN

The utilization data presented in Table A–4 may be compared with earlier statistics from Chinese sources. In 1957, the chief of the Chinese Forest Service was quoted (Liang, 1957) as giving an average percentage breakdown for the years 1954–56 while Deng (1959) also gives a partial utilization chart, though without establishing a base year. These are presented in Table A–5.

Significant differences between these earlier statistics and the postulated use pattern in 1962 (Table A–4) relate to the construction requirement (reduced from 69 to 50 per cent) and pit props (increased from 13 to 18 per cent). With regard to the former, the reduction undoubtedly reflects both a reduced building program, following a slackening in the pace of industrialization, and an increase in the use of timber substitutes in construction. The rise in pit prop requirements suggests that mining has been less affected by retrenchment than other sectors of the economy—a contention in accord with other evidence (Hughes and Luard, 1959).

Little change is noted in the percentage allocation to pulp and fiber products (5.0 to 4.2 per cent); undoubtedly, however, there has been an increase in the capacity for fiberboard production. Output in 1959 was considered to be only 10,000 tons (*World Pap. Trade Rev.*, 8/15/60) compared with 70,000 tons in 1962. Even so, China is yet produc-

Table A–5. Previously Published End-Use Patterns in Percentages

End Use	Liang (1957)	Deng (1959)
Construction	69	69
Pit props	13.0	13.2
Railroad ties	7.6	10.6
Pulp or fiber	5.0	2.4
Wagon-building	1.125	
Ship-building	0.660	
Scaffolding	0.425	"other" 4.6
Piling	0.360	
Poles	1.650	
	98.720	99.8

ing well below capacity which, according to one source (NCNA, 4/5/60), was 130,000 tons in 1960 and is likely to be higher now. The quality of board produced is not high and the conditions under which it is made are technically primitive (see Chapter V). It may be, therefore, that consumer resistance to a new and poor quality product accounts in part for this underproduction.

With regard to pulp products, there has been a big increase in paper production since 1957 but its effect on total wood use is small because of the extensive use of bamboo, rice straw, bagasse, shavings, and other vegetable matter. In 1957, wood pulp provided only 30 per cent of the raw material for paper manufacture and about half this quantity came from branches and foliage (Li, 1959). By 1962, less than 20 per cent of the raw material was in the form of wood pulp. The state of the pulp and paper industry in China has recently been reviewed by Solecki (1964), who emphasizes the extent to which postwar development relied upon Russian and German technical assistance. It seems unlikely that the withdrawal of such assistance will significantly affect paper production, however, since the Chinese are skilled in this field and have already themselves provided expert technical assistance to other countries (NCNA, 4/9/57).

The production of plywood is also increasing; according to the manager of Shanghai No. 1 wood factory, national production increased from 10,000 m.³ in 1957 to 270,000 m.³ in 1961. Unlike fiberboard, the product is of a high quality and the drop in production during 1962 was, in this case, attributed to a scarcity of suitable large-sized logs.

No mention has yet been made in this appendix of fuelwood. According to the Ministry of Forestry, no records of fuelwood use are maintained in China and the only published statistic is a reference to an annual requirement for Inner Mongolia of 3 million m.³ (NCNA, No. 014526, 1960). FAO has published estimates from time to time (see e.g. FAO, 1962) but they are of doubtful value. No forest areas are maintained specifically for fuel in China and the bulk of the requirement is satisfied by loppings of branches, dead trees, and debris from the forest floor. As of right, peasants can remove dead trees from forests and plantations and can prune dead branches at two-year intervals. These practices have serious implications for plantation management, in that the people have a vested interest in early mortality of newly planted trees and, also, they disfigure established trees by reckless pruning. Mutilated and unsightly saplings, even in the forest-rich areas of Manchuria, bear witness to the widespread nature of these practices. They indicate the need for plantations established specifically for fuelwood.

Because of the wide variety of conditions in China and the lack of precise information regarding population distribution, no attempt has been made here to estimate fuelwood requirements. It is worth recording, however, an indication of the order of magnitude that may be involved in a vast but resource-poor country. A recent survey in India, reported to the Asia-Pacific Forestry Commission, estimates that country's fuelwood consumption at almost 159 million m.³/year.

TRADE IN FOREST PRODUCTS

Compared with the situation before the war—when she imported much of her timber requirement—and in the sense that she now draws upon outside sources to a negligible extent, China may be termed virtually self-supporting in forest products. Such published data as are available on imports and exports are collected in Table A–6; they are collated from trade returns of countries reporting to the FAO and are incomplete. Thus, from the writer's knowledge, hardwood peeler logs are imported into China from North Vietnam and Burma, while *Pinus radiata* sawlogs (doubtless grown in New Zealand) have been imported from Japan. It is not possible to estimate the extent of such trade but, in terms of timber volume, it is negligible in relation to national production in China. It is of some interest, however, that on the evidence of Table A–6 imports of sawlogs and wood pulp increased significantly from 1961 to 1962.

FUTURE REQUIREMENTS FOR FOREST PRODUCTS

Any forecast of forest products requirements in China on the basis of the data presented here would be little more than an exercise in speculation and it will not be attempted. The following factors, however, need to be taken into account in any discussion of timber trends and prospects.

1. Net population growth in China is currently just short of 2 per cent a year. If it continues at this rate, the population by 1990 will approach 1,220 million and by the year 2000, 1,500 million. With the present per capita consumption of forest products, total industrial wood requirements would be: 50,000,000 m.³ in 1990 and 62,000,000 m.³ in 2000.

2. The Chinese have published at least two wood-requirement forecasts; these are illustrated in Figure A–1, together with a graph show-

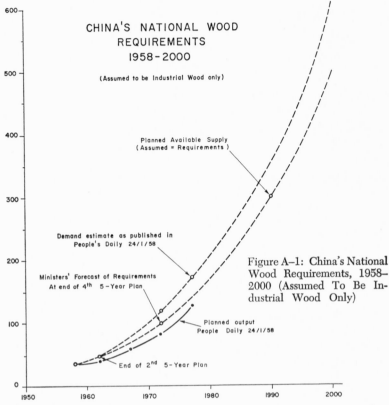

CHINA'S NATIONAL WOOD
REQUIREMENTS
1958-2000

(Assumed to be Industrial Wood only)

Planned Available Supply
(Assumed = Requirements)

Demand estimate as published in
People's Daily 24/1/58

Ministers' Forecast of Requirements
At end of 4ᵗʰ 5-Year Plan

Planned output
People Daily 24/1/58

End of 2ⁿᵈ 5-Year Plan

Figure A–1: China's National
Wood Requirements, 1958–
2000 (Assumed To Be In-
dustrial Wood Only)

ing the planned output to 1977. The requirement to 1990 is that promulgated by the Ministry of Forestry in January, 1956, as a preface to the twelve-year plan for afforestation (NCNA, 2/5/58). The alternative demand forecast and planned output to 1977 was published in the *People's Daily* of 1/24/58 and is also used by Kuo *et al.* (1959) and Kapalinsky *et al.* (1959). The forecasts have been projected to the year 2000.

From this figure, per capita requirements and the percentage annual growth in per capita requirements are as follows:

Year	Requirement m^3 Lower	Higher	% Annual Growth Lower	Higher
1958	0.0560	0.0560		
1962	0.0686	0.0686	5.5	5.5
1967	0.0905	0.1035	6.4	10.2
1972	0.1171	0.1306	5.8	7.4
1977	0.1507	0.1825	5.7	5.9
1990	0.2462	0.2937	4.9	4.7
2000	0.3365	0.3971	3.7	3.5

Table A–6.   Chinese Trade in Forest Products

IMPORTS	Sawlogs 1961 1962 000 m.³ (r)		Sawnwood 1961 1962 000 m.³ (s)		Woodpulp 1961 1962 000 m.t.		Fiberboard 1961 1962 000 m.t.	
Exported by:								
British N. Borneo	11b	21b						
Ghana								
Cambodia, Malaysia			0.5					
Hong Kong								
Finland					31.0	43.0		0.1
Norway					2.9	—		
Sweden					15.0	17.0		
New Zealand					6.2	4.1		
Canada					4.5	—		
U.S.S.R.	133a	222a						
Totals	166	293	0.5		39.6	64.1		0.1

EXPORTS	Sawlogs 000 m.³ (r)		Sawnwood 000 m.³ (s)		Plywood 000 m.³		Newsprint 000 m.t.	
Imported by:								
Hong Kong	4.6a	4.1a	10.0a	4.2a				
Japan	0.1	2.0						
U.K., Thailand, New Zealand			0.4b	0.1b				
U.K.					0.9	3.3		
U.A.R. (Egypt)					2.7	3.8		
Ceylon					0.2	0.4		
Malaya, Hong Kong					5.1	8.3		
Norway							0.3	
Hungary								
U.A.R.								
Burma							25.0	21
Malaya								
Hong Kong								
India								
Totals	4.7	6.1	10.4	4.3	8.9	15.8	25.3	21.0

Source: *FAO Yearbook,* 1961, 1962.
Note: All figures are from countries reporting in Trade with China.
a Coniferous.   b Broadleaved.

Assuming a continued population growth rate of 2 per cent and the growth in per capita requirement indicated above, total annual volume requirements by the year 2000 would be 500,000,000 m.³ or 610,000,000 m.³. Even by 1975, the requirement is only slightly less than that for all the FAO regional divisions of continental Southeast Asia, insular Southeast Asia, South Asia, and East Asia (FAO/APFC, 1964). In Table A–7 this estimate is shown in relation to the rest of the Asia-Pacific region.

3. If Chinese economic plans materialize, significant changes in the national timber-use pattern will emerge; by 1967 a coal output of 510

million tons is planned (Solecki, 1964) which, at the present rate of consumption, will require more than 18,000,000 m.³ of wood for props and sawn mining timber. A doubling of the present length of railways by 1975 is proposed which, on present standards, will need nearly 9,000,000 m.³ roundwood for new tie manufacture and an annual maintenance requirement of 3,500,000 m.³. It can confidently be expected, however, that wood preservation will improve over the years and that the life of ties will be at least doubled by 1970. At this rate, the annual consumption of roundwood by the railways (new construction and maintenance) will be of the order of 3,000,000 m.³. To counteract these increases in solid wood requirement, it may be expected that substitute materials will continue to gain ground for construction purposes. Fiberboard and plywood production will undoubtedly increase, but it would be folly to do more than hazard a guess as to the levels that will be reached.

4. Perhaps the biggest increase in demand for forest produce in China will come in the field of pulp and paper; Solecki (1964), from Russian and other sources, shows an increased paper output in China from 108,000 tons in 1949 to 2,240,000 tons in 1960 and a growth in publications between 1950 and 1956 which is three-fold for newspapers (798 to 2,611), ten-fold for periodicals (35 to 353), and more than six-fold for books (275 to 1,786). Later increases have probably been exponential. A policy of universal education, massive propaganda campaigns (particularly since 1963, when the ideological dispute with Russia came into the open), and a vigorous language reform campaign (see e.g. Snow, 1963) will ensure that the rise in demand continues at an increasing rate. The use of wood substitutes in paper manufacture will also, of course, continue but, as Solecki (1964) points out, in an

Table A–7. Estimated Future Requirements of Wood for Forest Products in 1975 (in Roundwood Equivalents)

Region	Requirements	Supply	Balance
			(million m³ r)
Continental Southeast Asia	12.4	20.0	+7.6
Insular Southeast Asia	22.6	35.0	+12.4
South Asia	19.0	9.4	−9.6
East Asia	108.0	88.8	−19.2
Oceania	23.4	20.0	−3.4
Subtotal	185.4	173.2	−12.2
Mainland China	150.0[a]	107.0[a]/[b]	−43.0[a]/[b]
Total	335.0	280.0	−55.0

[a] Interpolation from forecasts for 1972 and 1977.
[b] Only supply from existing forests (i.e. excludes any output from recent or planned afforestation).

economy of scarcity it is not easy to find unused natural resources without incurring heavy expenditure on transport and development.

5. The extent to which the forest resources of China can contribute to the fulfillment of her demand for forest products is an unknown factor. On the basis of the statistics outlined in paragraphs 1 and 2 above, and ignoring increment, the existing natural forest resource will last about thirty years. Disregard of increment is legitimate since with present methods of exploitation it will contribute virtually nothing to the timber harvest for many years. Primary forest is in areas populated only by peripatetic prospectors and hunters (whose wood requirements can be ignored) and the bulk of the present timber requirement is met by clear-felling in primary forest. It is unlikely that the Chinese will exploit the secondary forest to any extent until the accessible primary resource is exhausted. If 50 million ha. is taken to be primary forest and 75 per cent of it proves to be accessible, it will run out by about 1977; the timber requirement will then have to be supplied from low volume (*ca.* 50 m.^{3}/ha.), "creamed" secondary forest and the average log size will be much reduced.

Similarly, it is not easy to forecast when and to what extent the afforestation projects will contribute significantly to the national timber requirement. In view of the widespread failures which have occurred (see Chapter IV), however, it is doubtful whether they will yield more than fuelwood, some pulpwood, and round produce for local use within the next two or three decades.

OPPORTUNITIES FOR TRADE IN FOREST PRODUCTS

In spite of the speculative nature of forecast wood requirements and the limited data on which they are based, it is apparent that within the next ten years China's needs will be so great (both absolutely and relative to her resources) that she may constitute a major market for exports from other areas. Present trade flows could be considerably disrupted and the aggregate imbalance between forecast future requirements and domestic supply within the Asia-Pacific region could widen by a large margin.

It has been suggested that the limiting factor in China's timber economy as it affects industrialization is the production of large-sized logs. Southeast Asia is reasonably well endowed with this category and is developing an export trade; since several countries of both continental and insular Southeast Asia are closer to the consumption centers of southern China than much of her own exploitable forest resources, China could become a major export market for these products. With respect to pulp and pulp products, on the other hand, the Asia-Pacific region over-all has a deficit and, apart from possible supplies from New Zealand, imports into China will need to come from other regions. The economic geography of China suggests northeastern U.S.S.R. and the Pacific coast of North America as the logical sources.

Solecki (1964) has drawn attention to the advantages which North America has over the U.S.S.R. as a possible source of supply. The timber resources of eastern Siberia are needed for processing plants recently established on the Angara and Yenisei rivers and, in addition, transport costs to Chinese centers would be prohibitive. The forests of the Russian maritime province, on the other hand, are low-yielding, undeveloped, and would be costly to exploit. The predominantly northern flow of the rivers would militate against water transport, while rail and port facilities are wholly inadequate. There is every possibility, therefore, that the Pacific Northwest could successfully compete with physically closer sources of supply. These considerations underline the need for a comprehensive study of North America's trade potential in Asia, vis-à-vis the U.S.S.R.

Significant participation by China in international trade depends on her political and economic ability to gain access to foreign exchange. Here, in fact, lies the crux of any discussion of trade opportunities in China. Detailed examination of her potential as an exporter to dollar and sterling currency areas is, however, beyond both the scope of this essay and the ability of the author. Nevertheless, some impressions of factors affecting prognoses in this area—and they can be no more than the opinions of a layman—may, perhaps, serve as indicators of the need for detailed investigations by economists, political scientists, and other clairvoyants.

Firstly, China has no overwhelming political objections to trade with the noncommunist world; in spite of her apparent preoccupation with ideology and her pedagogic attitude toward alleged deviationists, her leaders are essentially pragmatists and as convinced as the Russians of the merits of "goulash-communism." Even more significantly, the Western world is becoming increasingly amenable to freer trade. Several countries of the British Commonwealth, France, West Germany, and Sweden have recently sent trade delegations to the People's Republic. Even in the U.S.A., interest in China no longer brands one as a rabid Marxist; the presence in China of American manufactures and a recent visit by U.S. businessmen (including, incidentally, some timber-merchants) to Hong Kong, to discuss trade with

Chinese from the mainland (*South China Times,* 1963), indicate a changing attitude that augurs well for increased commercial contact. Given a suitable political climate, the question arises as to what commodities the Chinese could offer in exchange for forest products. The state of her economy makes it probable that for several years to come the bulk of China's exportable products will be primary and, as such, of limited interest to North America. It must be remembered, however, that China has available a vast range of products; of her agricultural commodities, many are tropical or subtropical. Apart from the traditional exports (rice, soya beans, peanuts, sesame seed, tea, spices, cotton, silk, wool, skins, and hides), others produced in significant quantities include maize, millet, tobacco, jute, hemp, citrus and other fruits, rubber, coconut, sugar, many vegetable oils, and a wide range of egg products.

Mineral production is as varied and, in the long term, may be of much greater significance. In terms of exploitable reserves, China ranks either first or second in the world with respect to lead, aluminum, tin, tungsten, manganese, molybdenum, and antimony, while she possesses more than adequate quantities of coal, iron ore, phosphorous, uranium, gold, mercury, and bismuth. Her traditional exports include tungsten, tin, antimony, mercury, bismuth, molybdenum, nickel, and sundry by-products of their production; in addition, and as a result of industrial retrenchment, she now produces exportable surpluses of copper, lead, zinc, aluminum, phosphorus, iron ore, and boron. Other metals produced in greater or lesser quantities include gold, silver, uranium, zirconium, hafnium, vanadium, selenium, indium, germanium, chromium, platinum, and the rare earth metals, while reports of several new minerals (e.g. jiningite, hsiang-hualite, bafertisite) and studies of the radioactive niobate and the tantalates have recently appeared in technical journals. Of the nonmetallics, many are of world significance, including salt, sulphur, magnesite, calcined magnesia, silica, fluorite, talc, graphite, asbestos, barite, mica, and industrial diamonds.

It might be argued that, in the field of food production, because of China's alarming population growth rate—and her susceptibility to natural calamities and famine—domestic consumption will absorb any future increase and so militate against the provision of exportable surpluses. In a communist country of more than 700 million people, however, domestic consumption can be manipulated much more easily—and with less hardship—than in affluent capitalist societies. It is unlikely that China's leaders will allow home consumption of nonstaple commodities to interfere with the demands of overseas trade and the earning of foreign currency.

China frequently advertises light industrial products for overseas sale. Such advertisements are doubtless partly in the interests of national prestige (and, as such, directed primarily toward her immediate neighbors and the underdeveloped countries of Africa); but there is evidence that, because of retrenchment in heavy industry, the planned economy has been thrown out of balance and productive capacity for some commodities (especially, consumer goods) is in excess of her revised requirements. The implications of industrial retrenchment and the withdrawal of Russian aid to China in relation to overseas trade, therefore, might also provide fruitful fields for economic analysis.

In discussing China's increased participation in international commerce, the question must also be raised as to whether forest products could in any way contribute to Chinese exports. *Prima facie*, it seems highly improbable, in view of her domestic requirements and expected deficits. Nevertheless, two considerations are relevant. Firstly, much of China's forest resource (in the northeast) is closer and more readily accessible to the major markets of east Asia than to her own domestic centers of consumption; and, secondly, the development of major wood-processing industries in China (to meet her enormous domestic requirements) could well allow exportable margins, even if based on the processing of imported raw materials. The case of Japan comes to mind as the most obvious precedent, in this respect. If, indeed, similar developments were to occur in China, the products which, on present evidence of industrial and technical development, are most likely to be involved are plywood and paper; within the Asia-Pacific region, the pulp and paper industry is already second only in size to that of Japan.

Finally, in evaluating timber trends and prospects in China, regard must be paid to her peculiar socio-economic structure. The control exercised by the communist regime over the populace is so strict that rapid and sweeping changes in any sector of the economy can occur almost overnight and, in relation to long-term projects such as forestry, any prognoses could readily be stultified. In addition, the political break with Russia must, inevitably, affect the way in which the economy develops and the outcome of this cannot yet be forecast.

APPENDIX II.

Texts of State Council Regulations and
People's Daily Editorial

REGULATIONS GOVERNING THE PROTECTION
OF FORESTS, PROMULGATED BY THE STATE
COUNCIL, MAY 27, 1963

Chapter I. General Principles

Article 1. These regulations are made for the purpose of protecting forests, guarding against forest fires, reckless timber cutting, and diseases and pests, so as to promote forestry production.

Article 2. Forests owned by the State and the collective and forests owned by individuals are all protected by these regulations.

Article 3. People's councils at all levels should strengthen propagandistic education on loving and protecting forests and should motivate the masses to do a good job of protecting forests and trees.

Chapter II. Organization of Forest Protection

Article 4. The people's councils of the provinces, autonomous regions, and municipalities directly under the central authority, and the *hsien* people's councils and *hsiang* people's council [that is, the people's commune management committee—this applies to the rest of the text] in the forest area shall organize the departments concerned to establish organizations to direct forest protection. The forest protection-directing organizations at all levels, under the leadership of the people's councils of the same level, shall implement laws and orders concerning forest protection, prescribe measures for forest protection, direct the putting out of forest fires, prevent and control forest diseases and pests, and exchange experiences in forest protection.

Article 5. The production teams or production brigades of the people's communes in the forest areas, and the State-operated forest farms, agricultural farms, pastoral farms, reclamation farms, and industrial and mining

177

enterprises in the forest areas shall establish mass-type, basic-level forest protection organizations. The basic level forest protection organization shall, under the leadership of higher level forest protection-directing organizations, implement the regulations concerning forest protection, unfold propagandistic education on loving and protecting forests, control personnel entering the forest areas and the making of fires in open fields, organize operations for putting out forest fires, prevent and control forest diseases and insects, and prevent all acts which could damage the forests.

Article 6. The production teams or production brigades of the people's communes in the forest areas and the State-operated forest farms, agricultural farms, pastoral farms, reclamation farms, and industrial and mining enterprises in the forest areas shall, under the leadership of the *hsien* and *hsiang* people's councils, delineate forest protection responsibility zones and install full-time or part-time forest protection personnel. The main duties of forest protection personnel in the forest protection responsibility zones shall consist of the following: (1) undertake inspection; (2) prevent all acts liable to damage the forests; and (3) send all elements caught in the act of starting forest fires, stealthily cutting timber, or damaging forests in other ways to the public security departments for disposition.

Article 7. Forest areas located in provincial and *hsien* boundaries shall, based upon actual needs and under the leadership of the people's councils concerned, establish joint forest protection organizations, mutually support each other, and do a good job in forest protection in the joint protection areas.

Article 8. The people's councils of provinces and autonomous regions shall, based upon actual needs, establish forest-protection and fire-prevention organizations in large State-operated forest areas, and install forestry police to strengthen public order and protect the forests.

Article 9. The forestry administration departments of the provinces, autonomous *chou,* municipalities directly under the central authority, or the *hsien* shall establish forest disease and insect prevention and control stations in major areas where forest diseases and insects have occurred, to technically guide the prevention and control work.

Chapter III.   Forest Management

Article 10. The ownership of forests owned by the State, the collective, and the individuals should be protected. The products and incomes from the forests and trees shall be managed by whoever owns the forests and trees and shall not be encroached upon by any unit or individual.

Article 11. State-run forest plantations are responsible for the management of forests owned by the State. However, scattered forests, which are unsuitable for management by State-run forest plantations, may be assigned to production teams of people's communes, to people's communes, or to production brigades for management by the local forest administration departments. The forests or trees owned by people's communes and production brigades generally should be assigned to production teams for management; those which are unsuitable for management by production teams should be managed by professional teams organized by people's communes or production brigades. The trees owned by production teams should be managed by the teams themselves if the trees are located nearby, but may be assigned to members for management if they are scattered, and income distribution contracts should be signed.

Article 12. The following provisions must be abided by in the felling of trees and in the procurement and transportation of timber, bamboo, firewood, and charcoal:

1. The felling of State-owned forests and trees is governed by the "Provisional Regulations Governing the Felling of State-Owned Forests and Trees," and other regulations concerned.

With approval, the amount, specifications, time, and location for the annual felling of the collectively owned forests and trees should be decided upon according to the condition of the forest resources and the forest growth. The felling of the collectively owned forests and trees by the State should be decided upon according to the State timber production plan. Such decisions should be relayed through the forestry administrative departments of provinces and autonomous regions and should be agreed upon by the owners. Contracts for the felling of such forests and trees should be signed. The annual felling of trees by a collective unit from its own forest for self-consumption (including the individual needs of commune members) is subject to approval by the township people's council if the amount is less than 10 cubic meters, and subject to approval by the *hsien* people's council if the amount is over 10 cubic meters.

2. After the felling of forests and trees, reforestation should be carried out during the same year or the next year, according to State standards. The local forestry administration department is responsible for the supervision of such reforestation. After the felling of State-owned forests or trees, the units assigned by the State are responsible for reforestation. After the felling of collectively owned forests and trees, owners are responsible for reforestation if advance negotiations are conducted and a contract is signed. No less than three saplings should be planted for each tree that is felled, and their survival should be guaranteed.

3. The application for entrance into a collectively owned forest to procure timber, bamboo, firewood, or charcoal must be examined by the forestry administration department of the province, autonomous region, or municipality directly subordinate to the central authority, and must be approved by the planning committee of the same level and included in the annual plan. However, the system and the approval procedures governing the procurement of these articles by local or nearby area organizations for self-consumption, or by local and nearby area handicraft units for use as raw materials are provided by the province, autonomous region, or municipality directly subordinate to the central authority.

4. A transportation certificate issued by the forestry administration department above the *hsien* level must be shown when delivering timber and bamboo to a railway, highway, or waterway transportation department. However, the timber directly supplied by the State may be transported according to the State-approved monthly timber transportation plan, and in this case transportation certificates are unnecessary.

Article 13. Trees in the following forest areas should not be cut, except for pruning and rejuvenating purposes to ensure the proper growth of trees: (1) forests in water and soil preservation districts and around reservoirs, as well as those planted for windbreaks to protect farmland, roads, and river embankments, and to control shifting sands; (2) forests to beautify urban and industrial areas; (3) forests in ancient historic sites; (4) forests in scenic spots; (5) forests for safeguarding public health; (6) forests in tree nurseries; (7) forests in districts where hunting is prohibited; and (8) forests of valuable and scarce timber trees.

Article 14. The felling of any trees is prohibited in natural protection zones demarcated by the State.

Article 15. The denuding of forests for land reclamation is prohibited.

Article 16. Based on natural conditions and the people's production and livelihood needs, the *hsien* and *hsiang* people's councils should practice periodic closing of mountains for afforestation, wasteland, sand wastes, and old forest grounds where afforestation is suitable, as well as the periodic closing of newly planted forests.

Article 17. Livestock grazing near forests must be strictly supervised to avoid damage to trees by animals. A fixed grazing ground should be set aside in forest zones with favorable conditions.

Article 18. Under the leadership of the local forestry administration, the inhabitants in State forests areas, where they have been assigned the responsibility to protect and nurture trees, are allowed to cut small pieces of timber and to pick up firewood for sideline production.

Article 19. People who enter a forest district to engage in production should be organized by a concerned unit and led by a person assigned to see that all regulations promulgated to protect forests are followed.

Article 20. Based on the State's regulations governing the protection of forests and the people's interests, and after discussion and agreement, production teams and production brigades in people's communes and State-owned forest farms, agricultural and pastoral farms, and reclamations farms, as well as industrial and mining enterprises in forest areas, should sign a mutual agreement and institute a responsibility system for the protection of forests to carry out mutual supervision and enforce mutual observance of the regulations.

Chapter IV.   Fire Prevention and Fighting

Article 21. In addition to the routine work of forest protection and fire prevention, the people's councils of the provinces, autonomous regions, and municipalities directly under the central authority should, based upon local natural conditions and other conditions conducive to forest fires, stipulate a forest fire prevention period, while strengthening leadership and fire prevention measures.

Article 22. During the fire prevention period, vigilance should be redoubled with regard to the use of fires in forest areas and the following rules should be strictly observed: (1) requests for the burning off of wasteland and pastoral farms, for the burning of materials into ashes for fertilizer, and for the preparation of mountainous areas for afforestation must be submitted for approval to the organizations assigned by the people's councils of the provinces, autonomous regions, and municipalities directly under the central authority; (2) the burning of wasteland and pastoral farms, and burning of materials into ashes for fertilizer, and the preparation of mountainous areas for afforestation must be well organized and led by a person specifically assigned for the job; (3) a fire prevention line must be delineated and fire prevention equipment well prepared before the burning off of wasteland and pastoral farms, the burning of materials into ashes for fertilizer, and the preparation of mountainous areas for afforestation; the use of fire for the above purposes is permitted only in winds under grade three and the fire must be completely extinguished afterward; (4) a fixed area must be set aside for burning charcoal and processing subsidiary forestry production and a fire prevention line demarcated around it; (5) cooking, heating, and smoking should be done in an assigned area or in a well-selected, safe spot, and the fire must be completely extinguished afterward; (6) the burning of paper while visiting tombs must be done extremely carefully so as not to set fire to the grass, and the fire must be completely extinguished afterward; (7) the use of torches is prohibited while travelling at night.

Article 23. While passing through a forest area during the fire prevention period, railway locomotives must be equipped with fire prevention apparatus, and cleaning of their furnaces should be done at designated places in order to be sure to prevent fires. While working in a forest area, operators of tractors and automobiles using firewood or charcoal as fuel must abide by the safety regulations to prevent fires.

Article 24. During the fire prevention period, the carrying out of shooting practice or demolition in a forest area must be reported in advance to the local *hsien* people's council and precautions must be taken against fires.

Article 25. The burning of mountain trees and grass to drive out wild animals or the use of other measures, which could easily cause forest fires, to hunt animals are prohibited.

Article 26. On the basis of actual need, forestry administration departments and other units concerned should systematically take the following fire prevention measures: (1) establish fire prevention observation posts or lookouts at locations where observation can be easily conducted; (2) set up fire prevention lines, making use of rivers and roads, in forest areas, areas adjacent to grassland, areas surrounding residential districts, along railways, along provincial and *hsien* borders, and within the State boundaries where the risk of forest fires is relatively great; if possible, trees that do not burn easily or crops should be planted along the fire prevention lines; (3) build more forest roads and install communications equipment in main forest areas to meet the needs of production and fire prevention; (4) establish on a selective basis fire prevention weather-forecasting stations and chemical fire extinguisher stations at conveniently located State-run forest plantations and at forest protection, forest fire prevention organizations; (5) according to local practical conditions, establish aerial forest protection stations in large forest areas to strengthen air patrol and fire extinguishing work over forest areas.

Article 27. Anyone who discovers a forest fire must immediately do his best to extinguish it, and report it as quickly as possible to the local people's council or forest protection organization. After receiving the report, the local people's council or forest protection organization must immediately take measures to extinguish the fire.

Article 28. In extinguishing a forest fire, measures should be taken to organize a team of experienced firemen, strengthen leadership to organization work, centralize and unify command work, and do a good job in communications connections, goods supply, medical care, and rescue work. Attention must be paid to safety work, and old and feeble persons, pregnant women, and children must not be mobilized to take part in the work of fighting fires.

Article 29. In fighting a forest fire, the transportation and communications facilities—railway, highway, waterway transportation, aviation, postal and telecommunications departments—may be used on a priority basis, and commercial, public health, and food departments should energetically render their support and assistance.

Article 30. After a forest fire is extinguished, the affected area must be thoroughly cleared to prevent rekindling. In addition, timely efforts should be made to investigate the cause of the fire, estimate the losses, sum up experiences, and report these to the superior offices.

Article 31. Persons injured or killed while fighting forest fires will be given medical care or compensation will be paid to the survivors by the State.

Chapter V.   Prevention and Control of Diseases and Pests

Article 32. The prevention and control of diseases and insect pests should be actively carried out in forests owned by the State and the collective and for trees owned by the individuals. Should diseases and pests of a devastating nature occur, the *hsien* and *hsiang* people's councils in the affected locality must immediately organize vigorous, crash prevention and control measures.

Article 33. Tree disease and pest prevention and control stations, forestry work stations, State forest farms, and the people's communes of forest areas should install full-time or part-time personnel to be responsible for reporting evidences of tree diseases and pests; and should organize forest farm workers and commune members to co-ordinate their work with production, investigate the cause and progress of tree diseases and pests, and undertake timely prevention and control.

Article 34. Forest management units should endeavor to improve the composition and sanitation conditions of the forests by cleaning the forest farms and cultivating the trees. Afforestation units should adopt appropriate measures suitable to each locality to cultivate mixed forests and prevent and control the large-scale occurrence and spread of disease and pests.

Article 35. Forestry administration departments of the provinces, autonomous regions, and municipalities directly under the central authority should determine the need for quarantine for tree seedlings, delineate affected areas and protection areas, undertake the quarantine of tree seed-lings, and prevent the propagation and spread of dangerous diseases and pests.

Article 36. In the event of the occurrence of diseases and pests in forests and trees owned by the collective or individuals who are unable to prevent and control them, the forestry administration departments should provide appropriate support in the form of prevention and control techniques, in-secticides, and other equipment.

Chapter VI. Awards and Punishment

Article 37. Those who have earnestly carried out these regulations and accomplished any of the following deeds shall be commended or rewarded by the people's councils of various provinces, autonomous regions, munici-palities directly under the central authority, or *hsien*: (1) those who have kept forest fires from occurring in more than three consecutive years, either in the administrative areas concerned or in the forest protection responsibil-ity areas; (2) in the event of the occurrence of forest fires, those who have adopted timely and effective measures to fight them with organized strength, or those who have displayed a leading role and scored marked achievements in fighting fires; (3) those who have made timely reports on the discovery of forest fires and endeavored to fight them; (4) those who have scored marked achievements in preventing indiscriminate felling and other acts injurious to forests; (5) those who have halted in time or reported to appropriate au-thorities acts injurious to forests; (6) those who have scored marked achieve-ments in actively preventing and controlling tree diseases and pests; (7) those who have scored marked achievement in forest rejuvenation and the closing of mountains for tree cultivation; (8) those who have conscientiously carried out their duties in forest protection, kept contact with the masses, and displayed a leading role in propagandizing and implementing the laws and orders pertaining to forest protection; and (9) those who have scored marked achievements in creatively and ingeniously carrying out forest pro-tection work.

Article 38. Those who violate these regulations shall be subject to ad-ministrative reprimand or punishment under the public safety regulations. However, minor cases may be exempted from reprimand or punishment but given education through criticism. These violations include: (1) State working personnel who have caused damage to forests through dereliction of duty; (2) those who have caused fires in forest areas due to the failure to observe regulations pertaining to the use of fire in open fields; (3) those who have caused damage to forests through indiscriminate felling, stealthy felling, and other acts; (4) those who have undertaken felling and forest rejuvenation not according to State regulations.

Trees or timber stealthily felled should be confiscated and those held re-sponsible should be ordered to pay compensation for the damages.

Article 39. Those who have committed one of the acts under Item 1 of the foregoing article, causing great damages to the forests or serious acci-dents involving physical casualties, shall be sent to judicial organizations for disposition. Those who conspire or incite others to set fire to mountain forests or organize a crowd to damage forests shall be severely punished by judicial organizations.

Artcile 40. Those who have caused forest fires, engaged in indiscriminate and stealthy felling, or other acts damaging forests, but subsequently confessed and expressed regret to the government on their own initiative, and have returned the stolen goods, or have actively fought the fire and contributed to the reduction of damages shall receive lighter punishment or be exempted, depending on the seriousness of the case.

Article 41. As to those who have entered into collectively owned forest areas without prior approval to procure timber, bamboo, firewood, and charcoal, those materials procured shall be purchased by the *hsien* people's councils in the concerned locality at prices lower than the State procurement prices. In the case of repeated offenses, the products shall be confiscated.

Chapter VII. Appendixes

Article 42. Detailed measures for the implementation of these regulations shall be instituted and promulgated by the Ministry of Forestry. The people's councils of various provinces, autonomous regions, and municipalities directly under the central authority may institute their own methods of implementation based upon these regulations, and detailed measures of implementation incorporating the concrete conditions of their own localities. The methods of implementation so instituted shall be submitted to the State Council for record.

Article 43. These regulations become effective on the date of their promulgation.

Approved by the 131st meeting of the
State Council on May 20, 1963

PEOPLE'S DAILY EDITORIAL OF JUNE 23, 1963

It Is Everybody's Responsibility to Protect Forests

The promulgation of the "Regulations Governing the Protection of Forests" by the State Council is a great event in our country's socialist construction. Forests occupy a very important position in economic construction of a *hsien* as a whole. The proper protection of forests has an important bearing on industrial and agricultural production as well as the people's daily life. Before liberation, under the reactionary rule of various dynasties and the irrational social system, the forests in our country suffered prolonged destruction which resulted in insufficiency of resources and poor distribution. As a result, in our country, not only did timber and other forest products fail to meet the needs of various departments, but many areas constantly suffered natural calamities.

Since liberation, the Party and the government have continually attached importance to the work of afforestation and the protection of forests: every year the masses have been organized to carry out afforestation and to protect forests; and cadres and the broad masses of people in many areas have persevered in the work of forest protection for the past ten-odd years. New trees have grown up in many areas and forest disasters have been reduced considerably, as compared with the earlier days. This is an important achievement in the course of our country's socialist construction.

However, many localities still lack experience in the work of forest protection and quite a few localities fail to pay proper attention to the work. Therefore, the work of forest protection should be extensively intensified for further improvement. The "Regulations Governing the Protection of Forests" sum up the experiences of the work of forest protection by our country over the past ten-plus years and these experiences have been put into the form of regulations. This will invite even more universal attention to the work of forest protection and enable those areas which have done a good job in this connection to do the work in an even better manner and enable those areas which have failed to perform the work successfully to improve their work in an effective way.

Generally speaking, it is easy for people to understand the direct relationship between the sufficiency or insufficiency of timber and other forest products to production, construction, people's livelihood, and the economic income of the people in the forest areas. But people at times either fail to understand completely or understand only a little the effect of good or bad forest protection and forest growth on the water and soil conditions and climatic conditions, on agricultural production and hydrographical conditions, as well as the indirect but vital bearing on production and construction and on the people's livelihood as well.

Engles pointed out: "The inhabitants of Mesopotamia, Greece, Asia Minor, and other places cleared their land of forests because they wanted more arable land. But they never dreamed that this would render the land barren today. This was because when the forests were cleared the centers for accumulating and storing moisture were no longer in existence. The Italians in the Alpine regions cleared the southern slopes of forests because they wanted to plant the northern slopes carefully with pine forests. They had never expected that this would have wrecked the foundation for Alpine animal husbandry in their region, much less that this would have deprived the place of mountain springs for the greater part of the year and brought floods to the basin in the rainy season" (*Dialectics of Nature*).

Under the capitalist system, even though people realize this problem it is hard for them to solve it effectively. The narrow individual interests of the private owners have caused the blindness in treating forests. During the thousands of years of feudal society of our country, the destruction of forests caused many fertile lands to become barren. The serious loss of water and soil in the loess plateau is precisely the result of long periods of destruction of forests in the past.

Now, our country's socialist system provides unprecedentedly favorable conditions for the development of forestry. Many localities have scored brilliant achievements in this connection by gradually increasing the acreage of afforestation. However, it should be noted that it is a tremendously painstaking task to change the phenomenon of the insufficiency of forest resources which has lasted for thousands of years. Only by bringing the superiority of the socialist system into full play and by organizing the broadest masses of people to persist for years or tens of years in the struggle can we meet our desired results.

People always think that the growth of trees depends mainly on nature; they are not like farm crops which require yearly cultivation and monthly management. They think that it is inevitable for the forests to suffer losses of one kind or another and that even after trees are damaged, they will be able to grow on their own.

As for the artificial formation of woods, they think that the trees, once planted, will grow up naturally and that there is nothing further to be done. These ideas should be corrected. It is to be noted that forests need management and tremendous efforts are required to protect and manage forests. It will be very difficult for natural forests to grow again if they are seriously damaged.

Land laid bare, when weathered by the sun, wind, and rain, will become barren; even if a new forest is built, it will require more than ten years or even scores of years before trees grow up again. Without proper management after they are planted, it will be very difficult for the trees to stay alive, and, even when they live, it will be very difficult for them to thrive.

Many peasants have learned from their personal experience that "without proper protection after the trees are planted, all previous efforts will have been in vain." This viewpoint is correct. Many years of actual experience gained by various localities have proved that it is vital for us to exert sufficient efforts to protect forests either in natural forest areas or in afforested areas. We should by no means reckon only in immediate, small accounts, but should reckon in terms of long-range, big accounts; we should not take into account interests only in part but interests of the whole. When the trees on the mountain are protected properly, a favorable condition is provided for agricultural production at the foot of the mountain. If new saplings are properly managed, income from the forests will be increased considerably after a few years.

The great significance of forest protection can be easily seen if we take a long-range view. It should also be noted that the protection of forests is not a simple task but a prolonged and complicated one. It takes years to grow a tree with good management. Even a slight negligence will ruin all previous efforts. The growth of a tree is linked with many outside factors. In order to ensure the healthy growth of trees, it is necessary to prevent forest fires and control insect pests, prohibit the destruction of forests, improper reclamation, and destructive lumbering. Further, the trees should be rationally felled and planted according to the natural laws of the growth of trees. Each of these tasks involves many others. Speaking about the prevention of forest fires, there are many things which can cause forest fires and which require our close attention. Different localities have different ways of using fire at different times in production and livelihood. Moreover, there are those fires caused by lightning and other natural factors. Furthermore, vigilance should be heightened against anti-revolutionary elements who set fires. In forest areas meticulous work should be carried out to deal with the different sources of fire so as to put them under strict control and thus prevent forest fires.

There are various tree diseases and pests. Certain trees may be affected by different kinds of diseases and pests. Every one of these diseases and pests should be examined and studied in order to control and eradicate it with different, effective methods.

Logical felling also involves many other aspects, and should be ensured in one way or another. Sometimes, the felling is logical, but is not followed up with timely reforestation. This may turn out to be equally as disastrous as the destruction of a forest.

To sum up, a practical and effective struggle must be carried out against the various factors which could damage the forests. For this, the units and people concerned must adopt a very solemn, sincere attitude, be vigilant, make thoughtful arrangements, work systematically, and exert long, tireless efforts.

Forests spread over a vast area. Some are comparatively large forests in a concentrated area, and there is a large number of small ones sporadically located, and the factors which may damage them are various and complicated. Therefore, in order to do a good job in forest protection and management the forces of the broad masses of people in various fields must be mobilized. The masses in forest areas and their vicinity must carry out agriculture, cattle-raising, wild animal-hunting, wild plant-collecting, and other production activities; the vehicles of transportation and communications departments must pass through forest areas; workers of commercial and handicraft departments must purchase forest products and raw materials in forest areas, and personnel of geological, water conservancy, and meteorological departments must make frequent visits to mountainous and forest areas. On the one hand, this may increase the complicated factors which could damage forests, but, on the other, this could provide simultaneously the favorable conditions for the protection of forests.

The normal growth of forest trees will be ensured if the ideological and educational work on forest protection is done well so that everyone understands the important relationships of forests with State construction and people's livelihood, has the necessary knowledge about forest protection, improves consciousness in protecting forest, and understands that forest trees should always be protected and that a resolute struggle should be carried out against natural and man-made factors causing damage to forests.

The basic way to fulfill the work of forest protection is to carry out the education on loving socialist public property and being concerned with the over-all socialist interests, to carry out education on the importance and knowledge of forest protection, and to enhance the consciousness of the broad masses toward protecting forests. In addition, laws concerning forest protection must be worked out and implemented.

In order to protect socialist public interests, mandatory measures must be taken to prohibit intentional or accidental destructive behavior. It is important that one does not forget the existence of the class struggle and the struggle between communism and capitalism through the whole period of socialist revolution and socialist construction. Such struggles may also often find expression in incidents of forest destruction.

In order to safeguard socialist construction, the people's democratic dictatorship as a means must be fully exploited. The unlawful conduct of forest destruction must be strictly dealt with according to the law. The "Regulations Governing the Protection of Forests" promulgated by the State Council is one of the State's important laws, and should be practically adhered to by everybody. Of course for the proper implementation of these regulations, first and foremost, efforts should be made to comprehensively propagandize and clearly explain to the broad masses of people the spirit and essence of these regulations and the significance of their stipulations and their implementation. In the course of their implementation, efforts should also be made to use existing examples for carrying out propaganda and explanations in order to bring about maximum results.

The various departments in different districts are generally related to forestry, and their leading comrades should assume a serious attitude toward the "Regulations Governing the Protection of Forests," and study, propagate, and adhere to it sincerely. First of all, they should review their local work concerning forest protection in relation to these regulations. They should also review the progress on the handling of forest rights problems, to find out what are the existing problems regarding the organization and equipment for forest protection, whether the responsibility of forest protection has been clearly divided, and whether all the activities of their departments correspond to the regulations.

Simultaneously, those who, according to the regulations, have done a good job in forest protection should be rewarded, and those who have damaged forest trees punished. The rewards and punishment should be fair and timely and should be propagated comprehensively. By making use of existing examples, efforts should be made to let everybody become familiar, within a short period, with the basic spirit and main articles of the regulations. Party and Youth League members and cadres of various levels should play an exemplary role in abiding by and implementing these regulations. The sincere implementation of these regulations, in fact, is an important expression of the ideological consciousness of patriotism and socialism.

The protection of forest resources is an extremely important aspect of the protection and development of socialist construction. It is the responsibility of everybody to protect the forests and implement the regulations. "To protect forests is an honor, and to destroy them a shame" should be gradually developed into a social style. For the successful development of socialist construction and the building of a brilliant future for our people, it is necessary for everybody to protect trees and resolutely safeguard and continually develop our forest resources.

APPENDIX III.

Estimates of Tree Cover and Stocking Made
during Air and Rail Travel in China

TABLE A–8 shows subjective estimates of tree cover and survival
made during air travel in China by spot observations every five minutes
of the field of view through the window of an Ilyushin aircraft. No
attempt has been made to calculate precisely the area of ground covered by each observation but it was probably of the order of 40 sq. km.
to 50 sq. km. at an altitude of 1,200 m. In columns 2 and 3 of Table
A–8 the percentage of land surface area in forest or plantation is
divided into "mature" (i.e. natural) forest and "young" plantations
(almost invariably less than ten years old). Column 6 gives an estimate
(to the nearest 5 per cent above 10 per cent) of the ground surface
within plantations obscured by the tree crowns. With the close spacings used in China since 1950 it may be assumed that crown closure
in fully stocked stands would be complete at age three years in provinces south of the Yellow river and at five to six years further north.
For most of the area covered, therefore, column 6 probably gives
actual stocking densities to within ± 10 per cent, though it is, of
course, impossible to measure limits of error.

It is not suggested that the estimates in column 6 are very precise,
or that the figures in columns 2 and 3 are representative of all China.
Nevertheless, the method is not as vague as may at first appear. The
aircraft used are not equipped with cloud-flying navigational aids; in
consequence, they fly at low altitudes and only when visibility is complete; the cabins are equipped with altimeters. The flight path is, as
far as possible, restricted to river valleys and, since most young plantations have been established on bare, eroding hills above the valleys,
the trees can easily be seen. Little weight can be attached to the fig-

189

ures for "mature" forest, of course, since, except in isolated pockets and in Manchuria, it is restricted to the higher mountain ranges; many of the areas noted in Table A–8 were, no doubt, associated with Buddhist temples and shrines.

In Table A–9 are data based on observation for ten minutes every thirty minutes over a thirteen-hour period of daylight travel by train in southeast China. Again, the figures give no reliable estimate of forest areas. Column 5 indicates the length of time during each ten-minute observation period for which trees were visible on one side of the railway, and, except where stated otherwise, the data refer to substantial plantations, not shelter or amenity plantings. In this table, the "stocking percentage" assumes 100 per cent stocking at approximately 2-m. × 2-m. spacing. Inasmuch as accurate observation is easier from a train than an aircraft, these data are more reliable than those in Table A–8, though the sample is more restricted both in area and in site type.

Table A–8. Estimates of Tree Cover and Stocking during Air Travel

Time of Sample	Tree Cover (% of visible land surface) Mature Forest	Young Planta-tions	Altitude (approx. m.)	Direction of Flight (approx.)	Ground Cover (% within planta-tions)	Remarks
			Kunming (Yunnan)–Chungking (Szechuan)			
1400		40	?	E	35	
1405		50	?	"	40	
1410		45	?	"	50	
1415		35	?	E	30	
1420	15	60	?	NNE	50	
1425	10	70	2,000	"	55	
1430	15		"	"		
1435	20		"	"		
1440	15		"	"		
1445	<10		2,500	"		
1450	10	35	2,400	"	<10	
1455	15	20	"	"	<10	
1500	10	30	"	"	<10	Dry, eroding hills.
1505	5	40	"	"	<10	
1510	5	15	2,000	"	<10	
1515	20	10	"	"	30	
1520	15	60	"	"	40	
1525	10	50	1,600	"	45	
1530	<10	<10	1,500	"	30	
1535	<10		1,300	NNE		Over Chungking, with land-
1540	<10		1,200	"		scape trees only below,
1545	10		?	"		but extensive plantations
1550	<10		?	NE		in hills to east and west.
1555			?	NE		

Table A–8—Continued

Time of Sample	Tree Cover (% of visible land surface)		Altitude (approx. m.)	Direction of Flight (approx.)	Ground Cover (% within planta-tions)	Remarks
	Mature Forest	Young Planta-tions				
			Chungking (Szechuan)–Sian (Shensi)			
1630	60	20	?	NNE	75	⎫ Eroding hills.
1635	85	<10	?	"	<10	⎬
1640	<10		?	"		⎭
1645	<10		1,800	"		
1650	<10		1,850	"		
1655	10		?	"		
1700	<10		2,100	NNE		
1705			"	"		⎫
1710			"	"		⎬ Cloud.
1715	<10		2,400	"		⎭
1720	95		2,550	"		⎫
1725	100		2,700	"		⎬ Tsinling mountains.
1730	100		2,700	NNE		⎭
1735	55		"	"		⎫
1740	70		2,400	"		⎬ Severe erosion.
1745	60		2,350	"		⎭
1750	100		1,950	"		
1755	90		1,500	"		
1800			?	"		
1805			?	"		
			Sian (Shensi)–Peking			
1100	10		?	E		
1105	10		?	"		
1110		10	?	"	75	
1115		10	900	"	90	
1120			"	"		
1125			"	"		
1130		<10	"	"	80	
1135		10	"	"	70	
1140		15	1,350	NE	65	Eroding hills.
1145		70	"	"	90	Yellow river crossed.
1150	20		1,200	"		
1155	25	25	"	"	60	
1200	30	20	1,500	"	50	
1205	20	30	"	"	55	
1210			"	"		
1215			1,650	"		
1220			1,800	"		
1225	<10	<10	"	"	70	
1230		10	"	"	60	
1235	80		2,250	"		
1240			2,400	"		Hu-to-ho river crossed.

Table A–8—Continued

Time of Sample	Tree Cover (% of visible land surface) Mature Forest	Young Planta- tions	Altitude (approx. m.)	Direction of Flight (approx.)	Ground Cover (% within planta- tions)	Remarks
1245			2,550	NE		
1250			"	"		Cloud.
1255			"	"		
1260			"	"		
1300			"	"		
1305			"	"		Scattered landscape trees
1310			1,500	"		only.
1315			1,350	"		
1320		10	1,200	"	45	Sand dune plantation along
1325		15	?	"	40	Hun Ho river.
1330			?	"		
1335			?	"		Over Peking. Many land-
1340			?	"		scape trees, and planta-
1345			?	"		tions.

Peking–Shenyang (Liaoning)

Time of Sample	Mature Forest	Young Plantations	Altitude	Direction	Ground Cover	Remarks
0645			?	Variable NE		
0650			?	NE		
0655		60	1,200	"	45	
0700		55	1,350	"	55	
0705		65	1,500	"	60	Eroded hills and winding
0710		45	1,650	"	65	valleys. Rivers much dis-
0715		50	1,450	"	70	colored. Plantations on
0720		55	2,100	"	65	vast scale in hills. Agri-
0725		40	2,250	"	75	culture in valleys.
0730		50	2,400	"	60	
0735		30	2,400	"	55	
0740		35	"	"	50	
0745	15	25	"	"	60	
0750		30	"	"	65	
0755	<10	35	"	"	45	
0800	<10	25	"	"	60	
0805	10	25	"	"	45	
0810		30	1,800	"	55	
0815		45	"	"	50	
0820		40	1,350	NE	60	
0825			?	"		Approaching Shenyang.
0830			?	"		Plains agriculture.

Shenyang (Liaoning)–Changchun (Kirin)

Time of Sample	Mature Forest	Young Plantations	Altitude	Direction	Ground Cover	Remarks
1030		10	?	NE	15	
1035		15	?	"	<10	
1040		20	900	"	25	

Table A-8—Continued

Time of Sample	Tree Cover (% of visible land surface) Mature Forest	Young Planta- tions	Altitude (approx. m.)	Direction of Flight (approx.)	Ground Cover (% within planta- tions)	Remarks
1045		15	1,050	NE	20	
1050		25	1,200	"	35	
1055		30	1,500	"	30	
1100		25	"	"	25	
1105			"	"		} Wide arable plains.
1110			"	"		
1115	<10	15	?	"	45	Eroding hills.
1120		40	?	"	55	
1125			?	"		

Changchun (Kirin)–Harbin (Heilungkiang)
No tree cover—entirely arable plains.

Peking–Tsinan (Shantung)

0650			?	Generally S		
0655			?	"		
0700		10	900	"	50	} Plantations on old river
0705		10	"	"	45	} beds.
0710			"	"		
0715			1,200	"		
0720			"	"		
0725		15	1,200	"	40	} Plantations on old river
0730		10	"	"	55	} beds.
0735			"	"		
0740		10	"	"	40	
0745			"	"		Plantations in hills to SW.
0750			"	"		
0755		10	"	"	30	} Plantations on old river
0800		15	"	"	35	} beds.
0805		15	900	"	55	}
0810			?	"		
0815			?	"		Yellow river.
0820			?	"		

Tsinan (Shantung)–Hofei (Anwhei)

0900			?	Generally S		
0905		45	?	"	60	
0910		15	1,200	"	15	} Plantations on hill terraces.
0915	10	20	1,350	"	25	} Older trees on Tai moun-
0920	<10	15	"	"	20	} tains.
0925			1,500	"		
0930		15	"	"	65	Plantation on river banks.
0935			"	"		
0940		25	"	"	15	Plantation on river banks.

Table A–8—Continued

Time of Sample	Tree Cover (% of visible land surface) Mature Forest	Young Planta-tions	Altitude (approx. m.)	Direction of Flight (approx.)	Ground Cover (% within planta-tions)	Remarks
0945		35	"	Generally S	20	
0950			"	"		
0955			"	"		Arable plains.
1000			"	"		
1005		45	"	"	40	Plantation in hills to the
1010		30	"	"	45	east.
1015			"	"		
1020			"	"		
1025			"	"		
1030			"	"		
1035			"	"		
1040			900	"		
1045			"	"		
1050			?	"		
1055			?	"		
1100			?	"		
1105			?	"		

Hofei (Anwhei)–Shanghai

1215			?	Generally E		
1220			?	"		
1225			900	"		Air dust-laden, visibility
1230			1,050	"		very poor.
1235			"	"		
1240		30	1,050	"	<10	Plantation in hills.
1245		25	1,200	"	15	
1250		30	"	"	10	Yangtze river. Discolored.
1255		75	"	"	25	Low hills.
1300			"	"		
1305			"	"		
1310	70	25	"	"	20	Steep local hills.
1315			"	"		
1320			900	"		
1325			"	"		
1330			"	"		Tai lake.
1335			?	"		
1340			?	"		
1345			?	"		
1350			?	"		

Table A–9. Estimates of Tree Cover and Stocking during Rail Travel from Hangchow (Chekiang) to Kwangchow (Kwangtung). Observation between Shanghai and Hengyang (Hunan)

Time	Mature	Tree Cover (species) Young Plantation	Direction	Duration (minutes)	Stocking (%)	Remarks
0600		*Pinus* sp.	S.	5	85	Red soil.
0630		*Cunninghamia lanceolata*	"	5	80	Railway planting, 5 rows deep.
0700			"			
0800		*C. lanceolata*	"	10	65	
0830		*Populus* sp. ⎫ *Acacia* sp. ⎬	S.	6	90	Railway planting, 5 rows deep.
		Pinus sp.	"	1	<10	Plantation 10 yrs old, replanted 2–3 years ago.
0900			"			Railway station.
0930		*Pinus* sp.	S.	10	40	
1000		Species unknown	"	10	?100	1 row deep.
1030			"			
1100		*Pinus* sp.	"	4	25	
		Acacia sp.	"	5	80	1 row deep.
1130		*Populus* sp.	"	6	85	2–3 rows deep.
1200		*Pinus* sp.	"	2	55	Rolling hills, all planted.
				8	15	Some bamboos also.
1230	"	"		8	15	⎫ Same plantation as pre-
				2	5	⎭ vious. Bare, red soil.
1300	"	"		10	35	Same as previous.
1330	"	"		5	30	⎫ Same as previous.
				5	60	⎭
1400		*Pinus* sp.	S.	2	10	⎫ Same plantation as
				5	30	⎬ previous.
1500	"		S.	3	25	⎭
			"	1	20	⎫ Same as previous.
				1	95	⎬ Poor survival sharply
				2	50	⎭ differentiated.
1530		*Pinus* sp. ⎫ *Cunninghamia* ⎬ *lanceolata* ⎭	"	8	50	⎫ Eroding badly.
				2	45	⎭
1600						Railway station (Chuchow).
1630		*Pinus* sp.	W.	10	20	
1700		? species	W.	5	15	⎫ West of Siang Kiang
				5	30	⎭ river.
1730		*Cunninghamia* ⎫ *lanceolata* ⎪	W.	3	5	⎫
		? species ⎬		2	95	⎬ 1963 planting.
		Pinus sp. ⎭		2	30	⎭
		"		1	10	
		"		2	75	
1800		*Pinus* sp.	W.	2	30	Eroding badly.
				7		Railway station.
1830		*Pinus* sp. ⎫ ? species ⎭	W.	10	20–30	Variable. 1962 planting.
1900						City of Kwangchow.

APPENDIX IV.

Notes on Some Species of Northwest China, Used in Sand Stabilization

THE SPECIES listed in this appendix are based on a report compiled by the Sand Control Team of the *Academia Sinica* and the Soviet Academy of Sciences on the desert regions of western Inner Mongolia and the Ho-Hsi corridor (*Acad. Sin.*, 1958).

This area lies generally above 1,000 m., is very sparsely populated, and is climatically very harsh. The maximum summer temperature reaches 40°C., while the winter minimum drops to −30°C. The diurnal range is of the order of 14°C. Winds are strong, dry, and blow mainly from the north. From east to west, the annual rainfall decreases from 400 mm. to less than 50 mm., much of it falling during a few days in summer. The lack of cloud cover gives rise to intense insolation amounting to more than 3,000 sunshine hours per year over most of the area. Salt lakes abound but, because of surrounding mountains, the ground water resource is considerable. The soils are sands, gravels, and loess and the solid geology mainly sandstones of the Cretaceous and Jurassic eras. The first 110 plant species are arranged in a tentative order of effectiveness in sand fixation in the region but, as the report indicates, both conditions and opinions vary so much that it is impossible to establish objective criteria for this purpose. Similarly, where natural distributions are indicated, these lack precision and lay no claim to be comprehensive; they are general locations only. The last six species are not indigenous to China, but are plants from Soviet Central Asia which, on the basis of trials under way at the Chinese center for desert introductions at Chung-wei, have considerable potential for use in sand fixation in China. Chung-wei is in the southeastern corner of Ninghsia; the sand dunes there form a continuation of the

Alashan desert and, according to Cressey (cited by Wang, 1961), are among the highest in the world.

1. *Artemisia sphaerocephala*

A semishrub with a capacity for extensive vertical and lateral root development, the species occurs naturally on moving sand in northern Shensi, Kansu, Ninghsia, and Inner Mongolia. It can be established by direct seeding in late autumn, and it is used in the construction of sand screens and as a fuelwood.

2. *A. ordosica*

Native to stabilized, low-lying sand dunes in Kansu, Ninghsia, and Inner Mongolia, *A. ordosica* has a more restricted root system than *A. sphaerocephala,* but seeds as readily and has a similar potential on rather wetter soils.

3. *A. halodendron*

A creeping and fastigiate shrub of the steppes of Inner Mongolia and Liaoning, this species layers readily and grows well in arid, semistabilized dune areas. It has some slight economic value as a fodder plant.

4. *A. salsoloides*

This plant is extremely drought-resistant and is found on the sands and dry gobi river beds of Kansu. It seeds abundantly and is a useful fodder species.

5. *Hedysarum scoparium*

Able to withstand repeated burial by sand, and exposure, this Inner Mongolian species has a high potential in sand stabilization. Its foliage is used as camel fodder, and it also produces fuelwood and edible seed. It is a legume.

6. *Caragana microphylla* var. *tomentosa*

Another legume, *C. microphylla* var. *tomentosa* occurs in northern Shensi, Ninghsia, and Inner Mongolia. It is a shrub with a dense, spreading habit, a strongly developed root system and early-ripening seeds. The branches and foliage are used for fodder, fuel, or green manure.

7. *Calligonum mongolicum*

This species grows well on soft sand, but poorly on gravel or gypsum gobis. As a sand plant, it needs to be mixed with other species since, although it produces an extensive root system, the shoots develop poorly. It provides fodder for camels, sheep, and goats.

8. *Salix flavida*

A plant of the moist (though mobile) dunes of eastern Inner Mongolia, northwestern Liaoning, and northern Shensi, *S. flavida* suckers readily and withstands sand pressure well. It grows from cuttings, is excellent for

planting on ditch banks and in dune bottoms, and is harvested for basket-
and mat-making, etc.

9. *Haloxylon ammodendron*
   Occurring in western Inner Mongolia and Sinkiang, this species grows
well on soft sands with a slightly saline ground water. A small tree, it withstands extremes of temperature, germinates easily, and produces camel
fodder and fuelwood.

10. *Tamarix ramosissima*
    Adapted to saline flats, *T. ramosissima* layers readily in moist conditions
but may need irrigation for successful establishment. The branches can
be used for craftwork.

11. *Hedysarum mongolicum*
    A shrub some 1.5 m. tall, *H. mongolicum* demands a minimum annual
precipitation of 15 cm. Otherwise, its properties are similar to those of *H.
scoparium* (q.v.).

12. *Zygophyllum xanthoxylon*
    This species grows well on coarse dry sands and gravel gobis but fails
on highly saline sites or fine textured soils. It produces useful fuelwood
but the foliage is toxic to camels.

13. *Piptanthus mongolicus*
    A leguminous shrub native to Inner Mongolia and Ninghsia, *P. mongoli-
cus* is a valuable shelter species because of its evergreen habit, unique in
these deserts. It needs moisture, however, and does not grow where the
rainfall is less than 100 mm. It yields fat and oil extractives and makes an
excellent smokeless fuel.

14. *Psammochloa villosa*
    P. villosa is a perennial herb which grows best on moving sand dunes
and can withstand extremes of aridity; it is a valuable fodder plant, while its
rhizomes can be used in basket-making and its leaves for rope-making.

15. *Agriophyllum arenarium*
    An annual found on the lower slopes of crescent dunes of the Ordos and
in dune bottoms where soils are not saline, this plant seeds in late autumn
and tolerates a wide range of moisture conditions. It is said to be the best
camel fodder in northern China.

16. *Pugionium cornutum*
    A biennial herb, with an extensive root system, *P. cornutum* has a low
drought resistance and, hence, is only suitable for planting in the lee of
sand dunes where there is a high water table. The seeds yield oil and the
foliage may be used as a vegetable or as camel feed.

17. *Corispermum patelliforme*
Another annual, similar in habitat requirements to *Agriophyllum aren-arium*, this species yields seed-oil and animal fodder.

18. *Nitraria tangutorum*
A shrub species of western Inner Mongolia and Sinkiang which effectively accumulates moving sand, this plant is extensively used in sand-sealing areas where the water table is within 2 m. of the ground surface. It tolerates salinity and yields edible fruits (which may be fermented or used to make vinegar) and hog feed.

19. *N. roborowskii*
Naturally occurring on sand dunes in northern Kansu and Sinkiang—to the west of the area occupied by *N. tangutorum*—it is similiar in ecology and utility to the latter species.

20. *N. siberica*
This species is rather less effective in sand fixation than that previously noted but tolerates a greater degree of salinity. It seeds earlier than the other *Nitraria* species but has much the same uses.

21. *Stelpnolepis centiflora*
A biennial herb of moving sand dunes, which survives long drought periods but has little economic value, it can be used in conjunction with other sand-stabilizing species.

22. *Atraphaxis frutescens*
Growing on dry river beds and coarse sands of gobis in the north of Ordos, this shrub reaches some 2 m. in height and is highly resistant to drought conditions. It can be planted on semistable dunes and gravel plains. The young shoots are rich in protein and yield a valuable animal fodder.

23. *A. pungens*
A thorny shrub of gravelly soils, A. *pungens* is resistant to browsing—except by camels—and can tolerate an annual precipitation as low as 100 mm.

24. *Salix cheilophila*
As might be expected, S. *cheilophila* requires a high permanent water table and low salinity. Native to Kansu, northern Shensi, and Inner Mongolia, it is an excellent sand-stabilizing shrub and is grown from cuttings along watercourses. The wood is used for craftwork.

25. *Phragmites communis*
An indicator of a high water table, this is a species of the lake basins in internal drainage areas, where salinity is high. Growing to some 3 m. in height, the foliage may be dried for cattle food and the flower stalks used for mat-making.

26. *Elaeagnus angustifolia*
Widely distributed in Ninghsia, Kansu, Shensi, Shansi, Inner Mongolia, Honan, Sinkiang, and Tsinghai, this species tolerates a wide range of site conditions and extremes of temperature. A fastigiate tree with an extensive root system and large root tubercles, it is a principal component of the "great green wall." It produces utilizable timber, cattle fodder, and fruits used in brewing.

27. *Hippophae rhamnoides*
Another species very tolerant of varied soil conditions, this tall shrub is also widely used in soil and water conservancy. It colonizes dunes rapidly if the water table is within 1 m. of the surface and is found in Kansu, northwestern Shensi, Inner Mongolia, and Shansi.

28. *Populus diversifolia*
This poplar grows on highly saline, moist soils (usually old watercourses) in Kansu, Sinkiang, and Inner Mongolia. Although it suckers readily, it is usually raised from seed for sand-planting. The timber is dense and is used for cooperage and basket-making.

29. *P. simonii*
Another poplar found along watercourses in Shensi, Inner Mongolia, and Ninghsia, this species grows rapidly where there is sufficient moisture but it cannot survive if the ground water level drops below 4 m. It is raised from seed but layers readily in sand. The timber is suitable for construction, furniture-making, and fiber production.

30. *Apocynum andersonii*
A species native to Kansu, Tsinghai, and Sinkiang, this woody herb grows to 2 m. in height on saline sands. It is effective in stabilizing slowly moving dunes but is more often used to reclaim abandoned farmland. It yields a fiber used for fabrics and is also used in glue-making.

31. *Pycnostelma lateriflorum*
This species is abundant on the dunes of northern Shensi and Inner Mongolia and on the desert steppes of Ninghsia. *P. lateriflorum* is very droughtresistant but is not widely planted because it is poisonous to stock and gives rise to allergies in humans.

32. *Sophora alopecuroides*
Widely distributed in Honan, Shensi, Kansu, Ninghsia, Inner Mongolia, and further north into western Siberia and Central Asia, this legume seeds easily and tillers strongly on mobile sand dunes even though slightly saline. It serves as a green manure, can be used as winter feed for stock, and has medicinal value in the cure of throat infections.

33. *Glycyrrhiza uralensis*
Bordering the Yellow river in Inner Mongolia, Ninghsia, and Kansu on semistabilized sand and abandoned saline farmlands, this legume is grown

extensively in China's northwest. It needs water to get established but stands saline soils well. The foliage provides a protein-rich feed while root extracts are much used in the treatment of bronchial and gastrointestinal disorders.

34. *G. inflata*
Very similar to the previous species, *G. inflata* is similarly used, though it has less medicinal value.

35. *Alhagi pseudoalhagi*
Another salt-resistant legume, this species extends from western Inner Mongolia, through northern Kansu and Tsinghai, to Sinkiang, on semistable sands and dry watercourses. It is deep-rooting and can be used in sand-sealing around grazing land.

36. *Eurotia ceratoides*
This plant of the Ordos and Alashan is highly drought-resistant but can also grow in swamps. It is a small shrub 20 cm. to 40 cm. high with a variable growth habit depending on the availability of moisture. It is a fodder plant which is particularly nutritious after the first winter frosts.

37. *Hololachne soongarica*
A dominant, deep-rooting fodder shrub of deserts and desert steppes, this species occurs naturally in the gobis of northern Kansu and on highly saline flats of Tsinghai, Inner Mongolia, and Sinkiang. But it also grows on moist sands, and layers readily when buried.

38. *Myricaria dahurica*
M. dahurica is native to river flood plains and moist sands of central Inner Mongolia and Ninghsia. It layers easily and is therefore used for sand stabilization, but it needs a high water table. It has no economic value except as fuel.

39. *Juniperus sabina*
A semirecumbent shrub from central Inner Mongolia and northern Shensi, this juniper needs stable sand for initial establishment, but can spread over drifting sand and prevent further movement. It has little economic use other than as goat fodder.

40. *Inula salsoloides*
This perennial composite grows at bases of mobile sand dunes in Inner Mongolia and Kansu. Reaching a height of some 30 cm., it is a useful camel fodder.

41. *Oxytropis aciphylla*
A legume occuring in the rocky foothills of the Chilien mountains, *O. aciphylla* grows like a cushion and will stop drifting sand in arid and cold conditions. It, too, can be used for camel feed.

42. *Iris ensata*
   As might be expected, this species requires a moist soil. It is, however, salt-resistant and occurs extensively throughout the north and northwest provinces. It has a strongly developed root system and, growing to a height of about 1 m. and very densely during the vegetation period, it makes an effective sand-break plant. It is used locally as a raw material for paper-making and the dried roots are made into brushes.

43. *Achnatherum splendens*
   Although nonwoody, *A. splendens* looks like a shrub and grows to a height of 1 m. on the second terrace of the Yellow river in Shensi, Inner Mongolia, and the Ho-hsi corridor, and in dry mountain valleys. It is a useful protective species around lake basins and reservoirs and is an important dry-season feed for livestock. It is also used for basket work and paper-making.

44. *Oxytropis glabra*
   A perennial herbaceous legume of lake shores, river valleys, and saline soils of western Inner Mongolia, *O. glabra* can withstand high salinity and drought. Although effective in sand fixation it is little used because it is poisonous to stock.

45. *Ampelopsis aconitifolia*
   This species is a vine native to dry sands in central Inner Mongolia and northern Shensi and is a useful stabilizing plant for steppe country.

46. *Caryopteris mongolica*
   Ecologically, *C. mongolica* is a plant of river valleys and terraces, widely distributed in Shensi, Kansu, Ninghsia, and Inner Mongolia. It grows well on slowly moving dunes, but has little economic value apart from an attractive flower.

47. *Panzeria lanata*
   Not a common species, this labiate is found in the mountains of southern Inner Mongolia and in Ninghsia on sandy terraces and semistabilized dunes. It can be planted between sand dunes and produces fodder for stock.

48. *Oxytropis psammocharis*
   This species grows on sandy river flats in central Inner Mongolia and Shensi. It is not very effective in sand fixation but it will survive arid conditions and is a useful feed plant.

49. *Ulmus pumila*
   One of the principal tree species of the arid regions, *U. pumila* has a wide edaphic tolerance though it needs a rather better soil than the desert willows and is usually found in dry watercourses. It has been planted extensively for sand fixation and has many economic uses; the leaves can be fed to goats and sheep, the timber is used for agricultural tools and construction, the branches make excellent fuel, the young leaves and fruits are edible, while the bark is made into fiber products such as rope, matting, and fabrics.

50. *Armeniaca sibirica*
This large shrub is widely distributed over the steppes and is also found on poor gravels and sands, if stable. It is used in conjunction with trees in shelter belts of northern Shensi and, like other members of the *Rosaceae*, the achenes yield a useful oil.

51. *Amorpha fruticosa*
A well-nodulated leguminous shrub, *A. fruticosa* has long been cultivated in Ninghsia, Kansu, and northern Shensi and, spreading out from abandoned farms, it has become established in many areas where it was not known originally. The foliage readily absorbs alkalis and so it is used as a green manure to reduce soil alkalinity. On river banks it effectively counters wind erosion, while the branches can be used in basketry.

52. *Kochia prostrata*
A small shrub with creeping branches, this halophyte of western Inner Mongolia and Kansu produces valuable fodder on saline sands.

53. *Populus sinica*
Distributed along the alluvial plains of the Yellow river in Ninghsia and Kansu, this tree needs a high water table or irrigation to become established as a sand stabilizer. Unlike many of the poplars in China it is grown from cuttings. It propagates easily and even large stems retain the facility to form roots when buried by sand. The timber is used in construction and as furniture wood.

54. *P. alba*
A large tree, *P. alba* is well known in Europe and North America as an ornamental. It is salt-resistant and suckers readily if adequate water is available. It yields building timbers, furniture, and pulpwood.

55. *Lycium chinense*
A shrub from the second terrace of the Yellow river, this plant is a useful sand-sealing species on fertile saline sands in the Ho-hsi corridor. It is cultivated in Ninghsia as a medicinal plant, extracts of the root being used to cure tuberculosis while the fruit helps the treatment of gynecologic disorders.

56. *Thermopsis lanceolata*
From swamps and saline sands of western Inner Mongolia, Ninghsia, and Kansu, this legume can be direct-seeded in lacustrine basins and used as a green manure in the reclamation of salt-laden soils.

57. *Karelinia caspica*
A composite from slightly saline soils of the Ninghsia plains and the Ho-hsi corridor, *K. caspica* puts down a strong tap root which grows laterally some 80 cm. below the ground surface. Its only economic use is as fuel.

58. *Ephedra przewalskii*
A rare member of the *Gnetaceae* found in the gobis of Kansu and on gypsum desert sands of Inner Mongolia, this shrub withstands a high degree

of drought and calcium sulphate, and effectively fixes moving sands. It yields the alkaloid ephedrine and has been used in China as a medicinal herb since 3,000 B.C.

59. *Tetraena mongolica*
T. mongolica is a small shrub found only between the Table and Yin mountains of the Ikhchao League. Densely branched, it is an effective shelter species on sands. A sentence translated from *Acad. Sin.* (1958) reads, "A rare plant species, it should be preserved and well protected; it is also a good fuel"!

60. *Pennisetum flaccidum*
This fodder grass occurs extensively in the very dry deserts; the subterranean stems retain their viability even when exposed to strong sun for several days.

61. *Calamagrostis epigeios*
Inhabiting the river flats and partially stabilized sand dunes of Inner Mongolia, Kansu, Ninghsia, and Liaoning, this is one of the main pasture grasses in desert regions. It is effective in erosion control, perhaps because it is only moderately palatable to stock.

62. *Aristida adscensionis*
An annual herb of sand dunes, gobis, and dry river beds in western Inner Mongolia and Kansu, this plant only grows well in years of higher-than-average rainfall. It is a good fodder plant but produces a thorny fruit which can injure stock.

63. *Bassia dascyphylla*
An annual of level sands and dune bottoms in western Inner Mongolia and Kansu, this sand pioneer can alter its habit according to the available moisture. In dry years it reaches only 2 cm. to 3 cm. in height, whereas in a wet season it may grow to 50 cm. and provide a useful fodder.

64. *Salsola collina*
A species of sands, gravels, and compacted soils of the Ordos and the Ho-hsi corridor, *S. collina* is an annual herb often planted alongside *Artemisia ordosica* in sand fixation projects. It is highly palatable to stock.

65. *Potaninia mongolica*
This common associate of *Reaumuria soongarica* and *Salsola passerina* (q.v.) is a shrub up to 50 cm. tall and with a 40-cm. tap root. A fodder plant, it can remain dormant for several years at a stretch if drought conditions continue.

66. *Caragana tibetica*
A cushion-like leguminous shrub, valuable in stabilizing drifting sand, *C. tibetica* is a mountain species yielding camel feed.

67. *Cleistogenes mutica*
An important fodder plant for sheep and horses, *C. mutica* occurs on gobis, stable sands, and swamps. It has some value in sand fixation because of its wide site tolerance.

68. *Stipa glareosa*
Another major component of gobis, dry river beds, and sands in Ordos and the Ho-hsi corridor, this annual herb can be seeded during the summer rains to provide highly nutritious winter fodder for domestic animals.

69. *S. gobica*
This species is essentially similar to *S. glareosa*.

70. *Aneurolepidium dascystachys*
Widely distributed through northern China, this perennial rhizomatous species thrives on slightly saline sands and on gravels. It is adaptable and forms good grazing.

71. *Agropyron cristatum*
This steppe plant occurs with *Artemisia ordosica* on the Ordos plateau and on steppes and mountain valleys elsewhere. It withstands drought but can only be grown on stable sand dunes. It is cultivated in northern China and Outer Mongolia as stock feed.

72. *Agropyron mongolicum*
A. mongolicum is a perennial herb up to 1 m. in height and well able to suffer arid conditions. Its distribution overlaps that of *A. cristatum* and it is similar in properties.

73. *Artemisia frigida*
Found on loess and sand plateaus from the Ordos to the Ho-hsi corridor, this small shrub spreads rapidly on stable sand and provides excellent fodder.

74. *Apocynum venetum*
Not an effective species for moving sands, this plant grows on the saline loamy sands of Ninghsia and the Ho-hsi corridor and can be used to protect lacustrine basins. The stems yield fiber for fabrics, while the young leaves are used as a substitute for tea.

75. *Gymnocarpos przewalskii*
A mountain shrub, reaching 50 cm. in height, with numerous branches but very small leaves, this species plays a limited role in sand fixation but is highly palatable to camels and worth establishing as a fodder plant.

76. *Populus hopeiensis*
A poplar found on the dry loess plateaus of central Kansu, in the Ho-hsi corridor and further east, this tree survives drought but needs moisture and

a relatively rich soil for growth. It thrives on loess overlain by sand where the water table is high. Often propagated from root suckers, it produces good construction and furniture wood.

77. Thalictrum squarrosum

Native to western Liaoning and Inner Mongolia, *T. squarrosum* is a perennial herb with feathery leaves. It is easily damaged by wind and, hence, is of limited value in dune stabilization. It is a favorite feed of camels.

78. Echinops gmelini

An annual composite of Inner Mongolia and northern Kansu, with thorny leaves, it grows on sands but is so restricted as to limit its value; the inflorescence is palatable to stock.

79. Scorzonera divaricata

Another composite of Inner Mongolia and the Ho-hsi corridor, but a perennial herb, this plant also has a limited value in sand fixation, but it is more generally used than *Echinops gmelini* as fodder.

80. Stellaria gypsophylloides

A 50-cm. tall perennial herb with a large root system, *S. gypsophylloides* is unpalatable even to camels and, consequently, can be used to stabilize sand where grazing cannot be controlled. Its dry foliage is dispersed in late summer by wind and may aid fixation.

81. Peucedanum rigidum

This plant is found extensively on alluvial sediments and mobile sands in Inner Mongolia and Ninghsia. Although a perennial, the shoot withers after seed ripening and it is of little value in accumulating sand. It is very palatable to camels.

82. Hologeton arachnoides

A species of gypsum flats and gravels, this species withstands drought but it is a small-leaved annual, and flowers in July, offering no resistance to autumn winds. It is a fodder plant.

83. Peganum nigellastrum

A species growing extensively on recently abandoned farmlands of Inner Mongolia, *P. nigellastrum* tillers strongly but is of limited use in sand fixation when its foliage dies down in late autumn. It is used as a feed and as a green manure.

84. Cynanchum pubescens

Another sand-sealing species, often found at the base of dunes carrying *Nitraria schoberi* (q.v.), this perennial herb has a prostrate habit, grows rapidly, and has a stabilizing influence until it dies in late summer. It is not palatable to stock.

85. *Swainsonia salsa*
Found in the Ho-hsi corridor, Ninghsia, and parts of Mongolia, this plant withstands salinity and forms a green crop; it is not palatable and, because of its small leaves and branches, is insignificant in sand fixation.

86. *Dasiphora parvifolia*
A locally common species of the valleys between the Table and Yin mountains, this small shrub withstands drought but can only grow on stable sands. Its young shoots are eaten by sheep but it is a poor feed.

87. *Caragana stenophylla*
Native to Ninghsia, Inner Mongolia, and the Alashan, this small shrub can grow at high altitudes and is used as camel fodder, but it is too small to have great significance in sand fixation.

88. *Lespedeza dahurica*
Widely distributed in Inner Mongolia, Shensi, Kansu, and Ninghsia, this leguminous shrub is very adaptable on partially stabilized dunes and is an excellent feed. It must be used in conjunction with other species.

89. *Allium mongolicum*
A common constituent of the desert steppes, *A. mongolicum* is an associate of the evergreen *Piptanthus mongolicus, Zygophyllum xanthoxylon,* and *Artemisia sphaerocephala* (q.v.). It withstands very dry conditions during the growing season, but withers rapidly in autumn; it is a good fodder plant.

90. *Tournefotia sibirica*
A perennial rhizomatous herb of Inner Mongolia and the Ho-hsi corridor, this species is partially halophytic though it needs moisture. It can be used to raise stock feed in dune hollows.

91. *Convolvulus fruticosus*
C. fruticosus occurs on sands and gravels between the Table and Yin mountains. It is a cushion-like thorny shrub, 50 cm. tall, which reduces surface wind velocity and filters blown sand.

92. *Kalidium foliatum*
A salt-resistant shrub of Inner Mongolia and the Ho-hsi corridor, this plant (together with the subspecies *K. gracile* and *K. caspicum*) probably has a greater potential in sand fixation than has so far been realized, since it is gregarious. It produces edible seeds and succulent leaves suitable for camel fodder.

93. *Clematis fruticosa*
This shrub is an inhabitant of gobis, low mountains, and dry river beds, and is well adapted to aridity, but hard to propagate.

94. *Buddleia alternifolia*
Ecologically a component of alluvial communities in Shensi, Kansu, and Ninghsia, this 1-m. tall woody plant has been used effectively in protecting the banks of the Yellow river. It has an attractive flower.

95. *Asterothamnus centrali-asiaticus*
A species of gravels and alluvial sands in Inner Mongolia and the Ho-hsi corridor, its hairy leaves enable it to withstand dry conditions on stable dunes. It provides a suitable feed for camels, but not for cattle and horses.

96. *Salsola passerina*
From Ordos and Alashan, *S. passerina* requires a moist loamy soil but, since its root system extends for 30 cm. to 40 cm. it can grow on soils covered by layers of wind-blown sand. It is a fodder plant.

97. *Amygdalus mongolica*
A woody member of the *Rosaceae,* with thorny branches and leaves, this denizen of rocky mountains and dry valleys forms a dense cushion on dry and nutrient-deficient soils. The achenes yield valuable oil.

98. *A. pedunculata*
A taller shrub than *A. mongolica,* this species is otherwise similar in value as a sand plant.

99. *Nitraria sphaerocarpa*
Highly resistant to salinity, this plant grows on gypsum and gravel gobis in the Ho-hsi corridor. Although it has some value in sand fixation it is considerably less than that of the other *Nitraria* species (q.v.).

100. *Astragalus melitotoides*
A. melitotoides extends throughout northern China from Manchuria to Sinkiang and grows on the alluvial plains, or slightly saline sands, of the Yellow river. A green crop and animal feed, it cannot be established far from moisture, but it can be planted on drifting sands around farmsteads.

101. *Iris tenuifolia*
An herb of moderately dry sands, the value of this species lies in its ability to withstand trampling by animals. The leaves are used to make rope.

102. *Asparagus gobius*
From rocky mountains, gobis, and stable sands of Inner Mongolia and the Ho-hsi corridor, *A. gobius* can resist drought but has limited fixation value because it grows singly.

103. *Cynoglossum divaricatum*
A component of stable dunes in the Ikhchao League, this perennial herb grows to some 80 cm. in height and produces wide, succulent leaves. Unfortunately, it withers quickly after seeding in June.

104. *Cleistogenes squarrosa*
A common associate of *Artemisia ordosica*, the species is found in eastern Inner Mongolia and Liaoning. It is drought-resistant but is very sensitive to salinity. It is highly nutritious to horses.

105. *Artemisia anethifolia*
A common species of the desert steppes, this biennial adapts to varying precipitation in its growth habit. It has only slight use in sand fixation but can be used as winter feed.

106. *Medicago sativa*
Cultivated from Manchuria to Sinkiang, this excellent fodder legume can prevent sand movement though it will not stop it once it has begun. It grows on loamy sands and slightly acid soils, and is used for green-cropping as well as feed.

107. *Pappophorum boreale*
Widely but sparsely distributed on sands, gravels, gobis, and swamps, this annual is edaphically very tolerant but of limited effectiveness in preventing sand movement. It is a highly nutritious autumn grazing species.

108. *Tragus racemosus*
A species of gobi ditches, intermontane plains, and sands of Inner Mongolia and the Ho-hsi corridor, this annual herb is too small to have much value in sand stabilization but it provides good fodder for sheep.

109. *Chloris virgata*
The habitat of *C. virgata* is one of dry stream beds and sand dunes in Ho-hsi and Inner Mongolia. It can be established only when rainfall is plentiful and, consequently, is not a major sand species. It has some value as stock feed.

110. *Artemisia capillaris*
A common constituent of desert steppes and loess, this species is found in Inner Mongolia, Kansu, and Ninghsia, and often constitutes a weed species on farmlands. Of only slight value against drifting sand, it has a medicinal use in the treatment of dysmenorrhea.

111. *Calligonum caput-medusae*
From Central Asia, this shrub is sturdy and develops a vigorous root system which is very effective in sand fixation once it is established. The fact that the seeds have a long dormancy requirement, which has so far proved difficult to break, militates against its current use in northern China. Due to its impressive growth on the crescent dunes of Kazakhstan and its obvious potential in northwest China, the species is under cultivation in Chung-wei for field trials in Inner Mongolia and Sinkiang.

112. *C. arborescens*

Another species of Soviet Central Asia, this woody plant is similar in its seed dormancy requirement to the previous one. A large shrub able to resist sand pressure in Kazakhstan, *C. arborescens* is also under cultivation in Chung-wei with a view to its large-scale introduction into China.

113. *Salsola richteri*

Yet another shrub from Soviet Central Asia, this one has roots extending into sand to a depth of up to 10 m. It has no inherent dormancy problems and will shortly be established in the northwestern provinces of China.

114. *S. paletzkiana*

Also from Central Asian sands, *S. paletzkiana* has an extensive root system and resists sand movement. The seeds, however, retain their viability only for a short period. It is said to be an intermediate species in the evolution of desert plants.

115. *Haloxylon persicum*

From the Tukuman desert of the U.S.S.R., this shrub can grow on dunes as high as 40 m.; it is a typical plant of mobile dunes with a strongly developed root system and cladodes instead of leaves. It is a good animal feed and fuel species.

116. *H. aphyllum*

A species occurring naturally on heavier soils in Central Asian deserts, this shrub is another plant possessing cladodes and can withstand both aridity and salinity. It too provides stock feed and fuelwood. Seedlings established at Chung-wei are said to be flourishing.

REFERENCES CITED

ABBREVIATIONS:

AAAS   American Association for the Advancement of Science.
APFC   Asia Pacific Forestry Commission.
CSIRO   Commonwealth Scientific and Industrial Research Organisation.
ECAFE   Economic Commission for Asia and the Far East.
ECMM   *Extracts from Chinese Mainland Magazines* (American; pub-
           lished in Hong Kong by the American Consul General).
FA   *Forestry Abstracts.*
FAO   Food and Agriculture Organization of the United Nations (pub-
           lished in Rome, unless indicated otherwise).
JPRS   Joint Publication Research Service, Washington, D.C.
NCNA   New China News Agency [*Hsinhua*]; (Peking edition, unless
           indicated otherwise).
NSF   National Science Foundation.
PBA   *Plant Breeding Abstracts.*
SCMP   *Survey of the Chinese Mainland Press* (American).
SSB   State Statistical Bureau, Peking.
U.K. BBC   United Kingdom. British Broadcasting Corporation.
UN   United Nations.
USDA   United States Department of Agriculture.

Abotin-Pavlov, R. J. 1952. Spruce originating from a pine. *Agrobiologiya*,
    5: 30. [Russian.] In *PBA*, 23: 1506.
Acad. Sin. 1958. *A report on the co-ordinated research on the desert region*
    (*no. 1*). Peking: Sci. Pub. House. In JPRS, No. 18658, April 11, 1963.
Afanasev, V. A. 1959. Lesnye Kultury Kunninghamii v Kitae. *Les Khoz.*,
    12(10).
Auslands Inf. 1960. *Auslands Informationene*, XIII(24): 6.
Biki. 1959. FAO document recording a statement from *Biki*, Moscow,
    April 2.
Bogdanov, P. L. 1946. Vegetative hybrids of poplars. *C. R. (Doklady) Acad.
    Sci. U.S.S.R.*, 54: 357. [Russian.] In *PBA*, 19: 546.
Bretschneider, E. V. 1898. *History of European botanical discoveries in
    China*, 2 vols. St. Petersburg.
Buchanan, K. 1960. The changing landscape of rural China. *Pacific View-
    point*, 1(1): 11.

Carter, J. 1958. China plans to raise timber output. *Timb. Trades J.*, **226** (Sept. 6): 74.

Chang, Chao. 1960. China's fast-growing tree cover. *China Reconstructs*, Sept.

Chang, C. Y., *et al.* 1962. *National atlas of China, vol. V, general maps of China.* Ed. Chang Chi-yun. Taiwan: National War College.

Chao, K. C. 1961. *Agrarian policies of mainland China, 1949–1956—a documentary study.* Cambridge, Mass.: Harvard Univ. Press.

Chen, C. S. 1945. The frost of China. *Bull. Inst. Geog. Nat. Central Univ.*, Ser. A, No. 7. Cited by Wang, 1961.

————. 1959. *Scientia*, **5**: 147. [Chinese.]

Chen, H. C. 1936. Forest flora of Lu-shan (Kiangsi). *J. Ag. and For.*, **13**(35), No. 443: 974. [Chinese.] Cited by Wang, 1961.

Chen, T. H. 1961. Science, scientists, and politics. In *Sciences in communist China*, AAAS Pub. No. 68, p. 59.

Cheo, Y. C., and Kuo, C. C. 1941. *Forests of China.* Cited by Wang, 1961.

Chien, S. S., Wu, C. Y., and Chen, C. T. 1956. A tentative scheme for phytogeographical regions. In K. F. Lou, *Tentative schemes for dividing natural regions of China*, p. 83. Peking.

Chi-hua Ching-chi. 1957. No. 12, Dec. 9. [Chinese.]

China Reconstructs. 1959. May.

Chu, K. C. 1959a. An expedition to inquire into the feasibility of transmitting water from the upper course of the Yangtze to the Yellow river. *Ti-lih chih-shih* [*Geographical Knowledge*], **10**(4): 145. [Chinese.]

————. 1959b. The fight against deserts. FAO typescript, Sept. 11.

Chung-kuo shui-li. 1957. No. 5, May 14. [Chinese.]

Chun, W. Y., and Kuang, K. Z. 1958. A new genus of Pinaceae—*Cathaya* Chun et Kuang, gen. nov., from southern and western China [*Genus novum pinacearum ex Sina australi et occidentali*]. *Bot. Zhurn. S.S.S.R.*, **43**: 461.

Cox, E. H. M. 1945. *Plant Hunting in China.* London: Collins.

Cressey, G. B. 1955. *Land of the 500 million . . . A geography of China.* New York: McGraw-Hill.

Current Events Handbook. 1955. Why is it still impossible to embark upon large-scale reclamation of waste land? *Shih-shih shou-tse*, Sept. 10. [Chinese.]

Dadswell, H. E. 1942. *Monthly Newsletter*, No. 125, p. 5. Div. For. Prod., CSIRO, Australia.

Dallimore, W., and Jackson, A. B. 1923. *A handbook of coniferae.* London.

Daniel, L. 1927. Variations de l'appareil sécréteur chez diverses plantes grefées. *Compt. Rend. Acad. Sci.*, **185**(233): 1296.

David, A. 1872–74. Journal d'un voyage dans le centre de la Chine et dans le Tibet oriental. *Nouv. Arch. Mus. Hist. Nat., Paris. Bulls.*, **8**:3 [1872]; **9**:15 [1873]; **10**:3 [1874].

Deng, C. H. 1959. China's Anstrengungen zur Aufforstung. *Holz-Zentralblatt*, July 4.

Dzei, C. H., and Cheng, K. T. 1957. Some methods in experiments of exchanging egg-white in fowls. *General Biology*, **1959**(7): 319. [Chinese.]

ECMM. 1956. The forests in our country. *Shih-shih shou-tse* [*Current Events Handbook*], No. 6, March 25.

————. 1959. Ten years of afforestation. *Ti-lih chih-shih* [*Geographical Knowledge*], **8**(Aug. 1).

Economic Research. 1962. May 17.

FAO. 1958. *Yearbook of forest products statistics.*

————. 1959. *Yearbook of forest products statistics.*

————. 1960. *World forestry inventory, 1958.*

————. 1961. *Timber trends and prospects in the Asia-Pacific region.* Geneva.

————. 1961. *Yearbook of forest products statistics.*

————. 1962. *Yearbook of forest products statistics.*

————. 1963. *Yearbook of Forest products statistics.*

————. n.d. Typescript, undated and unreferenced, in FAO files.

FAO/APFC. 1964. *The implications of mainland China's situation for regional timber trends and prospects.* [Paper tabled at 7th session of Asia-Pacific Forestry Commission, New Zealand.] FAO/APFC–64/4.1.

Far East. Econ. Rev. 1950. **IX**, 23(Dec. 7).

————. 1958. Jan. 23.

Fong, C. H. 1956. Some realizations upon attending the genetics conference. *General Biology*, **1956**(10): 66. [Chinese.]

For. Lang. Press. 1956. *Labour laws and regulations of the People's Republic of China.* Peking. [Chinese.]

Franchet, A. 1883–88. Plantae Davidianae ex sinarum imperio, pt. I. *Nouv. Arch. Mus. Hist. Nat. Paris. Bulls.*, **II**(5): 153 [1883]; **II**(6): 1 [1883]; **II**(7): 55 [1884]. Pt. II: **II**(8): 183 [1885]; **II**(10): 33 [1888].

Freeborne, M. 1962. Natural calamities in China, 1949–61. *Pacific Viewpoint*, **3**:2.

Frei, S. 1959. Erfahrungen bei der Begrundung von Nesterkulturen. *Arch. Forstw.*, **8**(11): 1017.

Greene, F. 1962. *The wall has two sides.* London: Cape.

Handel-Mazzetti, H. 1930. The phytogeographic structure and affinities of China. *Abstr. Vth Int. Bot. Cong.*, p. 315. Cambridge, Eng.: Int. Bot. Cong.

Hou, H. Y., Chen, C. T., and Wang, H. P., 1956. The vegetation of China with special reference to the main soil types. *Rep. for VIth Int. Cong. Soil Sci.* [English summary in *VIᵉ Cong. Int. Sci. Sol.*, Vol. A, p. 55.]

Hsu, Chien. 1959. China aims to turn its land green. FAO MS., Sept. 20.

Hsu, Y. C. 1950. A preliminary study of the forest ecology of the area about Kunming. *Contr. Dudley Herb.*, **4**(1): 1.

Hughes, T. J., and Luard, D. E. T. 1959. *The economic development of communist China, 1949–1958.* London: Oxford Univ. Press.

Huxley, J. 1949. *Heredity, East and West.* New York: H. Schuman.

Hwang, P. W. 1940. Regions of natural vegetation in China. *Rev. Hist. and Geog.,* 1(3): 19. [Chinese.] Cited by Wang, 1961.

————. 1941. Regions of natural vegetation in China. *Rev. Hist. and Geog.,* 1(4): 38. [Chinese.] Cited by Wang, 1961.

Hwang, T. T. 1944. On the Turfan depression. *Science* (Sci. Soc. China), 27:(4): 7. [Chinese.] Cited by Wang, 1961.

JPRS. 1960. No. 2447, March 30.

————. 1960. No. 5224, Aug. 15.

————. 1963. *Water and soil conservation, communist China.* No. 17046, Jan. 8.

Kapelinsky, Y. N., *et al.* 1959. *Razvitie Ekonomiki i Vneshneekonomisheskikh Svyazei KMR* [*Development of the economy and external economic relations of the Chinese People's Republic*]. Moscow: Vneshtorgizdat [For. Trade Pub.].

Karapetjan, S. K. 1952. A hazel originating from a hornbeam. *Agrobiologiya,* 5:3. [Russian.] In *PBA,* 23:1501.

Kenji, A. 1961. Measures to increase China's agricultural production in 1961. *Ajia Keizai Jumpo,* No. 461. In JPRS, No. 9229.

Kinmond, W. 1957. *No dogs in China.* New York: Nelson.

Kuo, C. C., and Cheo, Y. C. 1941. A preliminary survey of the forests in western China. *Senensia,* 12:81. Cited by Wang, 1961.

Kuo, L. H., Hsieh, H. F., and Kuo, C. M. 1959. Economic geography of the Hu-lun-Pei-Erh (Mongol) league. *Geog. Res. Dept. Acad. Sin.* In JPRS, No. 11125.

Kuang Ming Jih Pao. 1963. May 9.

Lai, J. Y. 1953. *Trade union work experience at the Wu-san factory.* Peking. [Chinese.] Cited by Hughes and Luard, 1959.

Lanner, R. M. 1963. Soviet forestry and the "new biology." *J. For.,* 61(1): 12.

Lee, T. Y. 1959. New achievements in producing faster-growing new hybrids through applying Michurin's genetic principles. *Scientia Silvae* (Peking), 3:259. [Chinese.] In *FA,* 21:4065.

Liang, Hsi. 1956. Strive for a better conservation system, more green hills, and the prevention of natural calamities. Statement of June 19. Recorded by Chao, 1961.

————. 1957. *Green age.* Japan.

Li, C. C. 1961. Genetics and animal and plant breeding. In *Sciences in Communist China.* AAAS Pub. 68, p. 297.

Li, F. C. 1960. Vice-premier Li Fu Chun's report on the draft of the 1960 economic plan. *Current Background* (Peking), 615, March 30.

Li, J. C. 1957–58. Fundamental principles of genetics. I–XIII. *General Biology,* 1957(3): 42; 1957(4): 41; 1957(5): 35; 1957(6): 28; 1957(7):

41; **1957**(8): 40; **1957**(9): 48; **1957**(10): 36; **1957**(11): 38; **1957**(12): 53; **1958**(1): 52; **1958**(2): 48; **1958**(3): 42. [Chinese.]

Li, S. W. 1960. Repeated pollination in poplar breeding. *Vestn. sel.-Khoz. Nauk.*, 5(2): 14. [Russian.] In *FA*, **21**: 4064.

Li, T. Y. 1959. China, home of paper making. *Ta Kung Pao* (Hong Kong), Oct. 6. Cited by Solecki, 1964.

Lindbeck, J. M. H. 1961. Organization and development of science. In *Sciences in Communist China*. AAAS Pub. 68, p. 3.

Lin, D. Y. 1956. Quoted in Am. Geog. Soc., *World geography of forest resources*. New York: Ronald Press.

Lin, Jung, et al. 1959. *Handbook of water and soil conservation in the middle Yellow river loess region*. Peking: Science Press. In JPRS, No. 19810, June 24, 1963.

Liou, T. N. 1934. Essai sur la géographie botanique du Nord et de L'Ouest de la Chine. *Contr. Inst. Bot. Nat. Acad. Peking*, **2**:423.

———. 1936. Plant geography of the south and the south-west of China. *Ephemeris Biologicarum Sinicarum*, 1(1): 21. Cited by Wang, 1961.

Lowdermilk W. C. 1932. Forestry in denuded China. *Ann. Amer. Acad. Pol. Soc. Sci.*, **152**:98.

Lysenko, T. D. 1946. *Heredity and its variability*. Transl. T. Dobzhansky. New York: King's Crown Press.

———. 1949. Direct sowing of shelter belts by the "nest" (patch) method. *Dokl. Vsesoyuz. Akad. sel-Khoz. Nauk. Lenina*, **1949**(10): 3. [Russian.]

———. 1950. Some new ideas in the science of biological species. *Dokl. Vsesoyuz Akad. sel-Khoz. Nauk. Lenina*, **1950**(12): 3. [Russian.] In *PBA*, **21**: 2500.

———. 1953. Letter to the editor. *Bot. Z. Moscow*, **38**: 91.

———. 1954. *Agrobiology. Essays on problems of genetics, plant breeding, and seed growing*. Moscow: For. Lang. Pub. House.

———. 1957. For materialism in biology. *Agrobiologiya*, **5**: 4. [Russian.] In *PBA*, **28**: 3727.

Merrill, E. D. 1945. *Plant life of the Pacific world*. New York.

Messines, J. 1958. Forest rehabilitation and soil conservation in China. *Unasylva*, **XII**: 103.

Mi, C. C. 1960. A critique of the mutation theory of evolution of modern Darwinism. *General Biology*, **1960**(1): 20. [Chinese.]

Michurin, I. V. 1949. *Selected works*. Moscow: For. Lang. Pub. House.

Ministry of Forestry. 1963. Personal communication, June.

Murzayev, E. M., et al. 1960. Prirodnyye usloviya sin'tszyana [Natural conditions of Sinkiang]. *Acad. Sci. U.S.S.R.* In JPRS, No. 15084.

NCNA. Releases of the following dates:
Sept. 13, 1952.
June 13, 1954.
Oct. 1, 1956, Suppl. No. 248.
April 9, 1957.

Sept. 25, 1957.
Jan. 2, 1958.
Feb. 5, 1958.
April 4, 1958.
April 7, 1958, CCP and State Council joint directive on afforestation.
Nov. 12, 1958, No. 111242.
Nov. 14, 1958.
Nov. 17, 1958. (See also *SCMP*, 1920.)
1959, No. 012515.
March 5, 1959, No. 030551.
Aug. 30, 1959. Hong Kong.
Sept. 18, 1959, No. 091833.
Oct. 28, 1959.
Nov. 1, 1959.
Nov. 22, 1959.
Dec. 22, 1959.
Jan. 22, 1960.
April 5, 1960, No. 040541.
1960, No. 082514.
June 1, 1961, No. 060123.
Dec. 1, 1961, No. 120107.
1961, No. 051214.
Aug. 8, 1962, No. 080803.
Aug. 11, 1962. Nanking.
Nov. 21, 1962 No. 112102.
1962, No. 020313.
1962, No. 031517.
1962, No. 082202.
1962, No. 080907.
1962, No. 091107.
1962, No. 101704.
1962, No. 112502.
1963, No. 021309.
1963, No. 032908.
1963, No. 041105.
1963, No. 041312.
1963, No. 042302.
1963, No. 052105.
Needham, J. 1964. Science and China's influence on the world. In R. Dawson (ed.), *The Legacy of China*, p. 234. Oxford: Oxford Univ. Press.
Nekrasov, V. I. 1958. Conf. on problems of forest selection. *Akad. Nauk. S.S.S.R. Izvestia Seriia, Biologicheskaia,* **23**: 628. [Russian.]
Nesterov, V. G. 1952. New methods of improving the quality and productivity of forests. *Les Khoz.,* **5**: 28. [Russian.]

————. 1956a. Michurin's ideas and experiments in forest growing. In *Michurin's theories and experiments in forestry*. Sci. and Tech. Inform., No. 18, p. 55. Transl. and pub. for NSF and the Dept of Ag. by the Israel Program for Scientific Translation.

————. 1956b. Progressive practices and backward theories. *Les. Khoz.*, 5: 4. Transl. M. L. Anderson.

Nikitin, I. N. 1941. On new ideas in arboriculture and silviculture. *Les. Khoz.*, 5: 4. Transl. M. L. Anderson.

————. 1958. New points on the biology of some tree species and stands. *Les. Khoz.*, 11: 18. [Russian.]

Orleans, L. A. 1961. Education and scientific manpower. In *Sciences in Communist China*. AAAS Pub. No. 68, p. 103.

Pai, C. C., Sun, Y. W., and Chang, W. T. 1961. Effects of rotation grazing on grassland improvement and soil and water conservation in the steppes of northern Shensi. *Tu Jang* [*Soil*], No. 6. [Chinese.]

Peking Review. 1958. April 22.

————. 1960. Jan. 26.

————. 1960. Feb. 23.

People's China. 1956. May 16.

————. 1956. Communiqué on fulfillment of the national economic plan in 1955. Supplement to *People's China*, July 16.

People's Daily. Peking issues of the following dates:

Jan. 24, 1958.

Sept. 9, 1959.

June 4, 1960.

Feb. 12, 1961.

Jan. 9, 1963.

April 10, 1963.

June 9, 1963.

Aug 6, 1964.

People's Education. 1958. May 1. Peking.

Petrov, G. 1952. Quoted in *de Houthandel*, 2(13), June 26, 1953.

Pobedinsky, A. V. 1961. *Trudy Institua Lesa i Drevesiny* [*Transactions of the Institute of Forestry and Timber*], 56: 91.

Ponomarev, A. D. 1963. The forest resources of the U.S.S.R. *Lesnoye Khozyaistvo*, No. 6. Transl. FAO.

Potanin, G. N. 1899. Sketch of a journey to Szechuan and the eastern frontier of Tibet in 1892–93. *Isv. Russk. Geogr. Obshch.*, 35: 363. [Russian.] Cited by Wang, 1961.

Premezov, N. P. (ed.). 1955. *Lesa i Pochvy Kitaya* [*Forests and soils of China*]. Transl. of Chinese book by Ma Chi and Liu Hai-peng. Cited by Solecki, 1964.

Radio Peking. 1957. Quoted in *Rev. Int. du Bois*, Dec., 1957.

Red Flag. 1958. No. 14, Dec. 16.

————. 1960. No. 24, Dec. 16.

Richardson, S. D. 1964a. Forestry in China. [Paper tabled at 7th session of Asia-Pacific Forestry Commission, New Zealand.] FAO/APFC–64/3.1, Annex 1.

————. 1964b. Production and consumption of forest products in China. FAO/APFC–64/4.1, Annex 1.

————. 1965. The forest industries of mainland China. *For. Prod. J.*, **XV**(1): 15.

Sai, F. T. 1959. Ten years of great achievements in the agriculture of Sinkiang. *Chung kuo Nung Pao,* **19**: 19. [Chinese.]

SCMP. 1960. Growth of China's fibreboard industry. No. 2293, p. 9.

————. 1961. Giant shelter belt project transforms formerly sand ravaged area of northeastern China. No. 2512, June 1.

Shui-li hsueh-pao. 1957. No. 4, Dec. 29. [Chinese.]

Snow, E. 1963. *The other side of the river.* London: Gollancz.

Solecki, J. 1964. Forest resources and their utilization in communist China. *For. Chron.,* **40**(2): 227.

South China Times. 1963. July. Hong Kong.

Sowerby, A. deC. 1922–23. *The naturalist in Manchuria,* 3 vols. Tientsin, 1923.

————. 1924. Approaching desert conditions in north China. *China J. Sci. and Arts,* Aug.

SSB. 1959. *Economic and cultural statistics on communist China.* [Chinese.]

————. 1960. *Ten great years—statistics of the economic and cultural achievements of the People's Republic of China.* Peking: For. Lang. Press.

Steven, H. M., and Carlisle, A. 1959. *The native pinewoods of Scotland.* Edinburgh: Oliver and Boyd.

Ta Kung Pao. 1962. Aug. 22. Peking.

Tan, C. C. 1957. On the physical basis of heredity. *General Biology,* **1957** (1): 8. [Chinese.]

Tan, C. L. 1960. (See NCNA release, April 6, 1960.)

Tao, T. T. 1955. Construction of preventive forests in new China. ECAFE typescript, FAO.

Tass. 1960. Release, Nov. 23. Peking.

Teng, S .C. 1948. A provisional sketch of the forest geography of China. *Bot. Bull. Acad. Sin.,* **2**: 133.

Thorp, J. 1936. Geography of the soils of China. In *Nat. Geol. Survey.* Nanking.

Tong, H. K. 1947. *China yearbook, 1937–45.* Chungking.

Troup, R. S. 1913. A note on the blue gum plantations of the Nilgiris (*Eucalyptus globulus*). *Ind. For. Rec.,* **V**(11): 34.

Tsou, S. W., and Chien, S. S. 1925. Vegetation of China. [Unpub. MS.] Cited by Yang, 1939.

U.K. BBC. 1958. Summary of world broadcasts, No. 346, Dec. 4.

UN. 1964. *Population, 1938, 1950, 1953–63.* Econ. Dept., Stat. Div., Census and Social Statistics Branch, Geneva.

USDA. 1961. Forestry and forest industry in the U.S.S.R. *Rep. of a tech. study group.* Washington, D.C.: Government Printing Office.

Walker, E. H. 1944. The plants of China and their usefulness to man. *Ann. Rep. Smithsonian Inst.,* p. 334. Washington, D.C.: Smithsonian Inst.

Wang, C. 1935. Forest zones of China. *Agriculture [Nung Hsueh],* No. 3, p. 41. Cited by Wang, 1961.

Wang, C. W. 1961. *The forests of China, with a survey of grassland and desert vegetation.* Cambridge, Mass.: Maria Moors Cabot Found. Pub. No. 5.

Wang, F. Y., and Chi, H. C. 1957. Afforestation and forest industry in south China. *Planned Economy,* 11(Nov.9).

Wang, K., and Chen, T. C. 1944. Table of estimated Chinese forest resources. [Unpub. MS.] Forest Products Laboratory, Madison, Wisc.

Watt, J. 1961. The effect of transportation on famine prevention. *China Quart.,* 6: 76.

Wen, Chieh. 1958. China's first five-year plan in forestry work. FAO typescript.

Went, F. W. 1948. Thermoperiodicity. In A. E. Murneek and R. O. Whyte (eds.), *Vernalisation and photoperiodism,* p. 145. Cambridge, Mass.: Chronica Botanica.

Wiens, H. J. 1961. Development of geographical science, 1949–60. In *Sciences in Communist China.* AAAS Pub. No. 68, p. 411.

Wilson, E. H. 1913. *A naturalist in western China,* 2 vols. London.

W. K. 1961. Communist China's agricultural calamities. *China Quart.,* 6: 64.

World's Pap. Trade Rev. 1960. Aug. 15.

Wu, C. H. 1956. The place of genetics in biological sciences. *General Biology,* 1957(3): 46. [Chinese.]

Wu, C. L. 1950. Forest regions in China with special reference to the natural distribution of pines. D.F. thesis, Duke Univ.

Wu, H. L. 1957. A discussion of the article "On what constitutes the physical basis of heredity." *General Biology,* 1957(7): 45. [Chinese.]

Yablokov, A. S. 1960. Prospects of selection of arboreal species in forestry. Questions of forestry and forest management. *Papers for the Vth World Forestry Congress,* p. 222. Moscow: Acad. Sci. U.S.S.R.

Yang, C. Y. 1937. The forest vegetation of Si-Shan and Hsiao-wu-tai-Shan. *Bull. Chinese Bot. Soc.,* 3: 97.

————. 1939. *Plant communities of China.* Cited by Wang, 1961.

Yang, M. T. 1962. Landscape characteristics of southern Kweichow and some problems of demarcation of natural districts. *Ti-li [Geography],* No. 4. [Chinese.] In JPRS, No. 20, p. 119.

Yu, K. Y. 1957. *People's Daily,* Sept. 4.

SUBJECT INDEX

Academia Sinica: timber resource surveys, 59; role of, in land use policy development, 59; technical handbooks on soil and water conservation, 59, 196; sand control team, 122; research commissions and institutes, 139

Academy of Forest Science: control of provincial institutes, 134; forest research centers, 134–35

Aerial reconnaissance, in forest protection, 58

Aerial sowing: advent of, 67

Afforestation: widespread failure of projects, 14, 58, 60, 63–66, 166; reduced emphasis on, in Regulations of May, 1963, 51–52; main lines of 1953 program, 56; objectives of program for, modified during its operation, 56–58; Russian influence on, 56, 148ff.; program for, in National Plan for Agriculture (1956–68), 57ff.; regulations limiting access to sites for, 58; program for, reduced in 1962, 59; resources devoted to, compared with forest management, 61; area data for, 62; vastness of, according to visitors, 62; statistics for, of little more than academic interest, 62; low standards of, 62, 65–66; targets for, based on trees planted, not area covered, 63; comparison of projects in, undertaken by state and communes, 64; intractable sites a large factor in failure of, 65, 66; timber producing species used in, in state projects, 77ff.; principal species currently used in, 79–81; roadside plantings in, 151ff.

Agriculture: area under cultivation, 5; as basis of the economy, 5; productivity of, dependent on water conservation, 5, 9, 11, 107ff.; intensive character of, 5–8; collectivization of, 6; first plan for, 7; establishment of output zones in, 7–8; eight-point plan for, 9

Arid zones: extent of revegetation problem, 58, 113ff., 120; devices to establish trees, 114, 121; species used in revegetation, 124, 196–210

Balsam poplars: In Yunnan and Kwangsi, 95

Biogeocenosis: Sukachev's concept of, in relation to Michurinism, 145

Botanical institutes: See *Academia Sinica*

Botanic gardens: location and types, 156ff.; functions, 156ff.; general layout and design, 157

Broadcast sowing: at Tailing nursery, 69

Canton: abundant labor force at, 71

Canton gum: exceptional growth, 91; use in state afforestation projects, 91; a proven exotic species, 92

Chain saws: use of, in tree felling in Manchuria, 98

Cheng Wan-chun: as a dendrologist, 77; influence on research, 136; and research co-ordination, 141

Chestnut: for roadside plantings, 151

China. See People's Republic of China

China Institute of Botany (Canton): vegetation survey of, 139

Chinese Academy of Sciences: See *Academia Sinica*

Chinese fir: natural distribution, 88; wide utilization, 88; planting practices for, 88; use in state afforestation projects, 88; general purpose timber, 88; successful plantation species, 89

Chinese pine: natural distribution, 86; use in state afforestation projects, 87; sites where planted, 87; periodicity of root growth, 87; survival and growth, 87

Chinese scholar tree: as a memorial, 151; for roadside planting, 151

Close planting: a Michurinist principle, 148; widespread application of, 148

221

INDEX OF LATIN PLANT NAMES

FORESTRY IN COMMUNIST CHINA
S. D. RICHARDSON

designer: Edward King

typesetter: Baltimore Type & Composition Corporation

typefaces: Caledonia and Perpetua

printer: John D. Lucas Printing Company

paper: Warren 1854 and Curtis Colophon

binder: William Marley Company

cover material: Columbia Riverside